Don't Let Me Be Misunderstood

American Music: New Roots
David Menconi, editor

Featuring work by journalists, music critics, scholars, and musicians themselves, this series aims to expand and challenge the way we think about American roots music genres, traditions, performers, and their ever-expanding contributions. Books in the series not only bring new perspective on familiar roots traditions like jazz, the blues, country, and folk music but also offer fundamentally new ways to consider where the roots of today's American music lie, what stories are told about them, and who does the telling.

A complete list of books published in American Music: New Roots is available at https://uncpress.org/series/american-music-new-roots.

Don't Let Me Be Misunderstood

NINA SIMONE, LANGSTON HUGHES & THE BIRTH OF BLACK POWER

W. Jason Miller

The University of North Carolina Press
CHAPEL HILL

This book was published with the assistance of the Blythe Family Fund of the University of North Carolina Press.

Manufactured in the United States of America

Book design and composition by Lindsay Starr
Set in Merope Basic, Thrillers, and Cervo Neue

LIBRARY OF CONGRESS CATALOGING-IN-PUBLICATION DATA
Names: Miller, W. Jason author
Title: Don't let me be misunderstood : Nina Simone, Langston Hughes, and the birth of Black power / W. Jason Miller.
Other titles: American music: new roots
Description: Chapel Hill : The University of North Carolina Press, [2026] | Series: American music: new roots | Includes bibliographical references and index.
Identifiers: LCCN 2026021858 | ISBN 9781469698212 cloth | ISBN 9781469696195 epub | ISBN 9781469698229 pdf
Subjects: LCSH: Simone, Nina, 1933-2003 | Hughes, Langston, 1902-1967 | Political activists—United States | African Americans—Political activity—History—20th century | Black power—United States—History—20th century | BISAC: BIOGRAPHY & AUTOBIOGRAPHY / Entertainment & Performing Arts | SOCIAL SCIENCE / Ethnic Studies / American / African American & Black Studies | LCGFT: Biographies
Classification: LCC ML420.S5635 M55 2026 | DDC 782.42164092 [B]—dc23/eng/20260505
LC record available at https://lccn.loc.gov/2026021858

For product safety concerns under the European Union's General Product Safety Regulation (EU GPSR), please contact gpsr@mare-nostrum.co.uk or write to the University of North Carolina Press and Mare Nostrum Group B.V., Doelen 72, 4831 GR Breda, The Netherlands.

CONTENTS

Prologue

The landing gear dropped before the pilot saw the bulldozers blocking the runway. The plane nosed skyward seeking an alternative place to land, heading west to Jackson, Mississippi. Nina Simone was on board with her husband, Andy Stroud, guitarist Al Schackman, poet Langston Hughes, and Art D'Lugoff, the famed proprietor of the Village Gate in Greenwich Village. Nina's name had appeared in concert advertisements under Art's famous cloth awning for the past six years, framed by lights. Each passenger must have shifted nervously in their seats while the pilot reoriented their course.

On the tarmac in Jackson, the travel party reembarked on a smaller plane that could clear the partially blocked runway back in Montgomery. On their reascent, however, the small plane's tail touched the tarmac because there was too much weight in the back. Passengers switched seats, and still the aircraft barely cleared the airport fence on takeoff.

Once the second plane successfully landed in Montgomery, against the wishes of white supremacists who did not want any more outside agitators descending on their city, the poet Langston Hughes and the singer Nina Simone had finally made their way to take part in a concert to celebrate the imminent success of the march from Selma to demand voting rights for Black people. On March 24, 1965, a crowd of more than twenty-five thousand spectators had gathered in a field to hear not only Simone but also singer Harry Belafonte, comedian Dick Gregory, and march leader Martin Luther King Jr. Stepping onto the bus that would transfer them to the concert venue, the two dear friends experienced this historic moment together.

What they encountered was a scene waiting to be filmed as much as lived. On one bus, all the stars descending onto the scene shared cigarettes. Open windows cleared the air as they handed down autographs written on found paper. Once the bus doors flung open, actor Anthony Perkins stepped off and tucked his glasses away in the front pocket of his suit jacket. Sammy Davis Jr. was immediately rushed backstage as Harry Belafonte fervently ordered commands to organize his impromptu program, "Stars for Freedom."

The number of assembled marchers had grown as the group got closer to Montgomery. This concert was one of their rewards. It meant the most to those who had suffered beatings while trying to cross the Edmund Pettus Bridge seventeen days earlier, an event so horrific it became known as Bloody Sunday. Many still had sores in their mouths: Billy clubs had chipped their teeth, forcing them to stagger with only handkerchiefs pressed helplessly into their lips. The less fortunate—fifty-eight in total, including John Lewis—had been sent to the hospital for treatment.

Those who continued the march, after President Lyndon Johnson assured their safety eight days later, were now standing with wet shoes in the rain-drenched field of St. Jude school. It was more distraction than acceptance that allowed them to forget those gas-masked policemen who had attacked them three weeks earlier. Tear gas had burned their eyes and choked their throats as cheers echoed from white bystanders who shouted "hurrah" when the chemicals were released.

Before any run of show for the evening had been settled, King prepared to address thousands of people expecting a concert, not a speech. Days before, as helicopters buzzed overhead so that news outlets could film the marchers along US Highway 80, he had called out new verse changes to "We Shall Overcome" while these same folk marched in the blinding sun, singing, "The Lord will see us through."

Such reminders buoyed the protestors. They knew that Sheriff Jim Clark had severely beaten Rev. C. T. Vivian in Selma after Vivian had demanded their right to protest peacefully. One of King's most faithful civil rights lieutenants, Vivian had secretly been taken into custody at the precinct using a back elevator. It was there, and not in front of the rolling cameras, that Clark's men started in. They permanently flattened every finger of the minister's left hand when he instinctively covered his head to protect his face and eyes from their clubs.[1] And it was common knowledge that civil rights activist Jimmie Lee Jackson had been murdered and that Rev. James Reeb, who was white, had been beaten so mercilessly that internal injuries took his life, too.

Instead of leading a freedom song, King took the microphone in his left hand and stared across the thousands of people shouldering in the dark of night. Not behind his accustomed pulpit, he began (without any rostrum to rest his hands on): "I just want to say to you"—the crowd quieted just enough to pretend to listen—"how much we are indebted to my dear and abiding friend Harry Belafonte, and to all the other famous artists and entertainers who have taken time out of their very busy schedules to be with us here in Montgomery, Alabama, as we march on the state capital tomorrow morning." A softer King added, "I know that our thanks will go out to them and will abide with them for years and years to come."[2]

Brighter stars than King were now descending into this controlled mayhem. Someone was leading Hughes and Simone through the crowd. One could imagine what they saw in this throng of tired but excited activists mixed with a bevy of celebrities. *Was that actress Lena Horne smiling despite the crush? Is that Odetta or Pete Seeger, a guitar or a banjo?*

The two friends felt forceful hands placed firmly above their elbows. National Guardsmen rolled fully lit spotlights attached to huge generators into place to keep them running through the night. Each one of the green army power sources had to be muscled across the muddy field by no fewer than five men, their chin straps loose and dangling from their helmets. Tire tracks unceremoniously imprinted their movements across the wet turf.

When Simone finally took the stage, she stood in front of her only accompanist, guitarist Al Schackman. Al hastily rushed to locate any outlet to plug in his amplifier. Searching madly with his head down, he was told to pull back a curtain just behind him. When he did, he stood in pure shock: The makeshift stage where they were about to perform had been built on stacked coffins. He immediately understood the rushed and improvised nature of this entire event. Once assured the wooden caskets were indeed empty, he and Nina began finding rhythm together as a lonely duo.[3] They fit right in, given that the crowd had earlier heard the folk trio Peter, Paul and Mary. Nina's white shirt and solid dark sweater might just as well have been borrowed from the adjacent Catholic school. Paired with a checkered skirt, it bore striking resemblance to the way "Eunice Waymon" had looked when Hughes first met her in 1949, back when she was still in high school.

Just a few feet from Nina's left hip, someone was shifting. She was beaming in admiration, with full knowledge that she had a front-row seat to the night's

Fig. 0.1. With Harry Belafonte seated in the front row (and Coretta Scott King standing directly to his right), Nina Simone performs "Mississippi Goddam" at the "Stars for Freedom" rally on March 24, 1965, at the City of St. Jude in Montgomery, Alabama, the night before the end of the Selma to Montgomery March. (Alabama Department of Archives and History. Donated by Alabama Media Group / Photo by Spider Martin, *Birmingham News*.)

most defiant attraction. Who had both the clout and the desire to secure such a position? Stationed directly to the right of Harry Belafonte, Coretta Scott King alternated between standing and kneeling, each flash of the cameras capturing her excitement. Only moments earlier, Harry Belafonte, sitting next to her, had coaxed Coretta onstage to recite Langston Hughes's poem "Mother to Son." It was a famous poem that celebrated perseverance, issued as a testimony whenever a mother wished to inspire her young son. Coretta's husband had also been invoking it from memory since the start of the Montgomery Bus Boycott in 1955:

> Well, son, I'll tell you:
> Life for me ain't been no crystal stair.
> It's had tacks in it,
> And splinters,
> And boards torn up,
> And places with no carpet on the floor—
> Bare.

Coretta was now back in the crowd. As a college music major, she could hardly believe she had been Nina's opening act.

Nina responded instinctively to the energy of the moment. Taking a risk known only to true artists, she came to the line in her song "Mississippi Goddam" where she was supposed to name the state of Tennessee. Instead, knowing exactly where she was, she thrilled the crowd with her spontaneous substitution: "Alabama's got me so upset / *Selma* made me lose my rest." The song had fulfilled Langston Hughes's hope that someone would finally write a "cool piece" of music about the movement in 1962. Too direct to ever be misunderstood, Nina had extemporaneously taken what Hughes had been whispering and turned it into a shout.

According to activist and former United Nations ambassador Andrew Young, Nina Simone had definitively "stolen the show." He said it was not her prowess as a vocalist but rather the fact that "her music so reflected the soul and the feeling of the people there."[4] That night, Al Schackman, Art D'Lugoff, Nina, and Hughes all slept in the same hotel room with federal marshals standing guard outside. Simone recalled that night fondly: "Langston told some stories."[5]

Simone's performance that night helped catapult her into a lead role in the civil rights movement, but Langston Hughes was the hidden secret to Nina Simone's success. Although playwright Lorraine Hansberry was one of Simone's closest friends until her death in early 1965 and writer James Baldwin a couth political ally, only Hughes's professional collaboration with Simone directly shaped Nina's career. In a sentence, this book shows how Nina Simone refined the strategies of resistance Langston Hughes pioneered during the Harlem Renaissance to create the soundtrack to the civil rights movement and inaugurate the birth of Black Power. The full story of their relationship is finally told here.

Hughes's strategies of resistance were many. Once he was established and respected as an artist, he knew he needed to travel outside the nation's borders to resee American racism. Not only was Hughes the only artist of the Harlem Renaissance to travel to Africa, but he also visited Haiti, Cuba, Russia, and Japan and traveled extensively throughout Europe. As it turns out, you have to leave a place to know it. Whether at home or overseas, networking with people beyond his primary discipline enabled Hughes to recognize that creative ideas come from everywhere—flowing both ways. The short list of those Hughes worked with includes photographers Henri Cartier-Bresson, Roy DeCarava, and Gordon Parks, visual artists Aaron Douglas and Jacob Lawrence, and of course numerous musicians, including Duke Ellington, Josh White, and Charles Mingus. Ella Jenkins carefully studied Hughes's *First Book of Rhythms* (1954) to create her breakthrough album *This Is Rhythm* (1961) and then go on to sell the most records in the history of Folkways Records.[6]

More subversively, Hughes used past histories of oppression to comment on present-day struggles. The illusion of the past as a framework provided safe cover from accusations of un-Americanism during conservative eras of red-baiting and the height of McCarthyism. Overtly acknowledging Black heroes and successful artists in his works overlapped with memorializing fallen martyrs, Hughes elevated numerous historical figures such as Frederick Douglass, Harriet Tubman, Malcolm X, and Martin Luther King Jr. He also wrote, between 1921 and 1967, nearly three dozen poems about lynchings.[7] In fact, in 1955 Hughes wrote both a poem and a song about Emmett Till, the first literary responses to his horrific death.[8] Over the course of their relationship, Nina would

Fig. 0.2. Langston Hughes captioned in *Ebony* (October 1959) as "famous poet, lyric writer, lecturer, and critic."

Fig 0.3. Nina Simone performing her tribute concert to Langston Hughes shortly after his death. Newport Jazz Festival, July 1, 1967. (Photo by Ursula Röhnert. James Weldon Johnson Memorial Collection in the Yale Collection of American Literature, Beinecke Rare Book and Manuscript Library, Yale University.)

similarly use each of these strategies in her own unique way, most visibly by spotlighting the victims of the Sixteenth Street Baptist Church bombing—Addie Mae Collins, Denise McNair, Carole Robertson, and Cynthia Wesley—who were murdered in Birmingham by the Ku Klux Klan on September 15, 1963. Following Hughes's example, Nina also started using her songs to memorialize such figures as Hansberry and civil rights activists James Meredith, Jimmie Lee Jackson, and Martin Luther King Jr. She repeatedly referenced Langston Hughes in her live performances.

How well did Simone and Hughes know each other? Nina's words lead us into a relationship that was far more than intellectual: "I was guided by Langston, who sometimes gave me books he thought I should read, but more often simply sat me down and told me what I should know. I'd go over to his place in Harlem and over dinner—southern style—we'd talk, recite songs and poems and drink wine until the sun came up. Then I'd catch a cab home, high on wine, music, and laughter."[9]

This book takes its title from a song Nina first recorded in 1965. Soon after, the song became a hit for the British band the Animals, which paved the way for Nina's first successful tour of Europe. Hughes himself deftly established Simone's reputation in 1960 on his way to forever shaping her image as the High Priestess of Soul. In narrating the full and detailed relationship between these two American icons, this book shows the human stories behind the duo who coproduced the soundtrack to the civil rights movement. It documents what drove Hughes to try so doggedly to write lyrics to hit records and why an esteemed musician like Simone would accept counsel from an older man with a literary, not musical, reputation.

Their relationship also stands in sharp contrast to intergenerational conflicts that often feel so strained today. These two artists show how the struggle for civil rights transcended eras to overlap each other rather than be a simple collection of like-minded people gathered at one dot on a timeline labeled a "movement." Langston Hughes and Nina Simone show us what is possible when generational differences result in true friendship and collaboration.

Yet, in some ways, they were an odd pair. Hughes was a cool cat dressed in a dark suit, with sensibilities that defined both the era of the Harlem Renaissance in the 1920s and the civil rights movement of the 1960s: His poetry directly influenced King's dream.[10] In a flattening-out of his full persona, he has come to stand for "Harlem." Nina's Afro and jewelry of the late 1960s proved that she had already expanded the emotional range of acceptable moods in music to include both rage and blasphemy. Nina's name alone is now a statement about aesthetics. She is rightly championed today by Black women of every age. Unvarnished, she personifies courage. Together, Hughes and Simone represent that rarely explored example of continuity in a world often defined by its divisions and fractures. Sadly, their combined eras must also be seen in the widest lens to underscore the undeniably slow pace at which the United States has shuffled, often stalling, toward fulfilling its constitutional promise of equality.

Don't Let Me Be Misunderstood also follows earnest inquiries to reassess how the poet and the priestess inaugurated the birth of Black Power. Knowing Hughes's and Simone's stories, we must revisit the detailed context of Stokely Carmichael's iconic cries of "Black Power" in June 1966. The fullest emotional register associated with the origins of the phrase "Black Power" now resonates as a collective stance, one that should include the formerly unregarded relationship of Simone and Hughes. It is now clear that the two directly contributed to the tone that marks what we know today as the Black Power movement. Would the world have witnessed John Carlos and Tommie Smith bowing their heads and defiantly raising gloved fists atop a podium at the 1968 Olympics without Langston Hughes's and Nina Simone's words and music adding early fuel to the movement?

In many ways, Langston Hughes and Nina Simone were destined for each other. Hughes wrote a poem about the singer after seeing her perform when she was sixteen. In this way, and in so many others during their lifetimes, it was fitting that as a last gesture of their deep and abiding friendship, Nina recorded Langston's song "Backlash Blues" mere months before he died. It became the poet's most important song, one he had spent the last eighteen years of his life trying to write. From their first encounter to the last time they met, the two were bound by chords that still resonate in the ears of those who are listening.

1

The Poet Laureate of Harlem

Hughes took one last drag from a cigarette most likely rolled a few miles from where he stood in Winston-Salem, North Carolina. His white pocket square was folded perfectly in his suit jacket. Since the late nineteenth century, the manufacturing city had been home to both the textile giant Hanes and the R. J. Reynolds Tobacco Company. The railroad made the city appealing to these industries, the same that carried Hughes here from his home in Harlem. Having sent hundreds of copies of his just-published book of poems, *One-Way Ticket*, before he arrived, Langston Hughes entered Forsyth County unaware that a throng of more than six hundred people was anxiously gathering. The problem? The venue at the George Moses Horton Branch of the public library held only one hundred seats. Discussing strategy with his well-prepared hosts, a plan was set in motion. Dressed in his typical dark double-breasted suit, he delivered a selection of his poems for the next three hours in five separate relays. After each fifteen-minute session, a new crowd faced Hughes. None of the six hundred was turned away.[1]

High schools, libraries, and colleges across the United States observed Negro History Week in 1949. Started by Black historian Carter G. Woodson twenty-three years earlier, the event had gained traction in post–World War II America. To honor two key figures, Woodson deliberately selected the week of February that spanned the birthdays of Fredrick Douglass and Abraham Lincoln. The seven-day window slowly expanded into a monthlong celebration in

Fig 1.1. Langston Hughes reading from *One-Way Ticket* (1949) during one of the five relays set up to accommodate the six hundred people who showed up for his appearance in Winston-Salem, North Carolina, on February 6, 1949. (James Weldon Johnson Memorial Collection in the Yale Collection of American Literature, Beinecke Rare Book and Manuscript Library, Yale University.)

the late 1960s, but it was not fully recognized as such until the nation's bicentennial year of 1976. Hughes had recognized the popularity of Negro History Week and sought out growing literary and cultural centers such as North Carolina as ideal places to both reach his audience and launch new publications. In 1949, Black intellectuals were in high demand. For Hughes, the money from these lecture stipends (and the book sales that ensued) made up a substantive amount of his salary. More than that, it allowed him to inspire the thousands of young people he encountered, engage local Black communities, and provide the physical representation of Black artistic success all too rare in 1940s America. The interaction was mutually beneficial: Hughes often found exciting new topics to write about during these journeys.

To capitalize on these numerous opportunities, Hughes had orchestrated a grueling schedule for February 1949. He began the first full week of the month with the stop in Winston-Salem before continuing west to Black Mountain College and then to Asheville.[2] He completed his week in the eastern part of the state in the small town of Wilson before heading to large events in Washington, DC, and Boston.[3] To fulfill a packed program of engagements in each of these six cities (over eight days), Hughes would cover a staggering 1,808 miles by train.[4] Most of the travel occurred overnight so that Hughes could speak and preside at multiple events each day.

At his first stop in Winston-Salem, Hughes spent the Sunday afternoon of February 6 detailing his earliest voyages to Africa and the first poem he wrote while in eighth grade. His smile stopped midlip rather than extending to the corners. He wore sharp double-breasted suits when it mattered most, tight-fitting sweaters when he worked. If his left hand held a glass of gin, it was Seagram's. He spoke as quickly as he thought, with a cigarette fluttering between his lips fast as the needle on a seismograph. He often placed it on the left side of his mouth to be sure his words came out right.

With a high-pitched register that slowly blurred into a laugh that most resembled a giggle, Hughes delivered his poetic response to having once seen a beautiful girl walk into a high school gym: "Sweet silver trumpets, Jesus." As Hughes regaled the crowd with stories of his travels, he did not tell them why he never married—he was a closeted bisexual. He was instead there at age forty-eight to remind them of what he had asserted in "My People," a poem written twenty-five years earlier at the height of the Harlem Renaissance of the 1920s:

> The night is beautiful
> So the faces of my people.

The stars are beautiful.
So the eyes of my people.

Beautiful, also, is the sun,
Beautiful also, the souls of my people.

Hours passed as books were autographed in black ink, and his "friendly technique" for contextualizing the poems came to a close.[5] With the ring on his left hand anchoring the book's spine, Hughes looked up from its red dust jacket through the frames of his tortoiseshell glasses. As a writer who gave more public readings than any other poet of the twentieth century, his experience showed. Selling more than fifty books, he collected a speaking fee equal to about $1,700 today.

In today's numbers, Hughes's appearance raised more than $8,000 for Nell Brooks Wright's library, which served a growing and energized African American community. These collective funds were used to purchase the library's first bookmobile, forever expanding the literacy of Winston-Salem's rural population. After Hughes met her in 1943, Raleigh librarian Mollie Huston Lee coordinated two of his stops in North Carolina in February 1949. The two Black libraries in Winston-Salem and Wilson purchased bookmobiles immediately after raising funds from Hughes's appearances that year. In this way, both Lee and Hughes played key roles in expanding literacy for thousands of North Carolinians.[6]

As would become the norm, a selection of music set the stage for Hughes's events. Librarian Vivian King Bright had carefully curated three Hughes poems set to music, with William Warren singing Hughes's poem "The Negro Speaks of Rivers."[7] Warren was following a national trend: Luminaries such as Marian Anderson had also turned the poem into a song. As Hughes wrote of this trip, the lighter side of North Carolina was also not lost on him that "once in Dixie that good old southern hospitality takes over and makes you feel right at home. . . . And nowhere are the biscuits hotter, the chicken browner, the sweet potatoes sweeter, or the pies more flaky and delicious."[8]

Hughes's intense week of speaking had begun hours earlier when he gave an interview to the Winston-Salem *Journal*. Though more page space was devoted to the Cleveland Indians re-signing pitcher Satchel Paige, Hughes shared details (for the first and only time) that he had more than passing ties with North Carolina: "All my grandmother's people came from near Fayetteville. It's an old family story that they were related to the 'Lowerie [*sic*] gang,' the Croatan Indian group which held out against authorities in a Robeson County swamp for some time."[9]

THE POET'S CHILDHOOD

The grandmother Hughes spoke of so warmly to a local reporter was Mary Langston. She was about seventy years old at the time she began raising her young grandson James Mercer Langston Hughes in Lawrence, Kansas. She and her North Carolina relatives had been affiliated with the notorious Lowry Gang, a loosely knit group of Black and Lumbee rebels who became infamous in Robeson County for both attacking the Ku Klux Klan and robbing area farmers only to then redistribute the bounty like modern-day Robin Hoods. Mary fled North Carolina in her youth when men tried to enslave her, and she inspired Hughes by telling him stories from the Bible and *Grimms' Fairy Tales* as they savored long evenings sitting on their front porch. She also spoke about current events gleaned from reading the *Crisis*. And, when she felt like reminiscing, she recounted the moments that defined her first husband, Lewis Sheridan Leary, who died fighting with John Brown at the raid on Harpers Ferry in 1859. The nine-year-old Hughes was deeply impressed hearing of Leary's valor in trying to free slaves in Virginia. Mary's second husband, Charles Langston, had a younger brother, John Mercer Langston, whose own success saw both a city and a college in Oklahoma named after him before he became a Virginia congressman in 1890. John Mercer Langston is so respected that a section of the former Robert E. Lee Highway in Virginia's Arlington County was renamed in his honor in 2022. Charles Langston's own father, Ralph Quarles, broke social norms. As a white man, he lived with former slave Lucy Langston as man and wife.[10] Hughes learned all this growing up in an era where history was passed by word of mouth.

Born in Joplin, Missouri, in 1901, Hughes was educated in integrated schools throughout the Midwest, shuttling between his mother and grandmother's homes in Lawrence and Topeka, Kansas. Hughes lived a blues lifestyle, learning early on that home was a place you left. Only in 2018 did the world learn that Hughes was born in 1901—a year earlier than originally thought.[11]

His mother, Carolina "Carrie" Hughes, had a challenging choice after she enrolled her only child for his first year of school. When Langston was sent to the segregated school in Topeka, she argued with the white school principal and won (four decades before the city would become famous for *Brown v. Board of Education* in 1954). Before Carrie returned him to Mary's home in Lawrence and headed off to work in Colorado Springs, Langston endured racial abuse at the hands of his schoolmasters—his first teacher warned the children that they should not eat licorice because it would "make you black like Langston."[12] He soon learned to resist such abuse. When his seventh-grade teacher segregated the few Black students in his classroom, Hughes created cards that read "Jim Crow Row" and placed them on each of his Black classmates' desks. Both gleeful and defiant, two traits he combined throughout his adult life, he ran up and down the playground telling the world his teacher had a "Jim Crow row." Though expelled for telling the truth, he was soon allowed back in school, where he saw with deep satisfaction that the Jim Crow row was gone.[13]

One weekend, Carrie took her son to see two stage shows in Kansas City. Walking along the streets of the bustling city in wide-eyed wonder, Hughes first heard blues music from a blind orchestra where the music "seemed to cry when the words laughed." Deeply moved, he wrote down many of the songs he heard, and some would inadvertently be attributed to him as poetry he himself wrote:

> I'm goin' down to de railroad, baby,
> Lay ma head on de track.
> I'm goin' down to de railroad, babe,
> Lay ma head on de track—
> But if I see de train a-comin',
> I'm gonna jerk it back.[14]

An only child, Hughes worked menial jobs most of his youth. When he wasn't delivering newspapers, he was shining brass spittoons at a local hotel where patrons emptied their mouths of cigarettes, cigars, and chew. The smell of tobacco juice stained both his hands and his memory. When his mother remarried, the family relocated to Lincoln, Illinois, and then Cleveland, Ohio, only to see Carrie and her new husband move on yet again soon after Homer Clark tired from the excessive heat of his job in the Ohio steel mill. Hughes remained behind. During his four years at Central High School in Cleveland, Hughes lived alone, stretching money his mother sent or brought back on her brief visits. Cramped in a small attic apartment during those lean years, Hughes would remember surviving night after night on not much more than rice and hot dogs. Nonetheless, the track and field team secured the city championship during his junior year, with a trim-waisted Hughes running his leg of the winning relay.[15]

Though Langston was resourceful and responsible enough to live alone as a teenager, he was, in many ways, still young enough to be afraid of his father. James Nathaniel Hughes was a forward-thinking businessman incensed by racism in the United States. He moved to Mexico to run a successful ranch shortly after Langston was born.

Upon graduating from high school in 1919, Langston traveled to Mexico to win a decisive argument with his father, which allowed him to attend (but then quickly drop out of) Columbia University. The confrontation was so intense, Hughes wrote about contemplating suicide immediately after.[16]

BLUES POETRY

Hughes began writing the poem "The Weary Blues" when he entered a stateside jazz club just before sailing for France in 1924. Being face to face with real-life jazz musicians in Europe expanded Langston's world, and he kept revising the poem because of these encounters while working in France. Scholar Tracy Sharpley-Whiting writes that Hughes was part of a thriving scene anchored by Black women, including Florence Embry and Ada "Bricktop" Smith, whom he met while washing dishes at Le Grand Duc in Montmartre.[17] Upon his return to New York, "The Weary Blues" won first place for poetry in the 1925 *Opportunity* magazine awards. Seeing jazz music elevated overseas culminated in verses that immediately linked the poet with a new movement.

The next day the *New York Times* reported that there was surely a "Negro Renaissance" happening.[18] Hughes became a leading figure of what is known as the Harlem Renaissance or the New Negro movement. Because his blues verses captured the burning energy and heartbeat of the city, Hughes became known as the Poet Laureate of Harlem. His work impressed leading publisher Blanche Knopf, with whom he signed a book contract in 1925.

At the age of twenty-four, Hughes was already famous.

Influenced by Black poet and writer Paul Lawrence Dunbar's use of dialect, Hughes was nonetheless quicker to name Walt Whitman and Carl Sandburg as personal influences for his approachable style. Whitman's flowing free verse and Sandburg's staunch defense of the working man left Hughes's verse simultaneously jagged edged and remarkably focused where one solitary idea often feels as much spoken as read.

Such an approach to poetry was Hughes's philosophical grounding, and his poems were often accompanied by stunning works of art by Aaron Douglas. Hughes expressed his approach succinctly with "The Negro Artist and the Racial Mountain" (1926), an essay regarded as the manifesto of the Harlem Renaissance. Though many other Black artists disagreed with him at the time, Hughes believed that predominantly white poetic forms, such as the sonnet, were ill-suited for creative Black expression. Many Black writers, such as Countee Cullen, tried to prove their legitimacy by assimilating white tastes; Hughes was among the first to assert that Black art should not embrace European standards: "We younger Negro artists who create now intend to express our individual dark-skinned selves without fear or shame. If white people are pleased, we are glad. If they are not, it doesn't matter. We know we are beautiful. And ugly too."[19]

Hughes would travel across the globe during his lifetime. He came to represent to the world what a Black writer looked like. His international advocacy as a spokesperson for writers took him to Paris on several occasions. He spent eleven months in the USSR in 1932–33, during which he shared extended time with Ernest Hemingway. He, too, risked injury by covering the Spanish Civil War in 1937 as a correspondent for the *Baltimore Afro-American*. Hughes was also the only figure of the Harlem Renaissance to travel to Africa. In 1922, he docked in more than thirty-two ports, starting in Dakar, Senegal. He joined the sailors in Lagos, Nigeria, when they went into the bordellos. He was also alone with at least one crewman onboard—throughout his life he would share intimacies with both men and women.

Nothing in his life up to then surprised him more than realizing that "the Africans looked at me and would not believe I was a Negro."[20] Citing his skin color and what he called his grandmother's Indian hair, Africans saw Hughes's light-skinned features as disqualifying. Though he was an experienced negotiator for a twenty-two-year-old, this colorism created sharp barriers. He was refused access to a drumming ceremony, informed by locals that the god being honored by the ritual would not "tolerate the presence of a white man."[21]

When, in 1931, the International Labor Defense, the legal arm of the Communist Party USA, came to the aid of nine African American teenagers wrongly accused of raping two white women in Scottsboro, Alabama, Hughes, like so many other Black people in Harlem, aligned himself as a fellow traveler or "pinko" among friends (and editors) deeply attached to the Communist Party. As Hughes would defiantly assert in "Freedom" (1943): "I do not need freedom when I'm dead / I cannot live on tomorrow's bread." Hughes was always an active political figure who "personally introduced [Ralph] Ellison to Richard Wright and the rest of the left" in 1936.[22] As a result, he was constantly labeled subversive and un-American, with the Federal Bureau of Investigation starting an extensive dossier on him in 1940. He was forced to testify before Joseph McCarthy in 1953. Despite his clear leanings, Hughes consistently and truthfully asserted that he had never been a member of the Communist Party.

HUGHES'S IMPACT ON BLACK CULTURE

Despite having his name on fifty-eight books, seventeen plays, five novels, two histories, and twenty-two years' worth of bylines for weekly newspaper columns, Hughes is still best known as the poet who documented the Black experience from the 1920s to the 1960s. He was most recognized for asking "What happens to a dream deferred?" in his poem "Dream Deferred" (first titled "Harlem" in 1951), and the poem's evocative first image became the title of Lorraine Hansberry's groundbreaking Broadway play *A Raisin in the Sun* (1959).

Martin Luther King Jr. would eventually invoke a half dozen of Hughes's poems in national speeches and sermons from the 1950s until his assassination. After Hughes penned a special poem at King's request, the reverend wrote Hughes, saying, "My admiration for your works is not only expressed in my personal conversations, but I can no longer count the number of times and places, all over the nation, in my addresses and sermons in which I have read your poems. I know of no better way to express in beauty the heartbeat and struggle of our people."[23]

His influence was larger than his modest five-foot-four-inch frame. Hansberry duly cited Hughes as a mentor, and he proclaimed proudly that he had been the first editor to publish a story by Alice Walker. He proved to be a major influence on poets Gwendolyn Brooks and Margaret Walker. Meeting Hughes at a young age, Brooks took what Hughes had done for Harlem and applied it to her Chicago neighborhood of Bronzeville. She listened to his feedback and advice on what would become her debut collection, *A Street in Bronzeville* (1945). Hughes celebrated Brooks's Pulitzer Prize in 1950 alongside her, attending the party at her home.

Memorizing Hughes's poems since the age of eleven, Margaret Walker recalled the impact of having her idol Langston Hughes visit her hometown of New Orleans in 1931. With Hughes's urging, Walker left the South to enroll at Northwestern University. She declared that the move to Chicago "made all the difference in my life."[24]

Hughes directly contributed to various arenas for Black performance beyond the realm of poetry. As his famous poem "Note on Commercial Theatre" (1940) suggests, Hughes founded three theaters across the country—the Harlem Suitcase Theater, the Negro Art Theatre in Los Angeles, and the Skyloft Players in Chicago—long before lamenting the fact that the Hollywood Bowl and Broadway took "my blues" and "mixed 'em up with symphonies" until "they don't sound like me." Equally important, Karamu House in Cleveland featured several of Hughes's plays. *Don't You Want to Be Free?* (1938), an assertive revolutionary call for equality, ran for a Harlem record of 135 consecutive performances starring Robert Earl Jones, a man whose son James would become the voice of CNN and Darth Vader. As its name suggests, the Harlem Suitcase Theatre was established during the Depression under the edict that everything needed for a performance could fit into a single piece of luggage. Hughes would also set a record of sorts when a bastardized version of his play

Mulatto: A Tragedy of the Deep South (1935), made more sensational in the hands of overaggressive producer Martin Jones, stood as the longest-running play on Broadway by a Black writer until 1959.

As a highly coveted mentor, advocate, and collaborator, Hughes developed lifelong stage friendships with Eartha Kitt, Ossie Davis, and Ruby Dee. Before anyone else recognized her acting potential, Hughes brought Claudia McNeil onto the stage in his *Simply Heavenly* (1957) before she starred as the quintessential "Mama" in *A Raisin in the Sun* (1959).

To his surprise, Hughes received a telegram from Elmer Rice in August 1945 inviting him to discuss something mysterious. When Hughes called the next day, Rice asked if Hughes was interested in the idea of reviving Rice's Pulitzer Prize–winning play *Street Scene* (1929) as a musical with the composer Kurt Weill. Having already been the first Black man to write for Hollywood in 1940, Hughes now accepted this invitation to work with two white writers, knowing that these circumstances were "so remarkable as to be virtually without parallel."[25] With twenty-four plays to his name, Rice was a top-tier dramatist. In charge of setting the poet's words to music, Kurt Weill wanted Hughes to write lyrics that "lift the everyday language of the people into a simple, unsophisticated poetry." Meeting Rice in Rockefeller Center, Hughes learned the catch: He was only being given the chance "to try out for the position as lyricist."[26] But by autumn, after submitting numerous samples, he had won the approval of both Rice and Weill.

The promise of a big payday seemed finally at hand for a writer simultaneously smitten with the stage and consistently rebuked that he once complained of wasting many hours "writing for the theatre and getting nowhere," so that he now preferred "literature between book covers."[27] At the Broadway opening of *Street Scene*, Kurt Weill felt as though he "were on [his] way to the scaffold."[28] After only a few scenes, his fears were greeted by applause. By the end of the show's run in 1947, Hughes's lyric "Moon Eyed, Starry Faced" was regarded as the signature song of the Broadway season.

THE LYRICIST

No year found Hughes trying to publish his own original songs more than 1949.[29] The first day of the New Year started with Hughes sending over lyrics for eleven songs to white cabaret singer Inga Andersen's hotel room at New York's Hotel Sheraton. An additional five songs he included were collaborations with Margaret Bonds, Hughes's friend and composer since they met in Chicago in 1936. Bonds wrote the music and sometimes coauthored the lyrics. Of the lyrics Hughes had written on his own, one stood out: He sent his sole manuscript copy of "Voo-Doo Man" to Andersen, only to have it returned to him in late August. Though Simone would heed his suggestion for a song about voodoo sixteen years later, in 1965, when she recorded "I Put a Spell on You," Andersen chose to return "Voo-Doo Man." She did keep a copy of "Little Old Letter," perhaps to have time to mull the tune over a bit more. Impatient for a response, Hughes fired off seven lyrics to the team of Lorenzo Fuller and Robbie Campbell. Once Andersen passed, Hughes sent another ten tunes to them two days later (four of them just rejected by Andersen). Andersen seemed unimpressed with songs already recorded by the likes of Duke Ellington and Kurt Weill.

Hughes was so invested in having his lyrics recorded that six months later, in August, he organized a personal portfolio of music into eight separate files that contained eighty-five of his original lyrics. A different set of eight tunes went out to Broadway singer Dorothea Freitag in October, with the poet trying to cross his blues poetry back over into its original medium with titles such as "Lulu Blues," "Grass Widow Blues," "Sorry Blues," "House Rent Blues," and "Do You Blues." The week before Thanksgiving, eighteen lyrics were handed to composer Albert Hague for arranging, and actor Dots Johnson received another nine tunes to choose from in March 1950.

Hughes's drive to hear his lyrics performed started organically when various musicians started recording several of his published poems. With Father of the Blues W. C. Handy composing music for his "Golden Brown Blues," and both Marian Anderson and Duke Ellington turning his ink into wax, Hughes immediately jumped at the possibilities.

Hughes's devotion to crafting song lyrics was intense. He studied three popular songs of the era by counting syllables, creating charts of rhymes, and adding measured dashes between words when typing out syncopations in delivery. His intricate study of Hoagy Carmichael's "Georgia on My Mind" resulted in typed lyrics with long dashes in "Geor—gia" to capture the elongated delivery. He noted in a typed summary that the song lyrics presented only "5 very clear and simple thoughts" with the "Title line repeated twice" noting the "end of last 8 bars the same as first eight bars." Focusing on the song "Blueberry Hill," Hughes noted the rhyme scheme, alternating syllabic lines of "4 / 5 / 5 / 4," then listed the alternating rhymes between "played" and "made" that are knitted together by "melody" and "be" in the bridge.[30]

Hughes's multiple-page study of "This Is Worth Fighting For" is truly mesmerizing, featuring typed tables and multiple colors. It was crafted with scientific precision. Hughes called this song a "Conventional 32 bar chorus" made of a "conventional 16 line lyric, divided into 4 four-line verses . . . with the title line repeated three times—at the end of the 1st, 2nd, and 4th verses." He seems to have been overly enamored with his discovery that the three verses where the title resurfaces have "exactly the same metrical and musical construction." Hughes hopelessly seemed to believe that the blueprint for a great song was merely to allow it to decompress and rise at the right speed, as one might engineer the design of a submarine.[31]

In spite of these ambitious (but misguided) formal studies, popular singers such as Burl Ives were indeed playing Hughes's song "Red Sun Blues" in both the studio and during his set at New York's Persian Room in 1949. As a result, a few years later, comedian Jackie "Moms" Mobley received ten songs to choose from, and multitalented Eartha Kitt perused a list of fourteen lyrics (seventeen years before she featured in her memorable turn as Catwoman in the TV series *Batman* in 1966). The practice of gladly recommending songs for other stage talents never ceased for Hughes, who sent eight verses off to actor Ossie Davis when the actor began planning a celebration for Martin Luther King Jr. in November 1960.

Six short months after his appearance in Winston-Salem for Negro History Week in 1949, Hughes asked the question that cemented his presence in the literary canon: "What happens to dream deferred?" As he was wondering if it would "dry up like a raisin in the sun, / or fester like a sore / and then run," Hughes did not know that his next book of poems would be his most famous collection. *Montage of a Dream Deferred*, a work he referenced that day in North Carolina as "a long book of poems about Harlem," was in fact becoming an extension of what happens when someone buys that one-way ticket from the South and finally faces the reality of living in Northern cities such as Harlem.[32]

By 1961, forty-five of Hughes's lyrics would be recorded by more than a dozen musical artists—including all the lyrics for Randy Weston's experimental Afro-spiritual album *Uhuru Afrika* (1961) and Abbey Lincoln's cover version of a song from that album entitled "African Lady." Nothing, however, brought him into contact with a talent equal to the pianist with whom he would soon share an auditorium in Asheville, North Carolina.

2

The Prodigy

The type of Sunday that found Langston Hughes appearing in Winston-Salem, North Carolina, in 1949 typically meant something significant for Mary Burnette. The eldest of three children, Mary had settled with her family in Black Mountain, North Carolina, after living in both Ohio and California. On Saturdays, she slept overnight at Allen High School, in nearby Asheville, to wake early enough to make the bus trips for the school's glee club events. For big occasions such as this Sunday, she often wore an elegant necklace to complement the flowing waves in her straightened hair. Throughout the winter of this, her senior year, she roomed with junior class president Eunice Waymon. Thinking of those Sunday excursions, Burnette recalled the exemplary piano player as a "marvelous talent that had exceled every piano teacher she had ever had." Once when sixteen-year-old Eunice was asked to produce an A-flat for her music teacher, "she gave her the sound [in her voice] without even touching the piano. She had perfect pitch."[1]

During the week, Mary's mornings were passed on the thirty-minute bus ride in from Black Mountain while Eunice, a boarder at the school, woke at 5:30 a.m. to practice piano in a private room. It was little wonder that many of her classmates were "a little jealous of her because of her talent. But they couldn't touch her: If they'd have practiced all night and all day, they couldn't touch Eunice. She was just a tremendously gifted person." At glee club events, Mary and her classmates sang while Eunice played: "We were inspired by her confidence and flawless performance at the piano. I assure you I was watching the pianist more closely than our director. . . . I watched Eunice so closely. I seem to remember her looking at us, her face expressionless, as a signal to say, 'Ok, get ready!'" How good was she? Mary asserted, "I believe she could have played 'Moonlight Sonata' blindfolded."

One Sunday visit to a little country church was particularly memorable. Eunice was always given time during the performance to demonstrate her prowess, and she found ways to showcase her skills while playing her piano solo. With her short, straightened hair, curled at the edges and covering her ears, Eunice was so trained for action that, even at rest in photographs, her fingertips pointed slightly up, ready to be pressed down on ivory keys. That afternoon, when she was playing a piece by J. S. Bach, her classmates all noticed that the church floor beneath the upright piano was uneven and warped. The singers could not turn away from her unrestrained approach to the keys as the piano rocked away and then back as if it were a boat floating in deep waters. The church hostess, observing with an even keener eye than her peers to note how her congregation was receiving such a demonstration, told the rest of the singers, "That girl's a-gonna turn that piano over on herself."

ASHEVILLE

Eunice Waymon sat in the Allen High School auditorium knowing that she had been given the honor of introducing guest poet and lecturer Langston Hughes. This moment was the culmination of the work she and her fellow members of the National Association for the Advancement of Colored People (NAACP) had put into organizing the event where Hughes would read his "Poems of Negro Life." As junior class president, NAACP chapter treasurer, and president of the drama club, sixteen-year-old Eunice was the obvious choice to take center stage, Burnette recalled.

Eunice was born and raised fifty-four miles away in tiny Tryon, North Carolina, where her mother, Kate, was a minister whose Baptist church was so close to the family's home that young Eunice walked the two blocks to play on Sundays as early as the age of six. Sneaking turns at more popular music whenever it was just her father J. D. at home, the sixth of the eight Waymon children was not enamored of either gospel or boogie-woogie; instead, her lifelong unwavering passion for composers such as Bach indicated her earnest intent to become a classical concert pianist.

One of the defining moments in young Eunice's life occurred when her instructor Muriel Mazzanovich arranged a public recital for her star student. Entering the Lanier Library in Tryon in 1944, Kate and J. D. Waymon were seated in the front row. Just as eleven-year-old Eunice took the stage to begin playing classical standards, however, her parents were relocated to the back of the library, moved to maintain racial norms. According to Kate, Eunice wanted her parents close enough to see her truly dynamic hands in action. Eunice announced to the entire audience that if her parents could not sit "where they can see my hands, I will not play. You can kick me, beat me, anything you want, I will not play."[2] With her parents returned to their original seats, Eunice began her program.

Her time at Allen would lead to an eight-week summer stint at the Juilliard School in July 1950 and to a formal audition in Philadelphia at the Curtis Institute of Music in April 1951. Half of Allen High School's instructors, all women, were white. And the students, numbering approximately 150 girls from grades nine through twelve, were all Black. Founded in 1889, the school was overseen by the women's division of the Board of Missions of the Methodist Church. Eunice boarded at the main dormitory, spending off-weekends visiting with her serious boyfriend, Edney Whiteside. Chaperoned constantly, the very compliant Eunice and her hometown sweetheart—sharing a soda with separate straws on their dates—had future plans for marriage.[3]

As Eunice surveyed the students from the auditorium stage at Allen, her focus likely strayed far from the absent Edney, who couldn't attend the all-girls school. She was about to meet her first example of Black artistic success. If she sought to calm herself before her introduction of Hughes, she could have called upon the same deep breaths required before playing fugues and sonatas. She had advanced so far beyond her school music teacher that she was supplementing her studies with two private instructors in Asheville, one of whom had studied formally in Europe. And she had clear ambitions to be somebody in this world, somebody as famous as the poet now sharing the stage.

While there isn't any concrete evidence documenting exactly what Eunice did or did not perform either that afternoon at 1:30 p.m. or that evening for outside guests at 8:30 p.m., a poem Hughes wrote in response to his visit clearly demonstrates that he heard Eunice play. It would have been natural for the school to showcase one of its star pupils to the community, given that Eunice was living on campus in the dorms with no home to return to for the evening. Furthermore, an unmistakable pattern emerges from the week: Every institution that hosted Hughes included music on the program along with his poetry. On the two days just before his time in Asheville, fourteen-year-old Fannie Lou Tomlin performed "Boy Like You" and W. M. Warren sang Hughes's poem "The

Negro Speaks of Rivers" in Winston-Salem, and Hughes remembered Delores Fullman as a "Negro Girl Singer from Chicago" from his stop at Black Mountain College.[4] Hughes himself expected music to be on the program in Asheville, having sent three of his own songs and suavely alerted the school: "There may be music both before and after my portion of the program if you so desire."[5]

Though Hughes kept meticulous notes documenting his appearances, it appears that the three consecutive events (and back-to-back red-eye train trips?) prevented him from recording any personal notes about his Tuesday in Asheville. This omission was remarkably rare. In fact, of the six appearances Hughes made that week in 1949, only his day in Asheville went undocumented by either an entry on his part or a substantive newspaper report chronicling any of his events. Instead, he did something better: He put all his energies into writing a poem about the young prodigy he encountered. Yes, even at sixteen years old, Eunice Waymon made an indelible impression on Langston Hughes.

Unlike at the school, anticipation in town had not been building all week. On Friday, February 4, a tiny notice in the *Asheville Citizen-Times* announcing Hughes's visit was buried on page 3.[6] Published for the newspaper's mostly white readers, Sunday's three sentences trumpeted an announcement from librarian Irene Hendrick that the "Asheville Colored Library will have special exhibits and displays of books by Negro authors" with a specific section "arranged of the books of Langston Hughes."[7] After speaking in Winston-Salem on Sunday and at Black Mountain College on Monday, on Tuesday Hughes was driven into Asheville by Barbara Drier for his three speaking events there. He would finish his week of engagements by speaking in Wilson, North Carolina, and in Washington, DC, before headlining a three-day celebration in Boston, where he would be the keynote speaker at the year's largest Negro History Week celebration in America. Such was the popularity and prestige of Langston Hughes in 1949.

Contrasting sharply with his reception in every other city he visited this week, no reporter was sent to cover any of Hughes's three events in Asheville, surprising given that admission to Hughes's night event (also in the Allen High School auditorium) required a five-dollar entry fee, roughly sixty dollars today, with all proceeds benefiting the "Colored Library."[8] Though Hughes spoke to Allen students at 1:30 p.m., the general public at 8:30 pm, and even in between at Asheville's Capital Press Club, where the guests included members of the International Fur and Leather Workers Union local chapter (meeting at their union hall), the town press was much more interested to share the news that local author Thomas Wolfe's home had just been officially acquired for preservation.[9]

Of all the locations Hughes was invited to speak during Negro History Week in 1949, Allen High School may have been the most surprising. The progressive school was governed by funds from the Methodist Church and deliberately featured a racially integrated staff. After Hughes's assistant Nate White reached out to the school by form letter, it was agreed that Hughes would give two performances at the school. His fee was $150.[10] School superintendent Claire Lennon wanted both her students and the general public to attend, and she knew that the "auditorium will not be large enough to accommodate all these at one time."[11] While Hughes was invited to stay on Allen's campus at one of the "guest rooms," he in fact ended up spending the night at the Lennons' home. As for the anticipation of Hughes's appearance, Hughes learned from Lennon that "our girls are very much excited."[12] Eunice's roommate Mary Burnette recalled that "Allen could acknowledge 'Negro History Week.' We were studying Negro History, and our text was written by Carter G. Woodson. This is weird because here in this thoroughly segregated city, where Black schools themselves are not mentioning Negro History, and are not teaching Negro History, this school, Allen can do it, openly. It was not mentioned at any of the integrated schools I went to [earlier] in California or Ohio, but this little school of Allen can do it openly . . . even in Black Mountain, NC, the teachers were very cautious." Allen High School's choice to celebrate Negro History Week made the institution unique.

Hughes stepped to the podium surrounded not only by Allen students, "a lively group of girls," and their all-female faculty, but also students from neighboring Black schools.[13] Hughes recalled "having been to almost every other large city in North Carolina," but this was his first and only appearance in Asheville.[14] Choosing spontaneity because he did not wish to "fall into a rut," Hughes did not present "a set routine of poems" but rather found a way to "weave them into my talk."[15] Hughes presented one of his most iconic poems, "The Negro Speaks of Rivers." It begins by asserting how a connection to the famous rivers of the world builds unity with one's race:

> I've known rivers:
> I've known rivers ancient as the world and older than the flow
>   of human blood in human veins.
> My soul has grown deep like the rivers.

Crossing time till the Euphrates, Congo, Nile, and Mississippi have each been surrealistically traveled by the voice of an "I" that is quietly becoming collective, the poem ends by once again reasserting, "My soul has grown deep like the rivers." For Hughes, "soul" would come to epitomize something far less

Fig 2.1. This senior class photo from Allen High School in Asheville, North Carolina, in 1949, shows the graduating class of those one year older than Eunice Waymon. As her signature indicates, Mary Burnette is in the front row, center. (Photo courtesy of Mary Burnette.)

spiritual and more complex. As esteemed scholar of both Hughes and music Tony Bolden has explained, "Decades before recordings of modern jazz and rhythm and blues popularized the concept of soul in the 1950s and 1960s, respectively, Hughes's contemporaries regarded him as an exemplar."[16]

Eunice, seated onstage rather than in the audience throughout the reading, observed how Hughes performed by substituting a podium for a piano. She may have struggled to believe that a man so short could arrive with such stature. Moreover, his singsong voice and ability to sprinkle in an occasional throat-giggle must have made the poet feel closer rather than distant. He was so unlike her idol, Hazel Scott, whose pictures hung on her dorm room wall. The famous Black pianist, who played everything from classical to boogie-woogie, parlayed her good looks and charisma into a career in film and onstage that earned her a salary equivalent to a million dollars a year today.

This very year, Hazel Scott would demonstrate that she had more in common with the politically inclined Hughes than might be imagined. She drew unwanted attention. In fact, when she and a companion were refused service in a restaurant in Pasco, Washington, in 1949, Scott brought suit and inspired civil rights organizations to successfully pressure the state of Washington to pass legislation outlawing discrimination in public accommodations.[17]

In listening to the music of Scott, and now greeting and hearing Hughes, Eunice was introduced to the idea that there were many ways to become famous. As a young Black woman, she was now learning this from her personal encounter with the first-ever successful Black artist she had ever introduced. Mary Burnette remembers watching Hughes from the front row of the auditorium: "When Langston Hughes was reading, it was customary for the reader to downplay any emotion. He's just reading and not putting any emotion into his reading. It was impressive to see someone of his caliber. I was impressed with his reading." Even without visible emotion, Hughes's language during this single appearance had a remarkable effect on Burnette. In fact, she later earned an MA in literature, for which she formally studied Hughes's poetry: "When I started to study English, I wanted to read all of Langston Hughes, I was particularly fascinated with his use of dialect." When Burnette's Black friends asked her why she loved poetry, she read aloud to them from the works of Langston Hughes.

BACH'S FUGUE IN C MAJOR: "LOVE ME OR LEAVE ME"

In performing at the school or evening events, Eunice, later taking the name Nina Simone once she began making music professionally, might have opened with any number of selections of J. S. Bach, her favorite composer. Simone's "Love Me or Leave Me" reveals her intellectual and physical approach to the classical music she was playing when she was known to all as Eunice. Recorded in 1957 and then released on her first album in 1959, this tune uses rhythmic lyrics as a frame around the center of a song that, unbeknownst to many owners of the vinyl, actually features a long passage from Bach's Fugue in C Major.[18] Simone performed the song in one of the most visible moments of her career when she appeared on *The Ed Sullivan Show* on September 11, 1960. Appearing on national television for the first time, fifty-two seconds into the tune, Simone coyly swerves off immediately into Bach's fugue, which she'd practiced since childhood.

For viewers, the foot-tapping, finger-snapping opening suddenly becomes a proper frolic as her right hand hits with the precision of a light mallet on the vibes. By the end of the song, the lyric "There's no love for anyone else" is extended and drawn out as the fugue resurges across the keys. One wonders if Simone was instead summoning thoughts of Bach himself when she played this tune rather than the lover seemingly addressed in the lyrics.

In Simone's mind, the connection between bop and Bach was more obvious than one might think. Speaking of Bach's music, she said:

> His form is like the blues, and it demands tremendous technique. Bach's music is structured like a good piece of architecture. And so are the blues. You can invert a section of Bach's music four times, five times, and each way it's perfect. It's like saying four times three are twelve and three times four are twelve and twelve divided by three is four. Well, you can do the same with the blues. Use the same notes, triple them and you have one feeling, change the lyrics and you have another if you like. Invert them and you have something else, but it's always the same.[19]

One of Nina's immense contributions includes bringing the works of classical composers into popular music, where everyday folks could access it. By eventually moving away from the traditional contexts for classical music, she inadvertently avoided a life of racial assimilation to instead infuse social justice into pop music. The role of voice in this move became essential: It moved Nina beyond the importance of representation to elevate her to the role of spokeswoman. It turned the early dream she had into a direction, not a destiny. Becoming a classical concert pianist would become an important part of a journey to uncover her full aptitude.

Though she was not yet aware of it, young Eunice Waymon would pursue a second dream: to create the soundtrack of the civil rights movement and become the world-famous Nina Simone.

During her high school years, the young phenom was always on public display. The previous March, in 1948, she had been paraded out to play Bach's French Suite in E-flat, Beethoven's Sonata in F Minor, three pieces by Frédéric Chopin, and two more challenging arrangements by Claude Debussy. During the encore, Eunice sat with her back to the piano as her teacher struck a single note, which Eunice then named by ear.

It is hard not to imagine Eunice performing at least one of the above solos as a fine prelude to the evening program featuring Langston Hughes. It would showcase the most accomplished of Allen's students to the community. Added to this repertoire could be any of the songs she played for the thirty-two-member-strong glee club that routinely spent Sundays at nearby churches and Asheville's Veterans Hospital. That catalog featured Eunice incanting the first movement of Beethoven's *Moonlight Sonata* while her classmates sang "Come to Me All Who Are Weary." This rendition featured a versified passage from Matthew 11:28–30 being played over the sonata so that audiences both felt and heard the line "You will find rest for your soul." In so elegantly grafting African American virtuosity with classical music, Mary Burnette would realize many years later, "our Glee Club was a living form of protest."[20]

If this was a bit too spiritual for the setting, a folk song used by the glee club such as "My Little Lindy Lou" (first crooned solemnly by Leadbelly before being shaped for the mainstream the year before, in 1948, by Paul Robeson) might have proved light and festive. However, no tune is more tantalizing to the imagination than the thought of Eunice playing the glee club standard "Mighty Lak' a Rose" solo. This song was so ingrained in young Waymon that she even included it (much as she might have sung it in 1949) as part of a medley of two lullabies released in 1964 under the title "You Can Sing a Rainbow."

As Hughes's two events in Asheville ended, Eunice received at least two critical life lessons: (1) There were multiple ways to be famous and Black, but (2) it was dangerous for any person to appear to be anti-American. She learned these two lessons firsthand from sharing a stage with the first successful Black artist she had ever met. The opportunity provided Eunice Waymon a rare glimpse of the real challenges to becoming a "somebody" in America.

THE ASHEVILLE CONTROVERSY

Hughes had no way of knowing, when he appeared in Boston five days later, that a controversy surrounding his appearance was now percolating back in Asheville. Representing the view of many similar local citizens like herself, Anne Hunter Jenkins had written a query published in the highly visible Sunday opinion section of the *Asheville Citizen-Times* that rightly wondered why no news outlet in the region had covered any of Hughes's three local appearances. "His talk, interspersed with readings of his poems," she wrote, "was so simple and unbiased, and yet so powerful, that if it could have been heard or even read about by enough people, it would advance 100 percent the cause of intra-national tolerance and understanding. There was no report." She ended with a flourish of biting questions: "I ask you the editor, why do . . . our only source[s] of local news fail so frequently to report adequately happenings which are obviously of interest and importance, not only to the majority of Asheville readers, but to all the people of Western North Carolina?"[21]

It is startling to realize that while Boston and Washington, DC, news outlets featured Hughes's appearances widely in large mainstream presses, stolid Asheville apparently had too many other happenings to concern itself with his readings.

While any reader might quickly suspect race as a factor—and that is the unsurprising reason why Hughes was originally overlooked—racial bias and the overwhelmingly white subscription base of the town's three newspapers only begin to answer the question. Pricked the following Sunday, another citizen, Halsey B. Leavitt, offered this take: "Your failure to report the meeting, in my opinion, was commendable if you did so because you know the record of the man invited to speak. . . . Hughes is publicized as a poet, but let me give you here a part of one of his poems for which he is most highly praised by the Communists." If spoken, several of its phrases might have been accompanied by air quotes.

After including no less than ten lines from Hughes's incendiary poem "Goodbye Christ," which FBI director J. Edgar Hoover himself had been distributing widely since 1947 to justify his probe into radicals such as Hughes, the lancing ends, "This man Langston Hughes is a member of many Communist front organizations." The writer's final question is perfunctorily rhetorical: "Is this the type of man to be invited to address any pupils of any American school let alone one that is supported by a church?"[22]

It is clear that by February 27 the entire region was burning with demands for more information about the accused Communist poet. Of the four (yes, four) published comments in the local paper's opinion section, the first was by none other than Allen High School principal Julia Titus, who calmly assured the community that her thriving institution, richly funded by God-fearing people, had no truck with reds. Readers found a defiant stance: "Anyone who did not hear Mr. Hughes is not in a position to criticism him. Had he heard either program he would have heard nothing that can be construed to be anything but good, sound, American patriotism."[23] The reason for this truth was that Hughes himself made the majority of his salary from such lectures, not royalties, and he could not afford to be anything but cordial and conservative when he spoke as a guest at such institutions.

Next, the editors themselves responded to the controversy directly by leaning hard into the possibility that such political fears were more than warranted. Citing Tuskegee Institute's 1947 *Negro Year Book*, they suggested that Hughes had at the very least been a Communist until perhaps renouncing his membership as recently as August 7, 1944. To keep the possibility of his affiliation with the Left more open than closed, they ended with what they wanted to be read as a level interjection of the facts: "All this is not conclusive evidence, but it has some bearing on the question."[24] The very misleading interanimating subjectivity of this phrasing simultaneously panders to all of the intensely interested readers: Either Hughes did in fact formally leave the party or he may have still been a member. That he never held party membership at all is not mentioned.

Still unsatisfied, Anne Jenkins wrote in again and "amplified" the original penetrating cross-examination that sparked this entire fury when it began three weeks earlier. The editors began directly addressing her three questions by feigning her jabs: "No newspaper can report every interesting program or event, even briefly." By the second question, the tone had shifted to the telling moods of sarcasm (and sexism?): "Is this present question to be understood as naiveté, or as a right-handed punch?"[25] Most indicting, in their third response, they publicly apologized for not covering Ruth Bryan Owen Rhodes's talk about the United Nations held at All Souls Church but made no such concession whatsoever for ignoring the internationally known Black poet.

The controversy was a continued topic of discussion at Allen High School. On February 24, Superintendent Claire Lennon reached out to Hughes directly to see if he could be of help. She sent him the newspaper clipping of principal Titus's published response and asserted that this was affecting the entire student body: "Our girls think you have been done a gross injustice, and they too are terribly sorry and ashamed."[26] She asked if he would be "willing to write a statement to the paper confirming the statement that we have already made that you are not a Communist."[27] She followed up by assuring Hughes in another letter of both his impact and her support. A copy of his newest anthology, *Poetry of the Negro,* had now been purchased from a local bookstore and was being used at Allen. Moreover, Lennon assured Hughes, he had a "standing invitation to our guest room whenever you are in town."[28]

Unbelievably, this debate traveled all the way to Harlem with Hughes himself writing to the *Asheville Citizen-Times* to defend both himself and Allen High School. On April 3, 1949, readers of the paper could turn to the Public Forum section on page 5 to find in boldface type: "Langston Hughes Answers Critics." Addressing Leavitt directly, Hughes assured readers that he had never advocated for "subversive movements" in any of his lectures spanning the nation, from, as Woody Guthrie fashioned, "Columbia University in New York to the University of California at Berkeley." Hughes also reminded readers that he was not the "I" in poems about the KKK or Negro mothers.[29] Lennon was relieved. "We haven't heard one peep from anyone since your letter was published," she later wrote.[30]

Beyond Allen High School's direct appeal, something else accounts for Hughes taking such an active role in what appears to merely be a distant local debate about one of his Negro History Week readings. On April 4, 1949, *Life* ran a four-page article incriminating people who it declared were "intimately aligned with the communist movement."[31] In photos resembling mug shots, Hughes was pictured alongside Albert Einstein, Aaron Copland, Leonard Bernstein, and Arthur Miller exactly one publication day after the *Asheville Citizen-Times* ran his response. With so much now at stake regarding his future lecture opportunities, Hughes wisely engaged in some necessary triage.

Eschewing vagary and shadowboxing, Hughes ended his response directly so there would be no mistaking his position: "I am not now and I have never been a member of the Communist Party."[32]

While Hughes's statement is literally true, his alignment with the Left is of course far more complex. In fact, two days before his visit to Asheville, Hughes had published a scathing edict on February 5 warning against what was to come in the wake of the trials that had started on January 17 against twelve Communist leaders. Hughes often wrote political attacks that he would never speak in auditoriums. He began by asserting a novel connection that is now worn out, suggesting that this trial of US citizens was just the start of something "very serious to us Negroes because it is exactly what happened in Germany. . . . At the moment in America they only burn fiery crosses on Negro lawns in Virginia, make us ride the back seats of busses in Mississippi and Alabama, lynch us in Georgia, and Jim Crow us in jobs in New York in spite of the nice law we have. . . . In a little while they will send Negros to jail simply for being Negroes and to concentration camps just for being colored."[33] Hughes's stance ran completely counter to mainstream coverage of a prosecution that had rounded up people who had served as both personal friends and editors at radical publications where he published. Nonetheless, it foreshadowed a climax that would force Hughes himself to testify on television and radio before Senator Joe McCarthy.

Faring far worse than Hughes, Eunice Waymon's heroine Hazel Scott would lose her immense annual salary and TV show in the wake of her appearance before the House Un-American Activities Committee in September 1950. She was forced to leave for Paris to star in French films during the prime years of her career. If Eunice was paying attention, she would have noted that protesting against one's country in any form could summarily be a double challenge, tainting red someone who was already Black.

To a very real degree, Eunice was learning something by following the trajectory of her music idol and even overhearing the repeated red rumors surrounding Hughes: Political statements were doubly dangerous for a Black artist. After weeks of following daily controversy about the poet at her own school, Eunice knew that Langston Hughes had paid a dear price for being subversive. In no uncertain terms, she was old enough to realize that anticipatory obedience would have to be factored into her future decisions about either remaining quietly conservative or fully accepting the challenging role of being politically outspoken. Her political education had begun.

What effect did Eunice Waymon have on the poet? Having just met the sixteen-year-old who played an upright piano, idolized Hazel Scott, and would go on to record "Little Girl Blue" on her first album, Hughes paid Eunice the best honor he could: He wrote her into a poem. Hughes used a school setting

TO BE SOMEBODY

by

Langston Hughes

Little girl
Dreaming of a baby grand piano
(Not knowing there's a Steinway bigger, bigger)
Dreaming of the baby grand to play
That stretches paddle-tailed across the floor,
Not standing upright
Like a bad boy in the corner,
That sends its music
Up the stairs and down the stairs
And out the door
To confound even Hazel Scott/Who might be passing!
Oh!

Fig 2.2. Langston Hughes's draft of the poem "To Be Somebody," published in 1950. (James Weldon Johnson Memorial Collection in the Yale Collection of American Literature, Beinecke Rare Book and Manuscript Library, Yale University.)

to note the ambitious dreams of a young girl who fits Eunice Waymon to a T in his poem "To Be Somebody."

The idea of being "somebody" was often invoked in speeches by Martin Luther King Jr. and, later, by Rev. Jesse Jackson. The idea was used to implore Black Americans to take pride and honor in their worth. However, the concept of "somebodyness" dates even earlier, to a poem written by another pastor, Rev. William Holmes Borders, in 1943. Borders often included his poem in sermons delivered at his Greater Wheat Street Baptist Church in Atlanta. Martin Luther King recited the poem as an elementary student the way many white children are often asked to deliver the Pledge of Allegiance.[34] The poem was so well received that it was published in the *Pittsburgh Courier* with the headline that it was destined to "Become a Classic in American History and Literature."[35]

The long prose poem by Borders begins each of its seven sections with the words "I AM SOMEBODY—" in capital letters and repeats the phrase in every line that lists the occupations and name of famous Black Americans. Hughes knew the poem because it began with his name and profession: "I AM SOMEBODY— / I am a poet in Langston Hughes." Given this larger context, Hughes's poem "To Be Somebody" is neatly predicting that young Eunice will someday join a list of accomplished Black artists and intellectuals who followed his own example. Hughes was right. In the years to come, millions of people who listened to Nina Simone realized the truth that is silently prophesized in Hughes's deft poem: "I AM SOMEBODY / I am a pianist and singer in Nina Simone."

Hughes published his poem about becoming "somebody" shortly after encountering Eunice. This fact tempts us to wonder further about exactly what words, glances, or even advice the two might have exchanged during their first encounter in February 1949. Sadly, those all seem lost to history. But there is a litany of other things we do know. Hughes seems to have instinctually sensed that Eunice was indeed going "to be somebody." That "somebody" would soon don another name. Hughes would never meet Eunice again: The next time they met, he would encounter "The Amazing Nina Simone." It would happen eleven years later—not in North Carolina but at the Newport Jazz Festival.

3

Riot at the Newport Jazz Festival

DAY 1

It was opening night of the 1960 Newport Jazz Festival, and most acts on the program had played to large crowds before. Musicians often felt baptized here in the intense lights pouring back from a night-dark crowd and the occasional feedback ringing because of the stage's multiple microphones. Over the years, this stage had welcomed every jazz legend—including Dizzy Gillespie, Ella Fitzgerald, Count Basie, Duke Ellington, Charles Mingus, Miles Davis, Thelonious Monk, and the world's most recognized jazz figure, Louis Armstrong. Even Billie Holiday, Mahalia Jackson, Ray Charles, and Chuck Berry entertained capacity audiences of thirteen thousand in Freebody Park.

Fig 3.1. Langston Hughes's personal desk calendar denoting his role as narrator of the blues session at the 1960 Newport Jazz Festival and time spent afterward in Rhode Island. (James Weldon Johnson Memorial Collection in the Yale Collection of American Literature, Beinecke Rare Book and Manuscript Library, Yale University.)

Shortly after 10 p.m. on June 30, a twenty-seven-year-old woman was seated on a stool behind a microphone stand that had been lowered to catch her voice. After arranging an all-white dress hanging to ankle length, she suddenly stood up said, "Where's my tambourine? Can't forget my tambourine, boy." A large silver headpiece at the top of her forehead held loose-curled hair in place—it was no longer straightened.

With her knees slightly bent, she quickly returned to the stool with her instrument in hand. She faced the audience: "This is a folk tune, and it's called 'Little Liza Jane.' We'll get some rhythm started here and see what happens." The initial rhythm issued from her bare hands as she started with one quick clap followed immediately by a finger snap. Bassist Chris White was standing behind his upright with a music stand in front of him, and drummer Bobby Hamilton was playing his kit with round felt tips. Once the two men found a tempo she liked, she glanced over her left shoulder toward guitarist Al Schackman and he confidently leapt into her song. The night was jet black, and Nina Simone looked out at the faces of her audience.

Striking the tambourine with her left hand, Nina brought immediate energy to her performance. A long series of claps followed by a finger snap, then Nina smiled with eyes closed while feeling the beat. She addressed the band in an aside: "Come on now, fellas." Just before the second chorus she dramatically pointed straight to the ground and belted, "I will take good care of thee." But no one in the crowd clapped to her rhythm. Sensing that she wasn't getting the response she'd anticipated, after a minute and a half, Nina declared, "I think they're shy." After another minute, the volume increased and she shouted, "Let's get 'em now!" When the concert recording was released a few months later, in August, these pleas were edited out. With the tambourine beating against her right hip, Nina's intensity was powerful even though, unfamiliar with such bright spotlights, she played much of her set with her eyes pressed closed.

After raising her left arm to signal the song's end, she sang a cappella briefly to serenade the crowd, floating Liza's name gently into the breeze above their heads. Behind this absolute musical silence, Al Schackman accidentally released a clenched left hand and unintentionally produced an open E note from the top string of his guitar. Nina glared at him for a full second before finishing. Twin arpeggios would soon be carefully overdubbed in the studio, the second extending the accidental open E that could not be erased. Nina's dramatic a cappella moment was forever smoothed over.

One man who did not need to wait for the release of the album *Nina Simone at Newport* was poet Langston Hughes. He was arriving at the very height of his popularity. Not only had he spent another ten days on a reading tour traveling exclusively through North Carolina from April 4 to April 14, but he had also just received the NAACP's highest honor. The day before the festival started, Hughes was awarded the Spingarn Medal, an award bestowed previously on such icons as Jackie Robinson and Martin Luther King Jr. The next day, as a board member of the Newport Jazz Festival since 1958, he welcomed three new members: Newport mayor Jim Maher, Al Grossman, and George Avakian. Avakian was a music executive with Columbia Records. In a few years, Grossman would be managing the as-yet-unrecorded Bob Dylan.

Given his deep love of Black music, Hughes's commitment as a board member was sincere, and he took his role seriously. In fact, after meeting as a group in Boston on August 20, 1959, Hughes and the board convened again in Newport on December 15, and on May 4, 1960, he met one-on-one in New York with board president and founder of the festival George Wein.[1] As a board member, Hughes had been intimately involved in setting this year's lineup of stars, and his endorsement of Simone was critical. In fact, on August 21, 1959, Hughes brainstormed an early list of fourteen acts who might appear. His handwritten list included Lionel Hampton and Quincy Jones.[2] In the end, Nina Simone was the only one of his selections to perform at Newport.

Simone and Hughes had been formally introduced in the spring of 1959 at the Village Gate in Greenwich Village by owner Art D'Lugoff. Nonetheless, the Newport Jazz Festival of 1960 was the first time they enjoyed an extended meeting.[3] They talked at length and in depth during the weekend. Hazel Scott's name likely came up. Simone's favorite performer during her high school years was meeting with Hughes regularly these days: She was back from Paris to headline his Broadway play *Tambourines to Glory*, then in rehearsal. Hughes's visit to Simone's high school in 1949 was undoubtedly a critical topic to establish a connection. During their conversation, the two discussed that "Nina Simone" was not her real name.

Once "Little Liza Jane" ended with Schackman's confidence-shaking miscue, what might Hughes have noted about the rest of Nina Simone's forty-minute performance? Nina had just survived the bright intensity of the spotlight shining directly in her eyes. Now she was facing the second issue that so often accompanied the challenges of playing Newport. Long before large amplification setups were the norm at outdoor venues, the technical crew always faced an immense challenge. They not only had to amplify a wide variety of acts with little to no transition time; they also had to mic a wide stage that was often full of an unusually large number of instruments. Just over a minute into her next song, "You'd Be So Nice to Come Home To," feedback started to swell after Chris White added the low register from his standup bass. For the next twelve seconds—a length of time that can feel like an eternity to any performer—Nina had to ignore this loud distraction as she slowly introduced the musical motif of Cole Porter's song.

Unlike her glare at Al, or her own absentmindedness in forgetting her tambourine, this time Nina found herself in her true comfort zone. She was seated at the piano, a place she knew better than any other in the world. Nina did not hesitate or get rattled as she continued playing—perhaps nothing would have moved her fingers off the keys. The rest of the band must have locked into this feeling as the tune climbed toward what sounds like an infinite apex. Using Porter's bossa nova beat as a point of departure, Simone's performance shows both the complexity of her mind and the exactitude of her hands. With Nina going back and forth with Schackman's lead notes, the crescendo begins as the first words of the song appear, a full three minutes and twenty-four seconds into what seemed to be merely a jazz instrumental. Hughes, who knew music well, must have been struck by Simone's unflappable demeanor in ignoring that ear-piercing sound. Furthermore, he likely concurred with the later assessment of Miles Davis, who marveled at her ability to in effect transmit voice, harmony, and melody and to "keep all those motifs going at once."[4]

Nina's next tune coalesced with Hughes's own African sensibilities. No one is quite sure where or how Nina arrived at the song "Flo Me La," words she repeats throughout the entire song—rooted in African pack bearers' chants, it means "to walk" or "walking along." Given Hughes's love of spontaneity and exoticism, the song would have piqued his interest. Nina's left hand rolls over the lowest bass section of the keyboard as drummer Bobby Hamilton sets a tempo that would have left the audience wondering if African dancers were about to appear from the wings dressed in native garb. Al himself set down his guitar to strike the claves, adding to the primitive feel of a song that widened the variety of Nina's repertoire and range.

Despite its title, "Nina's Blues" is a cool jazz instrumental perfect for any club. In a traditional jazz move, the entire ensemble takes a quiet turn, with White even running a bow across his bass four minutes into this six-minute tune. Nina's rolling right hand deftly takes the song home with style and verve.

Nina ended her forty-minute set with "In the Evening by the Moonlight." If audience reaction is any indication, Hughes likely also assumed that the references to fiddle playing and cornbread were autobiographical. Songs such as this would also eventually lead him to reference the "folk quality" of her music as one of the traits where she was most suited. Firmly settled and in command, fifty seconds in Simone laughs playfully in reaction to an unidentified audience comment. Nina ended by extending a full and drawn-out "moonLIGHT" so loud that more than one microphone onstage suddenly projected the final syllable in stereo. Nina's set was a success. Music critic Bradford F. Swan called her "the festival's first pleasant surprise," and of all the opening night's performers, only Nina was pictured on the front page of a local newspaper above the caption "Nina Simone, her tambourine and 'Lil Liza Jane' send this couple 'way out' at the Newport Jazz Festival."[5]

Langston Hughes quietly observed this set with a level of musical expertise never before associated with any poet. To invent the genre of blues poetry, as he had done in the 1920s, meant more than transcribing a few phrases or mimicking cadences. Hughes had become one of the world's foremost experts on the subject, and his forty years of experience had brought him face to face with those now considered legends. The breadth of his knowledge included not only countless Harlem rent parties and Chicago nightclubs but even the cafés of Paris, where he regularly interacted with singers such as Florence Embry and Ada "Bricktop" Smith. He would have noted that Simone's virtuosity at the piano was outdone only by the sheer variety of her songs.

Beyond the genres of folk and jazz and her African rhythms, Simone showed her remarkable range, playing both a Broadway hit as well as a classic blues song. "Trouble in Mind," a moving blues track, had lyrics that must have struck a deep nerve within Hughes. When Simone reached the fourth verse, Hughes heard echoes of something with which he himself was forever associated. Simone sang that she was going to lay her head

> On some lonesome railroad line
> Let the 2:19 train
> Ease my troubled mind.

In a radio interview with Hughes in Chicago two weeks after Simone's performance at Newport, Studs Terkel noted, "I'm thinking of something here that is too rarely said, that there's a humor, there's an affirmation in the blues, too, as well as a sadness." Without hesitating, Hughes immediately responded: "Oh yes, you know, the verses I often quote, which I heard many, many years ago in Kansas City as a child illustrates that. The one about

> I'm going down to the railroad,
> lay my head on the track.
> Going down to the railroad,
> lay my head on the track.
> But if I see the train a-coming,
> I'll jerk it back.[6]

Hughes has been so associated with this refrain that it has often been credited as if he wrote it himself. The poet was still thinking about the imagined suicide in the song performed by Simone when he published his Newport summary two weeks later in the *Chicago Defender*. Recounting the musicians who played on that Sunday, Hughes called back to both Simone's performance and his earliest encounters with the blues: "They all plunged into that stream whose source is deep in the heart of the people who made it up, 'Trouble in mind. I'm blue—but I won't be always. The Sun's gonna' shine in my back door someday.'"[7]

As a poet who had also championed dialect, Hughes certainly would have noted that Simone was authentically creative in her portrayal of African American Vernacular English. Four consecutive iterations of the song's redeeming assertion of hope reveal Simone dropping the preposition "in" when she instead slides straight from one line to the next with: "'Cause the sun's gonna shine / my back door someday." The casual nature of Simone's thoughtful delivery lets the final "ine" of "shine" double as the "in" which she imaginatively omits. To the ears of a writer like Hughes, Simone is invoking the same types of poetic strategies that made him famous.

Hughes likely gained even deeper respect for Simone as an artist when she updated her most popular song with an astute nod to its deeper history. Selling more than a million copies, the song "I Loves You Porgy" had been Simone's first breakthrough the year before, in 1959. Written by George and Ira Gershwin, the song featured in the 1935 standout Broadway play *Porgy and Bess*. Because the song had also been a hit for Billie Holiday in 1948, Simone was inadvertently linked to the famous singer. As a Black woman, the connection seemed obvious to casual listeners, but it was a lazy assertion that bordered on racist. To distance herself both from Holiday and from two white composers sometimes linked with appropriation and sensationalism, Simone instead introduced her Newport rendition of "Porgy" as the one written in 1928 by Dorothy Fields and Jimmy McHugh.

Hughes had a deep and abiding connection to the version Simone chose to sing. His favorite singer, Ethel Waters, had sung it in 1930. In his extensive collection of phonograph records, he had no less than seven copies of Waters's recordings of the song.[8] Nina had unconsciously connected with him by tapping the two deepest roots of his sensibilities: She knew both his beloved blues and his absolute favorite singer. The former Eunice Waymon was someone he could connect with on multiple levels. Like the crowd that applauded her, Hughes also likely "would have had Nina stay on for more."[9]

DAY 3: RIOTS

Hughes, Simone, and thousands of others spent the second day of the festival enjoying the sounds of artists such as Louis Armstrong and balloon-cheeked Dizzy Gillespie. On the third night, Saturday, July 2, Ray Charles raised the atmosphere inside to the heights of a dance party, singing lines from "Let the Good Times Roll," and fans were heeding only the second half of his final chorus: "Get yourself under control. / Oh, let the good times roll." No moment at the entire festival drew louder audience response than when he leapt into his scorching "What'd I Say." Police were sent roaming the front rows to keep everyone at least near their official seats. By the time the four backup singers were repeating, "Baby, shake that thing," most folks in the crowd were swinging hips and shoulders. The temporary wooden fences between sections shook as the man onstage sang his final song, "I Believe to My Soul":

> You were dreaming, darling
> I heard you say "Oh, Johnny!"
> but you know my name is Ray.

His assistant arrived from the wings to cloak the star dramatically in a long trench coat. Charles was then escorted away like royalty. But just before this, he had uttered the final two words to end his forty-three-minute set: "That's it!" No one knew at the time just how prophetic those two words would become.

Langston Hughes remembered this evening differently from those who enjoyed dancing to Ray Charles. As a board member, he felt the weight of responsibilities for everything that happened. His reminiscences two weeks after this moment started the same, but then other details surfaced: "The program was quite wonderful. There were people like Ray Charles and Horse Silver Quintet playing and a very wonderful crowd inside the park enjoying the music, but outside there were young people, and they were not teenagers on the whole, they were college age and older, who decided to have fun by throwing beer cans over the fans and hitting people in the head who were sitting there."[10]

Not empty, these were full and heavy aluminum cans with their tabs in place. Were this the extent of the disturbance, day three of the Newport Jazz Festival would not have become the unforgettable event in city lore that it is today. By the time Ray Charles took the stage on Saturday evening, Freebody Park was filled to capacity with fifteen thousand sitting in attendance and another twelve thousand without tickets who were desperately trying to get in. A full riot broke out when those outside knocked down the gate entrance separating the park from the city's streets. Police rushed in and a fire truck was parked to form a new barrier where the gate had been lost. The white rioters "hurled beer cans, stones, and whiskey bottles at the police" and soon after they "started tearing up the town, knocking over cars and smashing windows."[11]

Tear gas and fire hoses ensued. The stakes were high. Newport was a posh resort town with expensive homes nearby on Millionaire's Row, where tire mogul Henry Firestone and even Dwight D. Eisenhower lived.[12] All told, an additional fifty marines and a hundred National Guardsmen were called in to restore order. Hughes later made it clear that "according to police records there was not a single Negro among them."[13] When half the mob was forced downtown, the other half found a public beach to sleep off their rage at being denied entrance. But this remarkable peak attendance had been constant for the past two years. What was now surprisingly clear to everyone was that privileged white college students regarded blues and jazz concerts as mainstream events no longer confined to the margins.

With more than two hundred arrests and 125 reported injuries, the city took a wide-reaching response, including banning alcohol sales for two days. It was another decisive step that deeply affected Hughes: The city council met on Sunday and decided to revoke the festival's license.[14] This didn't merely cancel the rest of the next two day's scheduled events; it effectively ended the festival's future in Newport, Rhode Island. Festival director Louis Lorillard immediately filed a $4 million lawsuit against the city asserting that Newport was to blame for not maintaining order when it knew so many young college-aged students would be coming to town.[15] George Wein wisely took a more effective approach. He quietly suggested to the city council that one unique group of musicians simply must be allowed to perform on Sunday afternoon. His pitch? The United States Information Agency was planning to film Sunday afternoon's special blues session so that it could distribute movie reels overseas in Africa. Its goal? To use the white audience's visible joy and mass attendance to show emerging countries how well America was succeeding with race relations during the height of the Cold War. Culture itself was at the center of a campaign to sway newly independent countries toward democracy and away from communism. It was one thing to not hear John Coltrane, Dinah Washington, Count Basie, and country star Chet Atkins at either of the two remaining evening events, but no one wanted to appear unpatriotic given the dire fear of the Soviets' imperialistic mission.

DAY 4: LANGSTON HUGHES NARRATES THE BLUES

Once the sounds of sirens turned to memories, Nina Simone took a center seat three rows from the front stage to watch Muddy Waters, John Lee Hooker, and

Sammy Price perform Sunday afternoon at the festival's inaugural session on the blues. The sun was pouring down on a very warm July day without clouds. To cope, one young man wedged a torn piece of cardboard below the bridge of his sunglasses to keep his nose from getting burned. Nina's tactic for such heat was more fashionable: She wore a large white scarf over her head, draping over both her temples and the sides of her black Ray-Ban shades. Knotted below her chin, the scarf hung clear to her midriff. As the official program advertised, the innovative session "Langston Hughes Narrating the Blues" was going to include a person who would soon have an influence on her career that neither of them could forecast.

Musical seminars were the norm during the day sessions, and Hughes planned to offer the crowd both background on blues, the musical form he considered to be the root of jazz, and performative examples of various blues styles. Most importantly, this was the first time the blues was performed on this scale to a predominantly white audience. No longer needing to sneak into a tiny club or cabaret, college students found the type of musical experience that they had rioted for the day before.

At 2:30 p.m., it was finally Hughes's turn to lead the educational session. Not only was he privately shaken with the knowledge of the festival's looming cancellation, but he had also planned a detailed set of events for this afternoon session that was now being drastically altered. Hughes had prepared fourteen pages of typed materials—revising them over three drafts—in which he had carefully composed a full call-and-response between himself and musician Sammy Price.[16] Hughes had also prepared to read one of his poems, "Blues at Dawn."

Just before the session, Hughes learned that Price and his trio were facing logistical problems and might not even arrive. In his meticulous preparation, Hughes had planned to begin this session with Price and bring on Muddy Waters at the end. Now, Waters's full band was being pressed into service much sooner than either man had planned. As the session was happening, a few tense requests must have been rushed backstage to bring Waters and his band on early. Such was the fragility and precarity of the session.

After directing Waters and his band to play an example of "gut bucket blues" while a car horn honked twice in the background, Hughes stepped aside for another of the singer's iconic works. "Catfish Blues" features one of the most foundational metaphors in American music: Waters sings that his mother warned his father before he was born that her boy child was "gonna be a rollin' stone." This image inspired not only the name of the band the Rolling Stones but also the magazine of the same name as well as Bob Dylan's song "Like a Rolling Stone" and "Papa Was a Rollin' Stone" by the Temptations.

Simone was no doubt keeping her eyes on pianist Otis Spann's right hand as he climbed further and further up the keys. She also heard Hughes sounding much more like a blues aficionado the next time he took the microphone. Waters left the stage, but Hughes promised the crowd that he would return. Before introducing a boogie-woogie style of blues, Hughes reminisced about hearing Leadbelly playing at a friend's house back in the 1930s. The forty nonstop verses he sang that night left a deep impression on Hughes, who noted that the blues have "some of the most beautiful lyric poetry in the world." He continued by announcing the logic behind his choice to center this session within the context of a jazz festival: "What you have just heard in these demonstrations is the root of jazz, the heart of jazz." Hughes was standing in a place of great privilege, directing professional musicians to do his bidding, while Nina was watching.

Hughes now steadied himself after his bumpy opening with Waters to establish himself as a musical historian. He offered up an extended seven-minute introduction to "The St. Louis Blues." Hughes wanted to highlight not only contemporary blues musicians but also some famous older composers and arrangers. He may have glanced knowingly at Simone when he named Cole Porter and the Gershwins side by side in a list of eight composers. Simone knew these figures as the source of her versions of "I Loves You Porgy" and "You'd Be So Nice to Come Home To," which she had performed just days before. From here, Hughes blended his knowledge of music with his famous penchant for humor. He recalled his intimate experiences with Father of the Blues W. C. Handy. In recounting the images in his arrangement of "St. Louis Blues," Handy took the symbols in the song from the world around him. Sleeping outside on the levee, he hated to see the sun go down because it was cold at night in late autumn. Moreover, the diamonds being worn were common in the city's underworld at the time. Hughes not only knew these facts but told the crowd that Handy had "told me this himself" when the two had met on more than one occasion years earlier. Hughes was not exaggerating. If anything, Hughes was being modest. The two men had collaborated on a few songs, and Handy had heartily endorsed Hughes's first book of blues poems in 1926.

Simone listened as Hughes explained that "St. Louis Blues" was the most popular song in the world—he'd heard it on jukeboxes in Japan, radios in Russia, and in clubs in South America. In France in the 1920s, Hughes had heard band after band play it immediately whenever Americans walked into a Parisian café. He concluded, "I think it's great poetry itself, as well as music."

Hughes ended with the story of how the French were able to play the song on the Nazi-run radio during World War II. The French explained to the Nazis that it was not really American at all but rather an old French folk song. St.

Louis was really Louis Quatorze, and the diamonds in the song belonged to Marie Antoinette. With everyone laughing, Spann played an instrumental version of the song. Hughes even added a few vocalizations, some guttural *ah-ahs*, while they played.

Like Simone in her performance three nights before, Hughes was gaining momentum throughout his session.

Hughes continued to combine his expertise and humor when the song ended. Pulling out advertisement cards he kept about Harlem rent house parties in the 1920s, he regaled the crowd with three examples of days when money was charged at the door to pay the rent. These parties always featured a band of musicians and cheap liquor. Hughes remembered being charged a quarter at the door and ten cents for a glass of gin. The funniest invitation indicated that the party would be held on "Saturday, May 9th from P.M. on . . ." Adding to the light vibe of the set, Al Minns and Leon James danced their one-foot spins and showed off their snake hips. Dressed in plaid jackets, they moved, danced, and clowned to a jump-tempo blues as the crowd laughed and clapped. With this, the educational portion of the blues workshop ended, and Hughes returned to his role as emcee, introducing John Lee Hooker.

In that introduction, Simone and the crowd learned that the guitarist before them had been recording since 1948 in Detroit. The audience did not know that Hooker had intentionally been using pseudonyms such as "Guitar Slim" in order to record the same song twice to make more money. Instead, they heard that he had recorded more records than any other musician, with 174 sides to date. Hughes knew him from his previous dates at the Village Gate, and Hooker's acoustic guitar playing ended when Hughes encouraged him after his marvelous five-song set to "Take a bow, John."

Everyone seated far behind Simone was anxiously awaiting a full demonstration of Muddy Waters and his band. Up to this point, Sammy Price had miraculously arrived (against all odds) to play a version of "The Price Is Right" that his trio wanted to be "loud as hell"; Lafayette Thomas had the nerve (or ignorance) to play Hooker's own standard "Things That I Used to Do" as Hooker watched from the wings; Butch Cage had fiddled while Willie Thomas strummed and then preached through introductions of their long thirteen-song set; and finally, Betty Jeanette, in her first public performance, sang "Backwater Blues." Likely tired from a bit too much fiddling, explication, and unrelenting heat, a small but noticeable portion of the crowd offered up an ironic cheer when Hughes finally announced that Waters and his band would soon reappear.

With the organizational session now officially ended, Hughes quick-stepped to the microphone, where he simply uttered two words: "Muddy Waters." Hughes then turned to his left, shook hands, and said, "Welcome, Muddy."

Opening with "I Got My Brand on You" and then "I'm Your Hoochie Coochie Man," Waters riffed about the historic nature of the moment, pointing toward the fact that the blues was being honored on such a large stage: "We're the Hoochie Coochie Boys / and the whole United States knows we're here." By the time Waters launched into the euphemism that was "Tiger in Your Tank," Simone's joy was impossible to miss. Bopping her head to the beat, Nina enjoyed the effects of Waters pulling the metal cylinder from his left pocket to play slide across the neck of his patented Fender Telecaster. She was not only grooving more than anyone else; she was moving to the beat with cool force.

Nina's presence was captured purposefully, for political reasons. The cameramen focused on presenting as many Black people in the audience as possible to build the narrative that these were happily integrated audiences. The United States Information Agency, a now-defunct government propaganda unit, wished to showcase racial harmony to the emerging democracies of Africa.

With the entire crowd on Waters's side, "Tiger in Your Tank" received a standing ovation. Women started screaming during "I Feel So Good." His full set was almost finished. Waters had won the audience by being deadly serious and ominous before turning playful as a kitten and then happy as a clam. Now he ended his set with two consecutive versions of "I've Got My Mojo Working." Perhaps there were thoughts toward releasing this song. One short version could be a single, while the longer first take could still be included on the album. Waters was now waving his knees and shaking his entire cheeks to give the word "Mojo" a bubbling vibrato. This was a stunning musical performance. The album he released of this show, *Muddy Waters at Newport*, became one of the 101 most influential albums in music history. It is known as the first live blues album of all time. It was nominated for a Grammy award in 1960 and established Newport as "a blues commerce center that attracted similar acts" for years to come.[17]

Standing right before Simone in a position of remarkable authority, Hughes now faced a challenging set of circumstances. A jam session among Waters and his band, John Lee Hooker, and Sammy Price was just ahead. At the same time, Willis Conover had an important message to deliver concerning the immediate fate of the festival. In addition, Hughes also had something else in mind to both commemorate the moment and model his own idea of the blues aesthetic. He framed the final collaboration to come at the end of this session as a moment to witness the "blues in creation." With three distinct competing emotions, he faced the crowd and said: "Willis Conover, who is coming to the platform after the jam session, to tell you something very blue . . . and very sad . . ." Hughes himself was surprised he had to pause and gather himself before the last three words. Tears started forming and his throat thickened. After divulging that he was on the board of the festival, he continued, "This is a blue afternoon for us. It's blues and it's blue, too."

After all the musicians assembled onstage, Hughes and Waters were once again out of sync. Hughes assertively suggested how the final jam session should go: "Muddy, if you will, why don't you come up to the microphone to do the first verse, and then let Sammy come in." At this, Sammy Price anxiously called Hughes twice. On the second "Langston," he proposed that Waters be allowed to do two verses on his own. Hughes quickly relented with "All right, or two verses, Muddy." Creation was indeed spontaneous: Somehow Betty Jeannette herself ended up sneaking in between Waters and Price to take her turn. Perhaps much of this had been worked out among the musicians themselves backstage before Hughes started conducting. Al and Leon extended the stage presence clear to the wings where Hughes was seated. Simone watched as the two men stepped forward, throwing hands and feet as if they burned. Soon their very chests were shaking, the audience wondering how their ribs held together. Once they had returned to a space usually reserved for background singers, Waters began to bring the song to a close. He had received the largest applause and had his very own band behind him—this was becoming a career-defining moment.

But just as Waters was beginning to sing the final chorus and bring the song home, Hughes signaled that it was time for a surprise. He leaned out and ushered an unexpected guest onstage so that everyone in the crowd could see him. When the huge man known ironically as Little Jimmy Rushing strolled out, moving with the slow confidence of a man who knew he was important, Betty Jeannette smiled so hard it shook her shoulders.[18]

Fully enthralled, Nina was snapping her fingers while a man next to her whispered something in her right ear. The cameramen then lost track of everyone except Rushing. Unlike the others onstage, Jimmy Rushing was an established star scheduled to appear on the prestigious final night of the festival. He had played Newport several times before, and his records had been heard by everyone onstage since he started recording in late 1936. In more ways than one, Little Jimmy Rushing was a huge star. The shortest man was also the widest one in all of Freebody Park. In fact, he was known as Mister Five by Five because he was five feet tall and five feet wide.

At first, Waters elegantly stepped aside. But this was a surprise in more ways than one. Rushing's opening verse reclaimed the very town Muddy was most associated with as he belted out, "Going to Chicago, sorry that I can't take you." Waters had made Chicago not only his home since 1954 but also the source of what would be known as the Chicago blues sound. When Rushing culminated his opening foray with "There's nothing in Chicago that a monkey woman can do," he was singing the lyrics to his own song, "Going to Chicago"—claiming his turf. In his second verse, Rushing belted out a new twist on the recorded verse, sending it twice as loud as Waters could ever shout: "When you see me coming, baby, raise your window high. / When you see me passing, hang your head and cry." For those unclear about the blues, this image now felt like a covert reference to Waters himself, who was sulking behind the giant Rushing.

Price and Rushing were now framing a wall in front of Waters, who was being eclipsed and overshadowed. However, Price appears to have wanted little part in this beef. Gently imploring Rushing to stop because both his suggestive images and total verses had gone too far, he placed both hands on Jimmy's left arm to escort him away from the microphone. The big man did not even consider moving; he had one more verse to deliver. All this was happening in front of Waters's very own band. Waters had to get out of the way with Rushing approaching as a flood.

The eight-minute jam concluded with a final stunning moment that would not have been lost on Simone. Rushing's last verse was simultaneously a salute to Hughes and a signal to all about who had pulled the strings to arrange this surprise moment. Rushing gave a telling look offstage, staring straight at Hughes before singing "Anybody ask you, baby, who was it sang this song? Tell 'em it was Little Jimmy Langston, he's been here and gone." Thanks to Langston Hughes, Rushing was reasserting that he was still the king of Chicago blues. Transcoding his feelings about the upstart Waters into the expected guise of a woman, the "baby" here in this blues is at once Waters or anyone in the audience: The song Waters started out performing on this stage was now reclaimed by Rushing. Waters never found his way back to the microphone again as the song "Bye Bye Baby" followed. The song itself made it seem Rushing was waving to Waters as he left.

Witnessing this live, Nina learned that Hughes was a musical force to be reckoned with. At the beginning of her career, she now learned that he not only chose the roster and defined varying types of blues by showing their relationship to jazz. He also found a way to bring in an old friend who summarily stole the show. When it came to music, she now knew, Hughes had clout and power rumbling beneath all that knowledge and humor.

With the cutting session now finished, Hughes stepped to the microphone with a somber tone. Only he and a few other board members knew what was about to come next.

Feeling the need to document the gravity of the moment, Hughes began, "This is the moment: It's 5:40, twenty minutes to six." He then introduced Willis Conover. The residual effects of the jam session were still coursing through the drummer Francis Clay's veins, and he struck a rim shot, completely unaware of the coming shock. Befuddled, Nina sat with thousands of others learning what Hughes had been choked up about earlier. Conover began, "There will be no concert tonight or . . . again." After several confused boos from a small group, he continued in deep earnestness: "The board of directors deeply regret that the true jazz lovers were denied the opportunity to hear their favorite jazz musicians, due entirely to non-ticket-holding people outside the park." Then, rolling up his prepared statement in his hands, he spoke from the heart, trying to align himself with the crowd's deep disappointment:

> I think it's a shame that the Newport Jazz Festival has to be killed because a bunch of pseudo beatniks and rock 'n' roll escapees [*applause*] who had no interest in jazz, who had no intention of coming to the concerts and were not inside the park at all, decided to use the Newport Jazz Festival weekend and the city of Newport as an excuse for giving vent to their healthy animal instincts in such a fashion as to qualify them for admission to a zoo rather than to a school. [*applause*] . . . It does seem to me that in attempting to cure the disease that infected the Newport Jazz Festival activities, they decided to shoot the patient without clearing up the germs.

This image, pointed like a dagger toward the Newport city council, got the largest applause of his brief announcement.

Hughes, like many others connected to the festival, believed that the event would never return to Newport again. The Newport Jazz Festival board had decided at noon on Sunday that the remaining events should be canceled. Apparently only George Wein's plea allowed the afternoon's blues session to be performed. Hughes learned of the cancellation a little after 1:00 p.m. when he arrived at Freebody Park. Honest to the spirit of the blues in every way, Hughes went into the press room searching for writing paper, where he found a Western Union blank (with its carbon copy page behind it) and, using a pencil, wrote out his own blues lyrics on the spot. His original song "Newport Blues" was what Hughes had in mind when he announced a final "blues in creation" moment.

With Waters now humiliated and Rushing's cutting done, Hughes put his plan into motion. Almost every account mistakenly suggests that Muddy Waters sang what would become known as "Goodbye Newport Blues," but this impromptu song penned by Hughes was sung by Waters's pianist, Otis Spann, a man Hughes had met mere hours ago. The poet handed the pianist his lyric. Waters apparently refused to sing, claiming he was "too drained." But Waters really had another reason not to perform Hughes's song: It was handwritten, and Waters had never learned to read.

As Hughes explained weeks afterward, "Otis Spann had arrived with the Muddy Waters band, and I asked if he would be so kind as to play it and sing it, and he had never seen it before, so quite spontaneously he gave this blues a melody."[19] Knowingly or unknowingly, Hughes may have regarded this as poetic justice. When he had first introduced Waters during the educational blues session, Hughes politely asked Waters to present the members of his band. Waters refused. Hughes may have regarded this as Waters wanting the bright spotlight to himself. Now Waters was cut, and one of his unacknowledged bandmates had the privilege of playing Hughes's song for the first time.

Hughes stepped to the microphone Willis Conover had just vacated and said:

> I heard the news only a little while ago myself. I had to leave the board meeting that was in session and come down here to the park for our program. When I heard the news, I felt as I'm sure all of you feel . . . and so I went into the press tent and looked around for some paper. There wasn't any there, nothing but Western Union blanks, and so I wrote a blues for Newport on Western Union banks. I gave it to Spann over there at the piano, and I asked Muddy Waters if perhaps we could create a blues right here on this stage. Spann has never seen it before, never sung it before, only saw it a little while ago. So, we're going to create for you, in honor of the Newport Jazz Festival, a goodbye Newport blues.

During the performance, Spann's hands walked slowly into "Goodbye Newport Blues" like an exhausted man. Butch Cage was still onstage, and his fiddle entered briefly after the first line in a moment of genuine spontaneous collaboration. Muddy Waters played a "sensitive" lead guitar on his signature Telecaster as Simone listened in the crowd.[20]

Spann's rendition of the song's four verses offers several alterations that improve Hughes's original lyrics. Simone heard the song begin: "Yes, what a gloomy day in Newport / Everything is sad, sad, sad." Spann added that second line on the spot.[21] This accomplishes two things. First, it replaces the overrepetition Hughes originally created with his unnecessarily redundant "It's a gloomy, gloomy day." Second, the improvisation picks up on the actual word, "sad," that Hughes himself spoke when he was brought to tears about the festival's cancellation. Clearly, Spann was listening. To document this genuine emotion, he substitutes what Hughes had written before with the word the poet had used onstage to express what he was feeling. It is not insignificant that Hughes sat directly to Spann's right as the two shared a piano bench while Conover made his lengthy announcement. What emotions might Spann have felt as he shared his seat with a despondent Hughes?

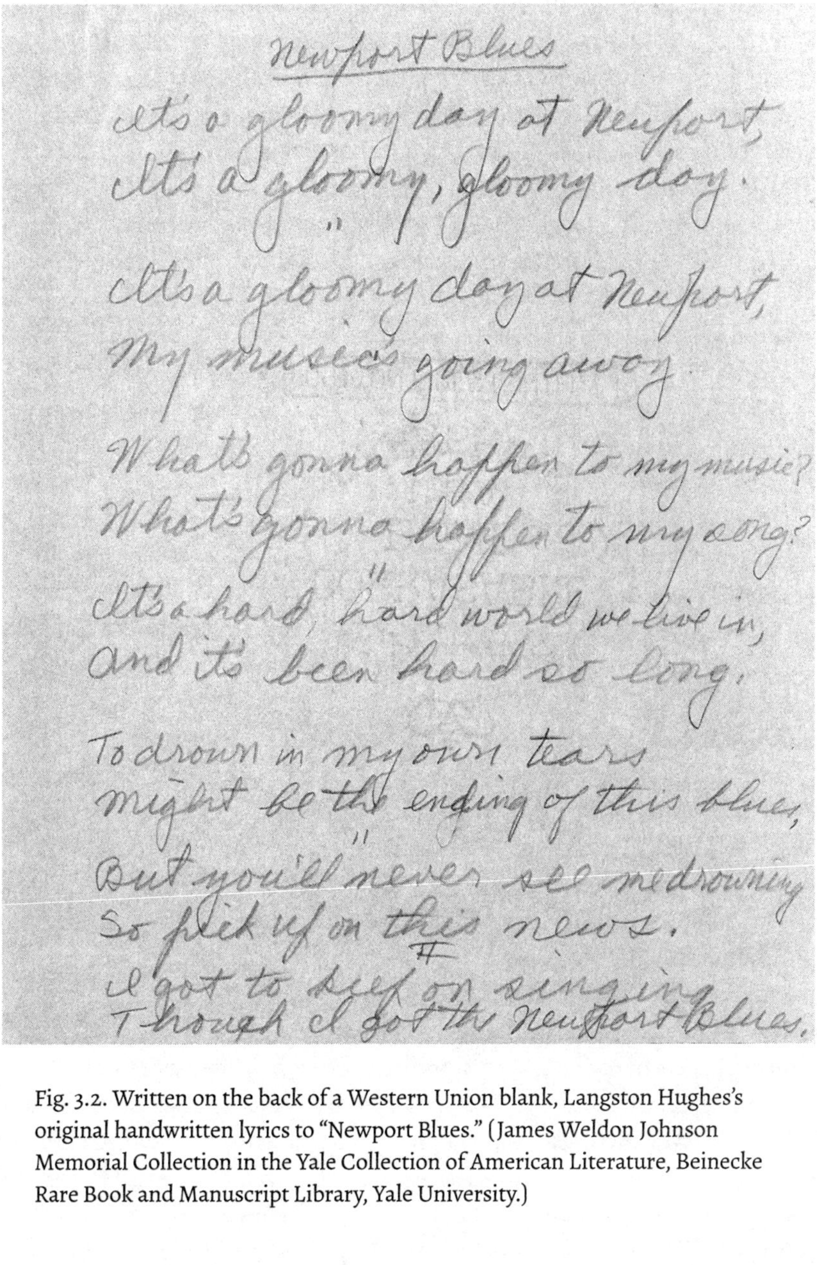

Newport Blues

It's a gloomy day at Newport,
It's a gloomy, gloomy day.
"
It's a gloomy day at Newport,
My music's going away.

What's gonna happen to my music?
What's gonna happen to my song?
"
It's a hard, hard world we live in,
And it's been hard so long.

To drown in my own tears
might be the ending of this blues,
"
But you'll never see me drowning
So pick up on this news.
II
I got to keep on singing
Though I got the Newport Blues.

Fig. 3.2. Written on the back of a Western Union blank, Langston Hughes's original handwritten lyrics to "Newport Blues." (James Weldon Johnson Memorial Collection in the Yale Collection of American Literature, Beinecke Rare Book and Manuscript Library, Yale University.)

Now needing a rhyme for "sad," Spann alters the final line of Hughes's first stanza, "My music's going away" ("away" originally rhymed with "day"), and instead ends this first verse by improvising a rhyme for "sad": "One of the worst of times I ever had." Spann is slyly inserting the actual emotions of Langston Hughes into a song in which Hughes had tried to imagine how this moment might feel to the musicians. Each of these men is seeking to sincerely harness an empathy that projects and privileges another's emotions so that their feelings might be accessed and preserved in place of their own.

Taking the persona of an actual musician such as Spann, something he is not, Hughes's song originally asks: "What's gonna happen to my Music? / What's gonna happen to my song?" Hughes's handwritten line, intended to end this verse, "And it's been hard so long," suddenly becomes "And to be here all along" from the lips of Spann. With this riff, Spann is now personalizing the song in such a way that documents Hughes's presence at the festival in its darkest hours. A song written for the voice of a musician has suddenly become a testimony to Hughes's vision, investment, and passion for inviting the blues musicians onto a stage where they could perform side by side with jazz.

While James Cotton's harmonica fills some of the open spaces in the music, the co-created song still presents Hughes's trademark surface simplicity to mask a key cultural cue. Stanza three connects ideas that should be repeated in parallel to quietly reveal how the riots have spoiled the festival. Line one asserts, "To drown in my own tears." Its sister, line three, would be expected to repeat this concept; however, Spann instead gestures to the significance of this opening phrase by hiding it and refusing to repeat it. After singing the second line, he presents a long string for the listener to unspool: A single and extended "Yeeeaaah" stands in for this image of drowning, followed immediately in line four by the expected return to "just might be the ending to all these blues."

If an attentive listener asks, "What has led to the end of all these blues?" here the answer is the riot that took place the night before. This little hint comes with realizing the significance of the first idea, which is not repeating or coming back as it should: Spann has disappeared the second reference to the idea of drowning "in my own tears." This is no accident. This specific line has disappeared here for a very significant reason. These words are also the title of a Ray Charles song. In fact, Ray Charles was singing a stirring version of "Drown in My Own Tears" in the middle of his ten-song set the very night before while the rioting occurred outside the festival. As the headliner of the most coveted evening session, Ray Charles decisively contributed to the demand for tickets that could not be met. Hughes's lyrical idea combines with Spann's effective execution to hint that the true source of sorrow expressed in "Goodbye Newport Blues" is the idea that rioting has caused the remainder of the 1960 Newport Jazz Festival to be canceled. Just as the festival will disappear, so this repeated line is also gone and absent from where it rightly belongs. The song has now become the artistic witness of both an organizer and a musician who were there "all along" to document the despondency in song.

The song approaches its end with Spann asserting that such actions by young white students will not deter him or his fellow musicians. Spann declares that he will "keep singin' my song" and "these blues." Before Hughes's lyrics turn yet another loss into victory by refusing to be defeated, they speculate what future print and media sources will say about Newport. Hughes is not optimistic about the press's likely focus. When Spann declares, "But you never see me drown / So you just pick up on the latest news," it gestures toward a narrative where vandals and the actions of white rioters will be sensationalized across multiple platforms, ignoring the devastating effect on these blues musicians. The news that readers will pick up will certainly favor stories about those who ruined this moment, not those affected. The song was never wrong: The front page of the *New York Times* featured a photo of police confronting rioters beneath the headline "Newport Jazz Festival Closed Because of Rioting."[22]

Spann ends the song's fourth and final verse with two substitutions that signal the remarkable co-creative act of producing this song. Here, it results from a mutually respectful dialogue between a lyricist and a performer. Spann returns to Hughes's word "sad" eight more times in his outro. Hughes's most moving moment onstage is codified here as the signature emotion of both the song and this day. The singer ends their song with a word that Hughes used in his introduction. Though the word does not appear anywhere in Hughes's handwritten lyrics, Hughes told the crowd that they were about to hear a goodbye Newport blues. Spann's final words of the song are:

> Goodbye Newport, goodbye
> Oh goodbye
> Goodbye.[23]

The very next day, July 4, 1960, Hughes typed up his written lyrics on a brown page of Western Union letterhead and added in Spann's key word to change the title from his own "Newport Blues" to the collaborative "Goodbye Newport Blues." At the bottom, he added, "As extemporaneously performed at the piano by Otis Spann of the Muddy Waters Band."[24]

Hughes, who had been earnestly seeking a hit record since at least 1949, sent the lyrics to Muddy Waters (he likely got Muddy's address from George Wein). By August 1960, Hughes had copyrighted the song, with due credit given: "Music by Otis Spann." Moreover, he kept tabs on the song's reception.

When he received an international press review reprinted in London of Muddy Waters's album, Hughes underlined (and bracketed) the following with a red pencil: "Spann, also a fine singer, is also featured on one number, 'Goodbye Newport Blues.' A lament for the fate of the festival, written impromptu by poet Langston Hughes, with Cotton and Muddy's guitar accompanying sensitivity, it's the highspot [*sic*] of the set."[25] Though this evaluation of "Goodbye Newport Blues" was far from universal, Hughes must have felt a keen sense of satisfaction in imagining that his song measured up critically to real hits such as "Tiger in Your Tank," "I'm Your Hoochie Coochie Man," and "I've Got My Mojo Working."

Muddy Waters's career reached new heights with the release of *Muddy Waters at Newport 1960* on November 15, 1960. Hughes listened to the final track on side B, then he sat down and began typing the actual lyrics Spann had performed to "Goodbye Newport Blues." He also tried to write out the actual notes being sung on a piece of sheet music. Did he realize how much emotional energy each artist had invested in trying to understand the other man? Despite Spann's remarkable contributions to both the lyrics and the actual music, he was not credited on the album. Worse, Hughes was listed as the song's coauthor, along with McKinley Morganfield (a.k.a. Muddy Waters). Did Hughes fully grasp how truly collaborative a song would have to be as it made the difficult move from the written sheet to pressed vinyl?

The final two words Simone heard from the stage came directly from a dejected Langston Hughes. Having listened carefully to Otis Spann, he stepped to the microphone to close not only his joyous session, months in the making, but the entire festival: "Goodbye, Newport." These two words belonged to both Spann and Hughes. "Goodbye Newport Blues" represents the generous act of decentering the self for documenting another's emotional story. We are left to imagine the conversations we have been robbed of: Only the rarest moments of our civil discourse mirror this type of sympathetic back-and-forth.

The lessons Nina learned directly from Hughes's 1960 blues session surfaced over the years in measurable ways. Just as Hughes had written what became "Goodbye Newport Blues," so Nina spontaneously wrote both the lyrics and music to "Montreux Blues," an improvisational tribute to Claude Nobs played for him live at the 1981 Montreux Jazz Festival. When she returned to the Newport Jazz Festival in 1966, she invoked the very language Hughes taught her on that day when she introduced "Blues for Mama," her collaboration with Abbey Lincoln, as a "gut bucket blues."[26]

Nina Simone left the 1960 Newport Jazz Festival with an unmistakable personal experience that allowed her to understand fully that Langston Hughes was much more than a poet. He was a powerful figure with limitless cultural capital and artistic influence who yearned to have his lyrics turned into songs. Hughes had direct connections to both established and emerging artists, including dancers, that blurred traditional lines demarcating what counted as performance. Here was the kind of figure Little Jimmy Rushing would call out to thank in the middle of a song before thousands of spectators. Most importantly, Simone learned that Langston Hughes wrote lyrics that led to collaborative songs performed by iconic musicians. In just a few years, Simone would unconsciously begin a welcome collaboration with Langston Hughes, a man who would spend the rest of his life devoting more time to musicians than to poets.

4

Ask Your Mama

After rioting caused the cancellation of the last performances at the 1960 Newport Jazz Festival, Langston Hughes nonetheless continued his stay in the city for several weeks in room 36 at the Hotel Viking. The Viking served as the official headquarters for the festival, and its conference rooms had hosted several musical workshop sessions in recent years. The historic hotel was not only the place to get tickets to the festival but also where many of the musicians stayed during it.

What we now refer to as the canceled sessions in 1960 genuinely seemed to be the very end of the festival. Hughes recognized two things after experiencing the crowd's response at the 1960 Newport Jazz Festival. First, the popularity of Black music—in the forms of both jazz and blues—was at an all-time high. Second, the continued challenges of merging this success with white audiences unleashed all the aspirations and challenges facing a nation grappling with the most important political topic of the day: integration. These somber facts left Hughes reflecting on the Black musician's tenuous role in American life at a time when civil rights were at the forefront of the country's consciousness.

It was the Fourth of July. He turned his small four-by-six-inch memo notebook sideways so that the spiral spine became a divider between the top and bottom sheets.[1] He began writing in quick bursts. In the many intense days of writing that followed, Dinah Washington and Louis Armstrong came to mind. He wrote the name Sammy Davis Jr., then crossed it out, replacing Davis with dancing duo Al Minns and Leon James, who took the stage during Hughes's blues session. Dizzy Gillespie. These blues and jazz musicians represented Black America's most esteemed cultural icons. These were not people Hughes read about; many of them were men and women he had just finished spending time with backstage. Clearly, the events at Newport were at the forefront of his mind.

He wrote across the barred pages in pencil, ignoring the blue lines as if the pinstripes were too small for his growing ideas. The opening image from the first page of his earliest notes suggests that the only photographs that can truly shake up the world are those "taken on the film of the heart."[2] Name after name kept coming to him. He was thinking back to those who had left a lasting impression. He eventually placed three names together in a list that suggested each deserved the other's elevated company: "Miles and Ella and Miss Nina." Though she had recorded only three albums, Langston Hughes earnestly believed that Miss Nina Simone was the equal of established legends Miles Davis and Ella Fitzgerald. Linking Simone to these figures at such an early stage in her career is a remarkable endorsement.

Hughes could place such confidence in Simone because he had seen her perform live on many occasions at the Village Gate before her debut appearance at the jazz festival.[3] Under the spotlight, Nina had proved her worth. Although Hughes had cultivated an uncommon gift over the years for identifying talent when he saw it, he didn't need any more time to evaluate Simone: Her proficiency with a variety of musical styles, captivating persona, and sheer expertise as a pianist meant that the dean of Negro letters could already assertively link her pending stardom with those who had long established their own lofty orbits. Without hesitation, he was declaring that Nina Simone sang as memorably as Ella Fitzgerald and attacked her piano as tenaciously as Miles Davis blew his horn. She was now "somebody."

Hughes invoked Nina Simone's name in a poem that appeared in his full-length book *Ask Your Mama: 12 Moods for Jazz* (1961). In *Ask Your Mama,* Langston Hughes took the cancellation of the Newport Jazz Festival and in turn created a record of contemporary luminaries in Black entertainment. The poem in which Nina is named, "Horn of Plenty," explores interracial dynamics. Taking up where the play *A Raisin in the Sun* ends, it addresses the question, "What happens when Black citizens move into white neighborhoods?" With

"Horn of Plenty," Hughes documents humorous responses to the painful experiences taking place in New York's newly integrated suburbs.

Nina herself would soon endure a confrontation in which race became a deciding factor in her response. After a concert performance at the University of North Carolina at Chapel Hill in February 1961, Nina, bassist Christ White, drummer Bobby Hamilton, and her acting manager Art D'Lugoff were heading back to New York by train. When a white woman's purse went missing at the Raleigh station, white police officers suddenly surrounded the group just before the purse was found. Ignoring the woman, Nina, and Art, with his eccentric beard, the police accused Bobby of stealing a purse he had not touched. Nina flew into a rage at the audacity of the officers, whose assumptions were based solely on race. She "read them the riot act" and, as Chris White recalled, "was just as Black as she could be with these guys, and they left us alone."[4] In other words, Simone all but told them that if they wanted to find the real person to blame, they should go "ask your mama." In many ways, the tone expressed by the speaker in "Horn of Plenty" (and several other poems in the collection) mirrors the attitude so often associated with that of Nina Simone.

FROM JAZZ TO POETRY

Longing since at least 1949 to produce a hit record of his own, Hughes now took the opportunity to write a new book of poetry so that it mirrored a record album in every possible way. Using as his model Duke Ellington's recent reissue of *Black, Brown, and Beige* (1958, featuring Mahalia Jackson), he reproduced many aspects of that album's design and color palette in *Ask Your Mama: 12 Moods for Jazz*. The number twelve suggests the total number of sections in the poem. It also clues in the listener to the idea of "playing the dozens." The dozens is a game of banter in which an argument intensifies until something derogatory about the adversary's mother is suggested in the phrase "Your mama!" to increase a sense of both humor and anger. Hughes's title invoked this refrain from "playing the dozens" to present another innovative form of jazz poetry fully intended to be accompanied by music. In the hands of Hughes, this iteration of jazz poetry became a "triumphant medium of protest" that spoke against racists by "giving them a dose of attitude."[5]

Each of the poem's twelve sections is dramatically set off by original artwork in the form of more geometric figures—he somehow convinced his publisher, Alfred A. Knopf, to pay for salmon-colored paper and beautiful blue and brown inks for the text, alternating these colors page by page. Imagining the way songs are often contextualized for listeners with liner notes, Hughes arranged for his own set of liner notes to appear at the end of the book. These were as puzzling as the poems themselves in that they did not explain meanings but offered only more information. Hughes was clearly having fun. He was also picking up on the immense popularity of Black music, which had moved others to riot. Finally, he secretly wanted to be the musician that others already expected him to be.

Sitting down with a lead pencil in hand in the spring of 1961, Hughes didn't hesitate: He began marking up the musical bars of blank sheet music. Getting no further than the staff, key signature, and first two notes, he scribbled out his errors. Without erasing, he continued his notations by starting on the blank staff below, adding slurs, three bars of music, and then erasing one sharp note to move it down a half step. By the end of the fifth staff, a completely new song had been written after a double bar. These lines were sketched so lightly and tentatively that they looked like a rough drawing that would never be painted. At the very top, across the opening staff where his hand had faltered, Hughes now wrote the letters: "HESITATION BLUES."[6]

Moving on to a second piece of sheet music, he typed a title. Hughes filled in this staff in black ink, later noting in red pencil where one rest and another grace note should be added. Finally, his lead pencil disagreed with something he had typed: The title of the second song, "SHAVE AND A HAIRCUT," now on its own staff and written dark and bold, received a "no," indicating that these words should be dropped. Hughes's third and final attempt inserted an opening mark right after the signature mark to indicate middle C. By placing a line vertically through its center, this resembled the cent symbol, ¢, no longer on standard keyboards. Re-creating the sheet music for this song revealed multiple intentions. In sending these works to editor Judith Jones at Knopf on April 30, 1961, Hughes indicated his plan to open his forthcoming book of poems with two staffs of sheet music.[7]

Hughes's mind was consumed by music. In fact, he was now bookending his previous act of writing out music. Hughes had typed the lyrics to the song "Goodbye Newport Blues" on the same day that he started to write the poems for this new collection. That happened while he was sequestered in Newport at the Hotel Viking. The appearance of written music here would also now mirror W. E. B. Du Bois's *Souls of Black Folk,* in which every chapter opens with a similar musical representation. Hughes knew this classic book well, having confessed to the author himself that he'd read it for the "10th time," and Du Bois's ongoing exile in Ghana for his communist leanings makes this connection very poignant.[8]

To be confronted immediately with written music challenges any reader. It presents the person opening Hughes's book with something that is both recognizable and alien.[9] This brings the reader to an impasse where what should be understood so easily, because it is simply recognized and named "music," ultimately ends in failure as a music that is not heard.[10] Where Du Bois's metaphor is the veil that separates Black people from white people, Hughes focuses on the social and cultural practices that are amplified when Black and white people become neighbors. As music and words seem to coexist as black images on white sheet music, the parallel here is that Black and white people who live on the same page of a neighborhood do not really know how to hear each other, block after block.

But Hughes was also engaged in a ruse. Unable to play a musical instrument, sing, or in fact read or write musical notation, Hughes had been copying the notes on these pages of sheet music to make it appear that he had written them by ear. In fact, Hughes had been working from a correct copy written by someone else.[11] "Hesitation Blues" was rightly credited to W. C. Handy. Hughes had secured a copy of the sheet music and was now staging the false production of an impure document intending to show that he had conjured these notes himself merely by listening to the record. Such are the desires of a wannabe musician.

Just before sending in his pseudo sheet music to editor Judith Jones, Hughes assertively answered two questions he had left for himself. Using a red pencil, he took a small sheet of memo paper usually reserved for shopping lists and wrote a reminder to himself: "Mama All in Caps? Cues on side?"[12] Each of these notes point to musical directives. Hughes noted in early drafts that he added these musical cues throughout the margins of his poem so that he could document for the reader the songs he himself heard and thought of while writing each section. Completely misunderstood today, Hughes's choice in 1961 to present the full poem entirely in capital letters displays his material attentiveness to how song titles of his era were typographically displayed on record labels. Not only had Hughes been typing songs and book titles in all caps in his newspaper articles and personal correspondence, but record labels—from Colpix to Columbia—always provided song titles on their record labels in all caps. What is often lost in Hughes's choice is that, like these record labels, the original edition set Hughes's text in SMALL CAPS so that they were not overwhelming to a reader's eyes, as they are in all reprint editions with full-size caps. Hughes clearly wanted every element of this book to echo the album he never recorded.

Hughes had additional joists framing this highly innovative collection. For one thing, his invocation of "playing the dozens," incorporating Black culture's penchant for the put-down and the comeback, gave a dual sense of frustration and humor throughout the work. When it came to what we might now call "talking trash," Hughes not only researched what little scholarship had been produced by intellectuals such as Yale University social scientist John Dollard and New York University English professor William R. Elton but also sought out living sources in Harlem. He informally interviewed at least one citizen and recorded the children's rhyme they remembered from their youth for inspiration.[13]

Most interesting of all, we are left to wonder whether Hughes had just heard musicians playing the dozens at either the Hotel Viking or backstage at the Newport Jazz Festival. Was there a beef between Muddy Waters and Jimmy Rushing after the final jam session, each claiming that Chicago was really his turf? Rushing's hit was "Going to Chicago," but Waters lived there and had defined a new electric style that would be known as Chicago blues. That Hughes began *Ask Your Mama* the very day after the cutting session took place onstage between Rushing and Waters raises this as a very real possibility.

Hughes also wanted to create a new genre of jazz poetry to match what he had established in the 1920s with his blues poetry. By offering riffs and rhythms that jumped from one motif into another (and back again), Hughes was following the same type of innovation that led him to become the first playwright to bring Black church music into the theater by inventing the gospel play. Third and finally, Hughes wanted to create a permanent record of famous Black musicians, intellectuals, and athletes who were now "almost as well-known as some flowers and trees."[14] The rioting at Newport asserted their popularity in no uncertain terms. But in offering mostly first names of Black celebrities, Hughes's ninety allusions throughout the book subtly demand that readers learn about the emerging icons of Black history on their own. Hughes asserts that they deserve to be known on a first-name basis. Moreover, readers are asked to reflect on what avenues of success are most visible (and thus seemingly accessible) to Black children in America in the early 1960s.

"HORN OF PLENTY"

In his poem "Horn of Plenty," Hughes lists either the partial or full names of more than thirty Black singers, dancers, choreographers, jazz and gospel singers, baseball and football players, and boxers. Hughes labored over the typographical layout of "Horn of Plenty": Its visual appearance is as important as its poetic language. To highlight these innovations is to understand fully Hughes's poetic choices, essential for interpreting the concurrent endorsement of Nina Simone that he was writing. The definitive article Hughes published in the *Chicago Defender* on November 12, 1960, to support Simone is best understood by first reflecting intently on how Hughes blurs and enhances many of the same creative strategies being artistically invoked here.

Something about "Horn of Plenty" made him think of another innovative poet, and he sent the poem off to LeRoi Jones to be published (on February 2, 1961) in the journal *Floating Bear*, where it was formally accepted but never saw publication.[15] The poem's most noticeable typographical element is the inclusion of $ (dollar) and ¢ (cents) symbols at the ends of an opening section that makes up the entire page on which it appears. Completely indistinguishable, the ¢ image here perfectly mirrors the musical symbol that denotes a 2/2 time signature in music known formally as alla breve. Trying to evoke the visual logic of the very sheet music he had labored over in copying Handy's "Hesitation Blues," Hughes's dollar symbols gesture toward the financial status of the numerous Black musicians, boxers, and baseball players named there who can afford to move to the white suburbs. He uses the cents symbol to visibly punctuate lines about the less fortunate who still live in the city's innermost neighborhoods and request quarters (not dollars) to attend films and performances.

Taking the link between money and entertainers one step further, Hughes shifts from dollar signs to the lesser denomination of cents when the famous names start to give way to unnamed citizens living in the quarter of the Negros. Here "quarter" is both a place and a coin. Writing with a poet's ear, Hughes repeats the phrase "In the quarter of the Negroes" throughout the book, resembling the rhythms of two consecutive turns made while dancing a waltz. The line twice presents two shuffle steps and then a spin. Each spin first rises, then falls. The formal name for this Greek poetic pattern is significant. *Tertius paeon* translates as "hymn of thanksgiving." Its two unstressed sounds, followed by a stressed and another unstressed syllable, are repeated back to back to signal the length of the words as much as their pitch. As this meter also drives the roots of dactylic hexameter used in both *The Iliad* and *The Odyssey*, Hughes's imaginative decision to invoke this rhythm in a book that includes only single names of famous Black Americans in 1961 is an audacious stance that casts Harlem as a contemporary Troy. This modern Homer forever documented living Black icons as heroes who deserved one-word names, just like Achilles and Odysseus.

This poetic measure for sound is also relevant to the era for other reasons. It is put to another, more contemporary effect here: "Horn of Plenty" refers to Louis Armstrong's trumpet, the title of a biography of Armstrong by Robert Goffin (1947), and the Thanksgiving cornucopia of fruits, vegetables, and grains. And Hughes was hardly finished with multiple meanings for "quarter": The end of the book features a child who asks his mother for the fare to see a show and needs quarters to be admitted.

Hughes had been listening imaginatively to records that included songs written by Billy Strayhorn with his intimate collaborator Luther Henderson, and every act involved in playing a phonograph record has been embedded in his collection, which opens more like an album than a book. Nothing is as profound as what Hughes activates at the start of his poems in this collection. In "Horn of Plenty," the first three lines are:

> SINGERS
> SINGERS LIKE O-
> SINGERS LIKE ODETTA.

Odetta is yet another folk musician with whom Hughes had collaborated. This stuttering introduction to the poem suggestively mimics the physical challenge of successfully dropping the needle in between songs to hear the entire introduction to a favorite tune. Hughes is bridging the world of song and verse in a way that consistently reminds the reader that they are reading what could be heard. He added this stuttering effect late in his revisions when he was applying every sonic possibility he could to make the sequence feel as though it were playing on a phonograph.

Of course, there are other ways that a phonograph jumps back to play the sounds from where it has already passed. To this end, Hughes provides another leaping needle later in the poem when he writes of those who have moved out "EVEN FARTHER FURTHER FARTHER." A metaphor so dead we often forget its origins today, a broken record can skip indefinitely once it is scratched. Moving forward only to be set back in place right where you were—that's exactly how it can feel to experience hesitation and impasses with those around you. All the implications of a skipping needle serve as the most resonate sonic metaphor for successful musicians living in integrated suburbs who find their dreams are still deferred. As recording artists, they circle endlessly without really getting anywhere.

This feeling comes from imagining how musicians like Nina Simone interact socially when they move into suburban neighborhoods, such as her very own Mount Vernon, New York. By re-creating the effect here, Hughes memorializes a skipping record as one of the most appropriate metaphors to convey the Black experience in America. In other words, racism itself is a repeating issue that the nation cannot get past—even in integrated suburbs. Regardless of any semblance of economic stability, Black people and white people are still living miles apart. To express its theme directly, "Horn of Plenty" presents those who have crossed community barriers to show the actual tensions, microaggressions, and misunderstandings that exist for Black people who attain the dream of reaching a higher-class status. By the end of the book, the metaphor of the record skip is extended beyond America. It reaches out infinitely to become a profound echo that travels across the diaspora of the international Black community.

Hughes names Mount Vernon specifically in the introductory poem to the collection. In a short time, Mount Vernon would be the home of Nina Simone and Andy Stroud soon after their marriage in late 1961. It was already home to such Black luminaries as Sidney Poitier, Harry Belafonte, Paul Robeson, Malcolm X and Betty Shabazz, and Ossie Davis and Ruby Dee. Hughes is clearly noting a trend of such celebrities moving to the suburbs, and his use of "St. Albans" as a potential replacement for Mount Vernon in this poem might be a way to create a veil for those dear friends he wished to shelter from direct comparison. Moreover, his first biographer, James Emanuel, also lived in Mount Vernon. Emanuel was the first to read the poetry collection when Hughes passed it along to him for comments early in January 1961. Emanuel would eventually write thirteen books of jazz poetry himself, and this was his first experience with a genre Hughes was just now creating. Not only is Hughes channeling Simone's future neighborhood in this poem, but the entire focus on naming mirrors what he would amplify in his article "Spotlight on Nina Simone." Just as that soon-to-come piece would focus on Eunice's new name, in "Horn of Plenty" Hughes taps into the feeling of being known all across the country and throughout Europe: "NOW A NAME! MY NAME—A NAME!"

However, in one draft, the three names "MILES AND ELLA AND MISS NINA" got dropped from Hughes's copy.[16] To be sure he had the rhythms right, Hughes, acting like a performer, recorded himself saying the book of poems out loud. He then carefully listened to the playback and made adjustments accordingly, removing elements that he did not think worked when spoken.[17] Simone, Fitzgerald, and Davis survived that cut. Hughes began performing poems from *Ask Your Mama* with longtime collaborator Margaret Bonds accompanying him on piano. When the two first performed sections of the poem at the Market Place Gallery in New York City on February 6, 1961, Hughes's red pencil removed two lines from "Horn of Plenty." Line seven of the poem named dancers Arthur Duncan, Carmen de Lavallade, Alvin Ailey, and Mary Hinkson. Both this line and Nina's callout along with Miles and Ella in line nine were removed wholesale. However, although they were cut on paper, in the end, Hughes and Bonds never even performed "Horn of Plenty" at Market Place Gallery. Furthermore, Hughes never removed these two lines again: They appear in the published book. Hughes merely considered omitting these lines for this one performance. Reading the poem to music, Hughes may very well have simply wanted to shorten his delivery to match the length of the song Bonds was performing. This would be a typical choice Hughes made on a presentation-to-presentation basis for performances, and his red pencil noted changes decided upon during rehearsals with fellow musicians.

"Horn of Plenty" suggests the fate that awaits the Black celebrity who enters a white suburb as a new resident. This occurs regardless of fame or wealth, two things Hughes understood did not always go hand in hand. White neighbors often ignorantly assume that all Black musicians must know each other and therefore can of course speak for their entire race. Hence, this imagined Black man is seriously asked, "DID I KNOW CHARLES MINGUS?" The response to such interrogations by white neighbors is one the reader has by now become accustomed to expecting. Asked where he got his money, the speaker in the poem responds with the triumphant and well timed: "FROM YOUR MAMA!"

Naming Mingus here is a much more significant gesture when compared with almost all the other musicians Hughes names in "Horn of Plenty." Upset with the Newport Jazz Festival, in 1960 Mingus and drummer Max Roach had deliberately staged their own antifestival—Mingus did not like either the growing crowds of white students the bigger jazz festival attracted or the feeling that he was being paid less than his white counterparts. Held on the exact dates of Newport's "official festival," their show earned Mingus and Roach the name—and future album title—"Newport rebels." Weeks before the riot closed the Newport festival, when his counter event's license had not been issued as quickly as expected, Mingus accused Newport founder George Wein of being the roadblock. The confrontation was intense, with Mingus declaring he would kill Wein "in front of 10,000 people."[18] Since Wein was the white organizational leader of the festival, Mingus's feud essentially elevated the idea of the dozens to its most dangerous levels. Though it is unclear exactly what they discussed, Hughes did meet with Mingus during his time in Newport. He was friends with both men, and his personal file contains his hand-drawn map to Mingus's concert location—Cliff Walk Manor—created while both men were staying in Newport.[19]

On the night of July 1, 1960, Hughes had a chance to speak with Mingus when he went to the Cliff Walk Manor to hear Nina Simone sing with Little Richard. Though she was not advertised on event billboards, from midnight to 4 a.m. a crowd of three hundred was treated to a "jumping and jiving affair billed as a 'concert by the sea.'" Bad weather had reduced the large crowd to less than fifty when the impromptu concert was finally moved inside. Simone had played her debut set at the official Newport Jazz Festival the night before. Now, at 1 a.m. the next night, police approached each entrance to the Cliff Walk Manor, determined to check whether alcohol was being served illegally after hours, but they were blocked from entering. One officer finally pushed through a dining room window, and after looking around, the police eventually left, satisfied the law was being obeyed.[20]

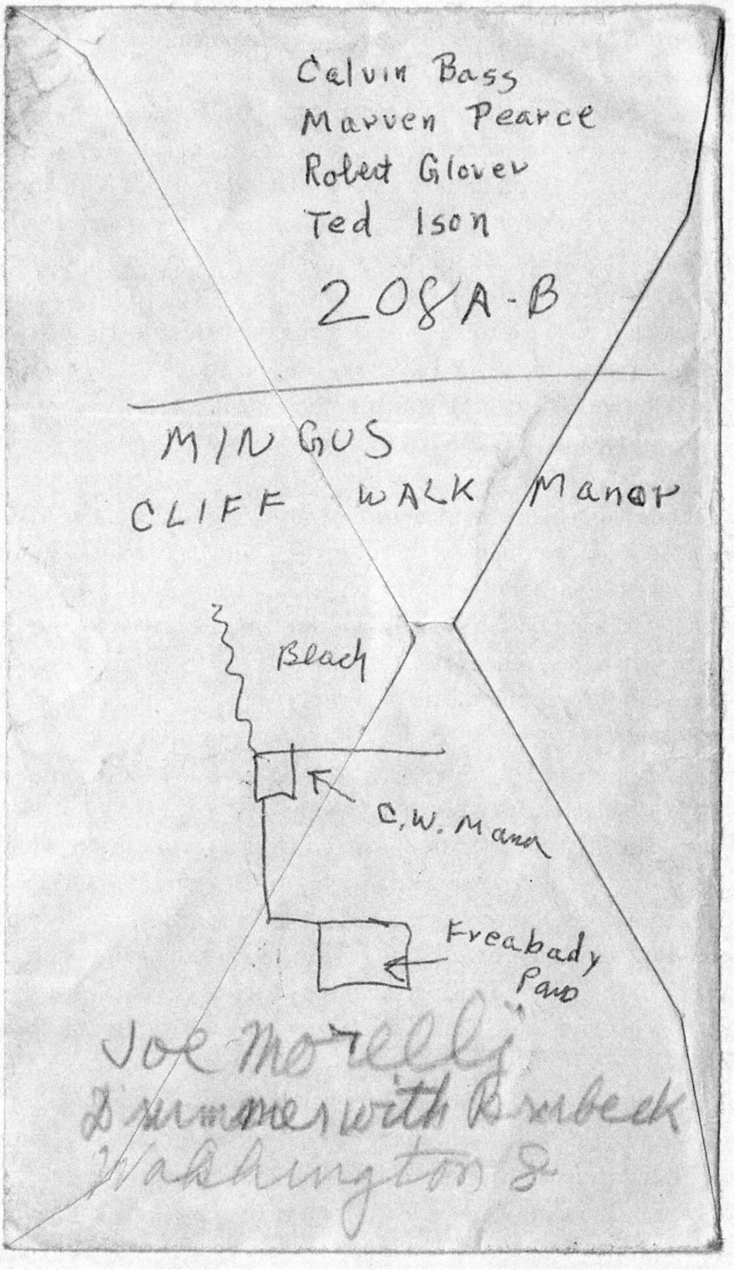

Fig. 4.1. Langston Hughes's hand-drawn map guiding him to the Cliff Walk Manor in Newport, where he met with Charles Mingus and watched Nina Simone perform with Little Richard into the late evening of July 1, 1967. (James Weldon Johnson Memorial Collection in the Yale Collection of American Literature, Beinecke Rare Book and Manuscript Library, Yale University.)

This was the setting that brought Hughes and Mingus together in Newport. The two had known each other ever since Hughes wrote a "glowing review" for Mingus in his 1956 column in the *Chicago Defender*.[21] To eventually meet Mingus this night, the poet walked south down Bellevue Avenue. To his right, he passed Newport Tower, an old stone mill located in Touro Park, and then the Muenchinger-King Hotel, the second-most popular overnight stay for festival headliners, after the Viking. Then, heading east on Memorial Boulevard toward the Cliff Walk, he found Freebody Park to his right before ascending up and then descending down the boulevard's subtle incline. With many blue hydrangeas already in bloom, the city's fernleaf beech trees along the mansion district gave way to the beachfront property that met Newport's famous Cliff Walk Manor, where Mingus was hosting his rebellious musicians.[22] Were any real jokes directed (or muttered under breath) against the police officers? Is it possible that the tension Hughes at some point witnessed between Wein and Mingus at the Hotel Viking (or later heard recounted) informed any of Hughes's poetic themes?[23] If George Wein or any of the white rioters had found the nerve to ask either Mingus or Hughes where they had been after the official festival ended, they would have replied, "Ask your mama!"

Hughes had originally typed, in earlier drafts of "Horn of Plenty," another line about a new resident being asked if their Blackness would rub off. But by his final revisions in February 1961, he asked his assistant George Bass, the man who would eventually become his literary executor, to move that line into the opening poem in the sequence. He instead ended this suburban interaction in "Horn of Planty" with a less naive but no less demoralizing conversation. The poem ends with the Black man being asked to recommend a maid to his white neighbor. Queried as such on one's very patio, how difficult would it be to avoid answering the door without "A CHIP ON MY SHOULDER." This image would prove muscular enough to be upcycled for even greater effect in Hughes's article "Spotlight on Nina Simone." Like the sheet music he worked on multiple times, Hughes would first highlight this theme and publish about the importance of names in his critical piece about Simone. Like a needle that kept skipping, the record turned on itself again when it came time to fully endorse Nina Simone publicly, a musician he compared to Ella Fitzgerald and Miles Davis without "hesitation."

5

Spotlight on Nina Simone

Still busy rewriting what would eventually be more than a dozen drafts to his book *Ask Your Mama,* Langston Hughes was also exhausted from reimagining his play *Tambourines to Glory,* starring Nina Simone's childhood idol Hazel Scott. Hughes reported his fatigue in reworking this stage production by noting that he was now redoing it for the "twenty-ninth" time in hopes of landing it on Broadway.[1] It was clearly time for a rest from everything. He showed unbridled joy about finally taking some deserved breaks as he wrote in his desk calendar. Its entries can be flipped day by day. Starting on Friday, September 30, 1960, and ending on Monday, October 3, each individual entry contains exactly one word per day. Turning through these one by one, they read:

Peace
It's
Truly
Wonderful!!![2]

Maybe he could find new energy by spinning a phonograph? He soon began writing a letter, opening it with a French expression—"La vie est difficile, tu sais." Hughes was sympathizing with a reader who was certainly learning that "Life is hard, you know." Connecting through Sam Cooke's current hit "Chain Gang," Hughes humorously expressed that he had been "working on the chain—GANG," his timely dashes communicating the lengthened beats between Cooke's own delivery of these words. His all-caps letters were something friends were used to interpreting as creative ways to raise points of emphasis. Then he continued with a very uncommon invitation to a unique event occurring at his home at 20 East 127th Street in Harlem:

> I've been thinking of you often and of our pleasant meeting at Newport, and listening often to the record made there which I like very much, and meaning to get in touch with you. But you know how hard it is to get ahold of anybody in New York, and I don't have a phone number for you. . . . The point of all this being, we are going to cook a coon—not a possum but a COON that a friend brought us from Down South. If you like coon, and are in town, are free, lemme know, and come up next Sunday around 6:30–7 to help eat said coon. If you don't like coon, come anyhow and eat whatever else there will be. If you'd like to bring someone, O.K come ahead. The Sunday I am talking about is Sunday, October 9. The place above address. My phone number: LE 4-2952 after 3 P. M. which is about when I wake up, since I work at night. If you can't come Sunday, hope to see you soon anyhow. And make your concert if I can. And say hello again, so phone me, please, m'am.
>
> Cordial regards, and sing on——*
>
> Sincerely,
> Langston Hughes
>
> *Sounds so good![3]

Said coon cooking was originally scheduled for August 28. Then it was moved to October 2 before finally being held on October 9. Hughes's desk calendar for that Sunday includes a concert he attended at 2:30 p.m. Then, written in his own hand, in green ink, it simply reads: "7—Coon Cooking Nina Simone invited."[4]

Simone responded to the invitation four days after Hughes's letter had been sent. She noted that this was something "which I thoroughly would enjoy." Hughes learned that her attendance was not possible the instant he beheld the letterhead: "Palmer House: Chicago." Simone's handwritten script confirmed as she began with a "Dearest Langston—" in black ink. She continued, "I'm in Chicago and we do not return until Monday evening—I'm terribly sorry. I know I'll be missing something—hope to talk and be with you soon." Hughes had earlier sent Simone a copy of his 1956 autobiography *I Wonder as I Wander* (likely after they were first introduced in March or April 1960), and Simone acknowledged that she had both received it and tried to call, "but you were out of town." It was clear, however, that they would meet again soon. She closed the letter with a "By [*sic*] for now—" then underlined only her first name in a signature that was merely "Nina."[5]

Rather than merely writing a single letter, Hughes would often post an additional note in the mail the very next day. This way the second missive would be sure to alert the receiver to what they had most likely postponed responding to the day before. On this occasion, Hughes ensured that he would not be ignored. After writing his personal invitation to the coon cooking on Sunday, he mailed Simone a copy of something of unmistakable value on Tuesday, October 4: a preview of his forthcoming article devoted exclusively to her music.

Hughes was the leading critic of Black culture in America, and his piece would immediately establish Nina Simone's national reputation. His stated need for "Peace" in his diary was apparently broken once he listened to Nina's latest album. It left him energized and ready to endorse her as a major artist. In his standard color of supershow green ink, written letters hovered above a preview of his typed column that would soon run across the country. The handwriting simply read: "Nina—I like your Nina at Newport LP! Langston."[6]

Falling victim to his coy strategy, Nina had indeed received notice of each of these two letters from Hughes before she responded from Chicago. More interested in meeting Hughes personally at his home, she referenced receipt of his article but said nothing more about it, as she had not yet seen it personally. As with almost all its readers, Simone had no idea that this single article by Langston Hughes would establish her reputation as a serious artist—at such a critical and early stage in her career. The piece still stands as the most definitive evaluation of her prowess.

Fig 5.1. Langston Hughes's desk calendar with his invitation to Nina Simone to join him at his home to eat a cooked raccoon on October 9, 1960. (James Weldon Johnson Memorial Collection in the Yale Collection of American Literature, Beinecke Rare Book and Manuscript Library, Yale University.)

HUGHES'S 1960 TONE POEM

"Spotlight on Nina Simone" appeared in the *Chicago Defender* on November 12, 1960. Hughes's weekly articles in the *Defender* had also been running nationwide in Black affiliates of the Associated Negro Press since 1942. The author's cultural clout in 1960 was equivalent to Oprah Winfrey's book endorsements early in the twenty-first century. This piece was unusual: Hughes rarely devoted an article to one person. The majority of his coveted endorsements received a sentence, often among titles of books to add to one's Christmas list. His public support of poet Gwendolyn Brooks is an appropriate analogue. Before Brooks won the Pulitzer Prize for poetry in 1950, Hughes had met one-on-one with her, edited her first collection in 1945, and even helped to place her first poem in *Negro Weekly*.[7] When it came time for Hughes to trumpet the accomplishments of Brooks, a poet he greatly admired, he wrote enthusiastically but not at length. In an article about interracial marriages, Hughes lists eight prominent interracial couples on his way to introducing Brooks's poem "The Ballad of Pearl Mae Lee." He effusively praises Brooks's debut book, *A Street in Bronzeville*, as "a sharp and dramatic book of poems by a zooming new talent on our literary horizon." After five paragraphs devoted to Black and white marriage, readers learn that Brooks's book will "give you something to talk about from now until Christmas."[8] Brooks's work is promoted and praised, but not on a verse-by-verse level. Hughes elevates the product rather than declaring that the world of literature has an unmistakable new star. Not even Gwendolyn Brooks received a full-length Hughes column devoted to her as she moved closer to her Pulitzer Prize–winning work.

Hughes's full-length column devoted to Simone almost had a different title: "Miss Simone: Songstress at the Piano." The idea for the improved title must have struck Hughes after he crossed out a large final section in which he had written, but not published, that she was "a colored girl from North Carolina" who was now "sitting in a spotlight at a piano."[9] The most distinguishing feature of the piece to those who have repeatedly cited it is the sheer volume of references to names. In fact, Hughes mentions no less than thirty-nine Black celebrities in this piece. These names appear because he was writing this article concurrently with his book of poems *Ask Your Mama*. As a result, the article feels as allusive as T. S. Eliot's *The Waste Land*. In this and many other ways, it is indeed worthy of being labeled by Simone's most thorough biographer, Nadine Cohodas, as a "tone poem."[10]

Always overlooked in the commentaries is Hughes's theme that Nina Simone has literally made a name for herself. Alerting the reader to something he discussed with Simone when talking to her at Newport, he writes:

> Her name is not Nina Simone.
>
> Why should anybody like Nina Simone simply because her name is not Nina Simone? Answer: Because she had the nerve to take a name like Nina Simone which bears no reference to anyone living or dead.[11]

Simone's story about the origins of her professional name was quite different. She would most often recount that her first name was invoked by a boyfriend she had in high school. As for her new last name: Simone always asserted that it came from French actress Simone Signoret, whom she had seen on the silver screen in the early 1950s. However, why she selected a different name was most important of all: She was too frightened for her parents, particularly her mother, Kate, to learn early on that she was not playing music for free in Sunday church meetings but instead professionally in Atlantic City nightclubs.[12]

Two more names are especially important in this article for communicating both Hughes's personal appreciation for Simone as well as his prime rhetorical goal. Hughes opens his piece with the attention-getting first lines: "She is strange. So are the plays of Brendan Behan, Jean Genet, and Bertold Bretch [*sic*]. She is far out, and at the same time common. So are raw eggs in Worcestershire and THE CONNECTION." Playwright Jack Gelber's production of *The Connection* in 1959 would soon become a movie in 1961. Its plot features a drug dealer waiting to prey on jazz musicians. The reference to Jean Genet is more interesting. When Hughes went to see Genet's hit play *The Blacks* on April 30, 1961, he promptly left after act 1 to go catch Simone's late set at the Village Gate.[13] Of the play, he confided to a friend: "Must say it baffled me."[14]

Billie Holiday's name is the only one that appears twice in the article. This reflects how Hughes is taking extra pains to clarify that comparisons between the great blues legend and this new rising star are unfair and erroneous. Hughes held a special place in his heart for Holiday—his writing desk held a portrait of her years after her death. No other image neared his typewriter. Because Simone's first hit was "I Loves You Porgy," a song made famous by Holiday in 1948, many unknowing listeners had linked the two artists in a move that made surface sense but also held an assumption that boarded on being racist.

Hughes was determined to show that one Black female singer was different from another. He did this by intentionally highlighting a remarkable artistic gift that Lady Day never had: Nina Simone played piano. Hughes asserted that Nina "plays FLUIDLY well, SIMPLY well, COMPLICATEDLY well, THEATRICALLY well, DRAMATICALLY well, and MADLY well. Not just WELL." The somewhat shocking "all caps" reminds us of two things. First, Hughes was writing before italicized letters appeared in newspapers. Second, he was trying out the same lettering used in his experimental book of poetry *Ask Your Mama*. Hughes's choice to use all caps here for the first time was actually a carefully chosen emendation. At one point, he had intended that the words "Ethel Waters WAS and Pearl Bailey IS, Bing Crosby WAS and Frank Sinatra IS," would be the first appearance of capitalized letters. These verbs were to continue through this paragraph and into his final comparison of George Walker and Sammy Davis Jr. However, in beginning the paragraph about how WELL Nina performs as the introduction of all caps, Hughes instead poetically draws emphasis to the true marvelosity of Simone's piano playing as something she does FLUIDLY and MADLY well.[15]

Only devoted readers of Hughes's weekly columns would understand what is at work in the tall letters that spell SIMPLY and FLUIDLY. Used for the first (but not last) time in the article, Hughes is alluding to one of the most beloved characters in his own prose, Jess B. Semple—or merely "Simple," as he is best known—who often humorously prodded readers to "listen fluently." His full name admonished highbrow readers to "just be simple." This character appeared regularly in these columns in the *Chicago Defender*. Even if Simone's music seemed as if it might "just be simple," Hughes was making his loyal readers smile as they understood that the streetwise Simple himself would endorse listening to Nina Simone every bit as much as the learned Langston Hughes.

Hughes continued his list of sharp contrasts to communicate Simone's verve. Focusing now on the repetition of the idea that she is "different," he asserted: "Nina Simone is as different as beer from champagne, crackers form crepes suzettes, Hulan Jack from Adam Powell." (Hughes's editor corrected the spelling Hughes submitted for the first politician named above by dropping the "d" from the end of "Hulan"). While "crackers" can read as the food itself, Hughes may also be winking a bit here since "cracker" is derogatory slang used by Black people when referring to white people. When "Spotlight" mentions that Simone has appeared on "TV shows," it is referring to her recent appearance on *The Ed Sullivan Show* on September 11, 1960, which drew a wide viewership.[16]

Because Hughes's article has been cited so often (and yet so rarely fully contextualized), two other points deserve to be underlined. First, Hughes wrote a wonderful statement about Simone that never made it into the published article. Near the very end of his first typed draft, he wrote, "What is Nina Simone? A comet out of a constellation. Doing what on Earth? Sitting in a spotlight at a piano."[17] This is the image readers should have in mind when they think of the title "Spotlight on Nina Simone." After hearing her album *Nina at Newport*, Hughes had originally imagined that the woman now "sitting at the piano" had just recently arrived on Earth from another world. This idea of Simone appearing from beyond traditional boundaries of place and time would remain as both a first and a lasting impression made on Hughes. Because of Hughes, this idea would soon become part of Simone's persona as she took on the moniker the High Priestess of Soul. Second, the letters Hughes spells out in the final paragraph, "l-i-v-e," do not relate to the fact that Simone's album captures a live performance. Rather, the omitted context right before the letters grow up into "LIVE" in the same sentence show that Hughes was instead thinking that Nina is and makes you feel "alive." He had at first typed, then omitted, these words just before his final paragraph: "She is like tomorrow morning. Bound to be here, if you live, and nothing happens. And nothing will, if you don't live."[18]

To dramatize the entire focus on how this new artist on the scene was indeed making a name for herself, Hughes ends with these final words to amplify a name he has included no less than ten times: "The letters l-i-v-e that spell LIVE mean exactly the same as the letters N-i-n-a that spell NINA. As for the word SIMONE——be cool, Jack, be cool!" The cumulative effect? Hughes is asserting in no uncertain terms that Nina Simone's name belongs next to each and every one of the famous personalities listed in his article—from baseball star Ernie Banks to the legendary crooner Frank Sinatra. Simone was now officially a "somebody." In writing such a praiseworthy and extended piece showcasing Simone, Hughes reminded the young artist that she was on the verge of fulfilling the promise he had seen in the sixteen-year-old eleven years earlier. His poem "Horn of Plenty" had a new companion in "Spotlight on Nina Simone." In every way possible, this is a prose poem written with the same creative energy Hughes was devoting to *Ask Your Mama*.

By 1961, Hughes and Simone had seen each other often enough to exchange contact information and birthday cards. Hughes's address book, one that often had as many as twenty to thirty new additions and updates per month, now had a new entry written in meticulous green ink: "Simone, Nina. Apt. 15- D / AC—2078 / 415 Central Park West." Simone also received an autographed copy of Hughes's latest book of poems in October 1961, responding in a handwritten card, "It still makes me want to laugh and cry at the same time." When February 21, 1962, rolled around, Nina thanked Hughes for the birthday card she received with a postcard noting, "It was sweet of you," before signing her name merely "Nina."[19]

After twenty years of writing exclusively for the *Chicago Defender*, Hughes started writing for the even more visible *New York Post*. Starting in June 1962, his weekly columns ran every Friday. Hughes devoted his second column at the *Post* to reprinting "Spotlight on Nina Simone." Having established her reputation with his praise, Hughes now sensed an opportunity to widen her acclaim. Below Hughes's own picture, emblazoned about the size of a postage stamp, the article was now simply titled "Nina Simone." This new title draws even more attention to the idea that Nina is an artist who made up her own name. The article also featured a headshot of Simone. She had ice-cold lips, long drop earrings, and an alluring dress that was surprisingly thin at the shoulders. Simone's hair, little changed since her first appearance at Newport, was cropped and curled, shaped by intense straightening.[20]

The 1962 reprint contained two changes. The article was now separated into three parts by a pattern of asterisks. These ran in sets of three between the long middle section of the piece where Hughes focused on folks who never liked Billie Holiday. The section ends with his quiet dig at James Baldwin for the "some" who read him compared with the "many" who read Frank Yerby. Typeface options had recently changed; hence, the capital letters that earlier read as SHOUTS from Simple were now softly reduced for emphasis as *italicized letters*. The way she played was now cool and lilting with a smooth lean to the side, and Nina's name was no longer blasted from a horn but merely emphasized with strutting elegance as *Nina Simone*.

Fig. 5.2a–b. Promotional poster (front and back) for Nina Simone's Carnegie Hall concert, March 21, 1964. (James Weldon Johnson Memorial Collection in the Yale Collection of American Literature, Beinecke Rare Book and Manuscript Library, Yale University.)

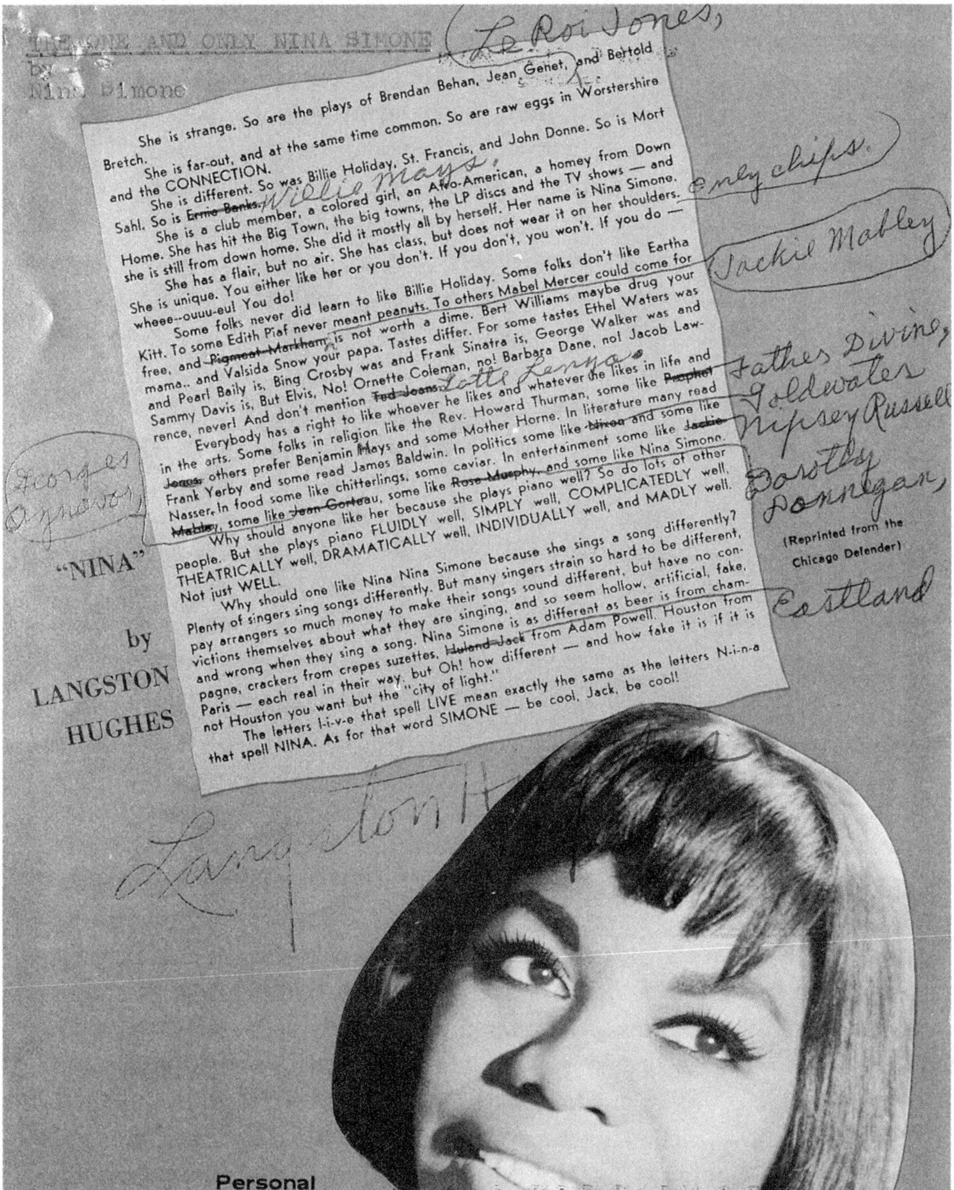

THE ONE AND ONLY NINA SIMONE
by
Nina Simone

"NINA"

by

LANGSTON HUGHES

She is strange. So are the plays of Brendan Behan, Jean Genet, and Bertold Bretch.

She is far-out, and at the same time common. So are raw eggs in Worstershire and the CONNECTION.

She is different. So was Billie Holiday, St. Francis, and John Donne. So is Mort Sahl. So is ~~Ernie Banks~~.

She is a club member, a colored girl, an Afro-American, a homey from Down Home. She has hit the Big Town, the big towns, the LP discs and the TV shows — and she is still from down home. She did it mostly all by herself. Her name is Nina Simone.

She has a flair, but no air. She has class, but does not wear it on her shoulders. She is unique. You either like her or you don't. If you don't, you won't. If you do — wheee--ouuu-eu! You do!

Some folks never did learn to like Billie Holiday. Some folks don't like Eartha Kitt. To some Edith Piaf never meant peanuts. To others Mabel Mercer could come for free, and ~~Pigmeat Markham~~ is not worth a dime. Bert Williams maybe drug your mama.. and Valsida Snow your papa. Tastes differ. For some tastes Ethel Waters was and Pearl Baily is, Bing Crosby was and Frank Sinatra is, George Walker was and Sammy Davis is, But Elvis, No! Ornette Coleman, no! Barbara Dane, no! Jacob Lawrence, never! And don't mention ~~Ted Joans~~.

Everybody has a right to like whoever he likes and whatever he likes in life and in the arts. Some folks in religion like the Rev. Howard Thurman, some like ~~Prophet Jones~~, others prefer Benjamin Mays and some Mother Horne. In literature many read Frank Yerby and some read James Baldwin. In politics some like ~~Nixon~~ and some like Nasser. In food some like chitterlings, some caviar. In entertainment some like ~~Jackie Mabley~~, some like ~~Jean Gorteau~~, some like ~~Rose Murphy~~, and some like Nina Simone.

Why should anyone like her because she plays piano well? So do lots of other people. But she plays piano FLUIDLY well, SIMPLY well, COMPLICATEDLY well, THEATRICALLY well, DRAMATICALLY well, INDIVIDUALLY well, and MADLY well. Not just WELL.

Why should one like Nina Nina Simone because she sings a song differently? Plenty of singers sing songs differently. But many singers strain so hard to be different, pay arrangers so much money to make their songs sound different, but have no convictions themselves about what they are singing, and so seem hollow, artificial, fake, and wrong when they sing a song. Nina Simone is as different as beer is from champagne, crackers from crepes suzettes, ~~Huland Jack~~ from Adam Powell, Houston from Paris — each real in their way, but Oh! how different — and how fake it is if it is not Houston you want but the "city of light."

The letters l-i-v-e that spell LIVE mean exactly the same as the letters N-i-n-a that spell NINA. As for that word SIMONE — be cool, Jack, be cool!

(Reprinted from the Chicago Defender)

Personal Management

ANDREW B. STROUD

419 Teoumseh Avenue
Mount Vernon, N. Y.

Of all the numerous references to the piece, it is worth revisiting at least two critical invocations of Hughes's article. Nina's husband and manager, Andy Stroud, used almost all his savings to secure Simone two high-profile engagements at Carnegie Hall. When the chips were down, he believed Simone could simultaneously fulfill her first dream of playing there as a classical pianist *and* increase interest in her new, extraordinarily popular music. For both of these risky performances, part of Stroud's gamble rested on the fact that he knew he had an "H" card up his sleeve: Hughes's article was the centerpiece of a very focused and well-staged ad campaign for each concert. For her career-defining concert on March 21, 1964, Hughes's entire article was reprinted on posters, and his evaluation "She is Unique" appeared on every newsprint ad above the full name "Langston Hughes."

Either Andy or Nina approached Hughes with another idea for using the article to gain Simone even greater stardom. Since Hughes's piece was cited in reviews so often, would Hughes consider allowing it to appear as the liner notes on her forthcoming album? With the idea of Simone singing not only folk tunes but also ballads, blues, and Broadway show tunes, Hughes's original 1960 endorsement would make the perfect addition. Stroud had already been republishing "Spotlight on Nina Simone" on countless inserts distributed inside programs at her concerts, making this a request to move beyond the stand-alone posters for Carnegie Hall (simply titled "'Nina' by Langston Hughes"). Tried and tested, could the article now be the official liner notes on the back of her next record?

Hughes was more than happy to oblige. His process speaks to someone who is glad to help despite being so clearly overcommitted. He did not go to his files and take out his own carefully written copy of the original work. Instead, Hughes followed the habits of a spontaneous bluesman. Provided a copy of the concert poster featuring his own writing, Hughes took out a blue ballpoint pen and simply began editing right on the glossy poster. Despite the approachability of his writing, Hughes often labored intensely over his words to find just the right combination of compressed meanings and rhythms. In this case, with physical space at a premium, he nonetheless wanted to update the original article. He was always current in his thinking. After all, many names had faded from newsprint in the four years since 1960, and a few other figures were now experiencing the media's rise.

Before he even finished the second sentence, Hughes knew he needed to add the hottest playwright in America. Hughes quickly made space for LeRoi Jones, whose new play, *Dutchman*, had debuted in March 1964 and was defining a new era in Black theater. Working quickly, Hughes wrote in "Georges

Aznavour" and moved Jackie Mabley from that space and up two paragraphs. Interestingly enough, Hughes met Aznavour at Simone's party after she performed at Carnegie Hall in 1964.[21] Somewhere in the publication process, an editor at Mercury Records noticed that the French singer was actually named "Charles" and corrected it accordingly.

By the time Hughes was finished, Mississippi's anti-integrationist James Eastland was the new counterpart to Adam Powell. All in all, ten new names were added in favor of more contemporaneous figures now in the news and minds of citizens living in 1964. Hughes punched the keys of his Underwood typewriter, then submitted a new typed copy to both Mercury Records and Andy Stroud on August 14.[22]

When he ended his new piece, it appeared on the back of Simone's album *Broadway-Blues-Ballads*, released on November 19, 1964.

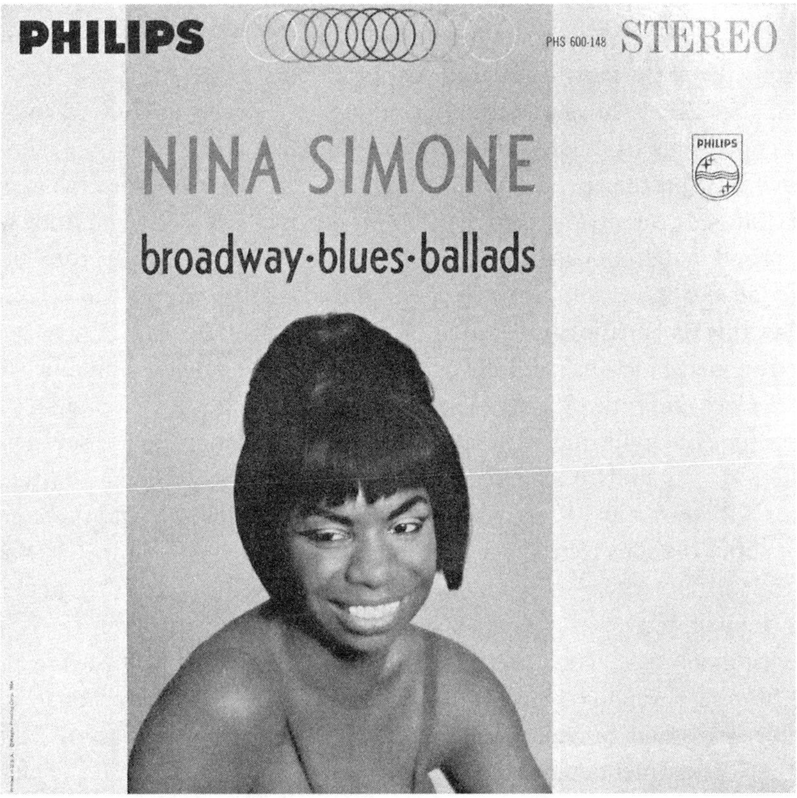

Fig. 5.3. The album *Broadway-Blues-Ballads* (1964). Langston Hughes's updated article appeared on the back as liner notes.

The old "Spotlight" was now titled "THE ONE AND ONLY NINA SIMONE, A Tribute by Langston Hughes." It featured only two further additions. The new final line was specific to the context. Hughes added at the very end, "And listen to this album," hoping that someone who lifted the record from a store's bin would walk straight to the cash register to count out their bills and coins. The other addition must have come to him from so many personal interactions. He included a new final image right after his most often quoted lines: "She has a flair, but no air. She has class, but does not wear it on her shoulder. Only chips." Those two little words spoke volumes about how well Hughes knew Simone by the fall of 1964. She carried not *one* chip on her shoulder but several. It also echoed all the way back to those who had "a chip on their shoulder" when Hughes wrote about Blacks moving into white suburbs in his poem "Horn of Plenty." It reads as if Simone herself could have been the citizen in that poem being queried about knowing Richard Wright or Charles Mingus. Even angrier, the plural *s* signals how many grievances Simone not only already had but would keep accumulating and then enunciating as their mutual engagement continued into the most significant years in Simone's career.

Hughes's summative assessment of Simone has been referenced so often it has now come to stand as the decisive evaluation of her talents. What is so often omitted is the crucial context that Hughes's assessment came so early in Nina Simone's career. Five months after his death in 1967, Nina and Andy were still proud to disseminate lines from "Spotlight" as part of their promotional materials. As one example among many, the advertisement for Nina's concert in Hawkins Hall on the campus of SUNY Plattsburgh on December 13, 1967, featured an image of Nina carefully placed just below an all-caps announcement of the place and time of her 8:00 p.m. appearance. The ad included only one other item, the following summation written by Langston Hughes seven years earlier: "A colored Afro-American, far out, strange singer who has hit the big towns, LP discs, and T.V. shows. She sings a song differently and has convictions about the songs she sings. The letters that spell LIVE also spell NINA. As for the word SIMONE—be cool, Jack, be cool!" Wisely, Hughes's original idea that she will make you feel "alive" was reanimated so that that it reads here as a reminder to see Nina perform "live" in concert. Starting at the inception and running through to the climax of Nina's career seven years later, the definitive assessment of Nina's talents was made by her friend Langston Hughes. Hughes's assessment endured precisely because he crafted it with the nuance and resonance invoked in so many of his best poems.

6

Honeymoon Sponsored by the CIA

Langston Hughes sat down at the White House for a luncheon with John F. Kennedy. He was relieved to have received his security clearance after suffering red-baiting at the highest levels in the past. For at least one moment, he might have relived some of the tension and humility of being called to Washington, DC, by Joseph McCarthy eight years earlier to testify on live television before Congress. But sometime between the appetizer course of smoked salmon and the mimosa salad (bright as the yellow flowers themselves, he noted), Hughes was able to relax. He could now be officially considered for an upcoming all-expenses-paid overseas trip funded by the US government.[1] As he savored the ice cream encased in the smooth outer shell, this bombe glacée Alexandra pairing well with his espresso, Hughes was also secretly acting as father of the bride to a performer he was now treating like his favorite daughter. In fact, by the time Langston Hughes left the capital on November 3, 1961, he had spent his Friday securing Nina Simone a honeymoon sponsored by the Central Intelligence Agency.

Hughes was invited to the White House via a special request made by the man President Kennedy was anxious to impress, President Léopold Sédar Senghor of Senegal. Senghor's own poetry and theoretical concept of Négritude were deeply indebted to Hughes, and when the American poet took his seat at the table, the other guests also moved into their places, knowing the importance of the official occasion. It was quite a cast of dignified characters. John A. Davis was there. Hughes knew him well. In March 1959, Davis had invited Hughes to speak at the first US meeting of the Congress of Negro Writers and Artists. At that conference, the American Society of African Culture (AMSAC) had been founded, providing the US government with the newest vetted channel for sending African Americans abroad. The first iteration of the Congress of Negro Writers and Artists took shape in Paris in 1956 after W. E. B. Du Bois and singer Paul Robeson were seen as too radical to represent a sanitized version of American democracy to the world.

Writer James Baldwin would not be enjoying hors d'oeuvres this afternoon at the White House because he was abroad. Louis E. Martin, though a close campaign adviser to Kennedy during the 1960 race for president, had his name deliberately removed (for reasons uncertain) on October 30 by White House staffer Evelyn Lincoln.[2] Being scratched from the list of invitees was exactly what Hughes needed to avoid. Those in his immediate orbit were using this formal occasion to test Hughes's ability to meet official government protocols. If he passed, it would clear the way for him to formally represent the US overseas. Best of all, Hughes did not have to avoid eye contact with Senator Everett Dirksen of Illinois during this luncheon. The man who joined McCarthy in interrogating Hughes before Congress in 1953 was "out of the city" owing to a prior commitment.[3]

The distinguished Horace Mann Bond arrived. His son Julian would eventually cofound the Southern Poverty Law Center, serve as NAACP president, and write poetry in his spare time, following the vein of his idol Langston Hughes. Horace Mann Bond was now president of AMSAC, which sought Black musicians to promote American democracy overseas in the fight against communism. In this way, the organization played a key role in a culture war that treated African countries as dominoes. Jazz was going to be put forward to the newly independent nation of Nigeria, with the supposition that countries such as Ghana and Senegal would look to their successful neighbor as a model of democracy. AMSAC was "the U.S. government's attempt to turn transnational citizen networks into weapons of anti-communist political warfare," and it essentially used "the Third World as a theatre of the Cold War."[4] The US government had already funded a dramatic coup to remove Congolese prime minister Patrice Lumumba in January 1961. This action resulted in the horrific murder of Lumumba, whom the United States considered the communist-leaning leader of the newly free Democratic Republic of the Congo.

At President Kennedy's table, Edward R. Murrow took his seat. After an illustrious career as a TV host and analyst at CBS, Murrow had recently joined the United States Information Agency (USIA) in 1961. This was work he was well suited for, having served as producer on the propaganda TV special *See It Now*, featuring Marian Anderson's 1957 tour through Europe. Murrow was also the first journalist to discredit Joseph McCarthy before the senator's death in that same year. Murrow's presence on this day signaled a silent level of collaboration between AMSAC and his office. In fact, Murrow would tap Hughes to travel solo to Ghana in 1962 to open a USIA library in Accra, Ghana's capital city. The building was stocked with Langston's own books. Murrow also made sure that Hughes traveled in 1966 to Dakar, Senegal, where he was so popular that "young writers from all over Africa followed him about the city and haunted his hotel the way American youngsters dog favorite baseball players."[5]

The State Department had already overtly sent reluctant musicians such as Louis Armstrong across Africa as early as 1956 on a mission of cultural diplomacy. The CIA took a different strategy, funding a front group made up of jazz musicians and stage performers whose Black leadership kept its covert goals on the down low. That front group was AMSAC. Along with William Fontaine, a philosophy professor at the University of Pennsylvania, and Mercer Cook, a Howard University professor of French, John A. Davis and Horace Mann Bond were AMSAC's four official leaders.[6] They were each currently seated with Hughes and President Kennedy.

By 1962, nearly every Black American luminary would participate in AMSAC activities in one form or another. Many were operating within its formal structure by trying to bend its mission to their own aims. Actors Ossie Davis, Ruby Dee, and Sydney Poitier had appearances that were followed by James Farmer, leader of the civil rights group known as the Congress on Racial Equality (CORE). A session in New York at the Hudson Hotel on May 2, 1962, featured photographer Roy DeCarava and painter Jacob Lawrence. It was preceded on March 14 with none other than LeRoi Jones presenting parts of his poetry sequence *Preface to a Twenty Volume Suicide Note*.[7]

Soon after their meal was finished, Kennedy lifted a glass of champagne to formally recognize what he imagined would be a bright and fruitful relationship between the United States and Senegal. President Senghor responded with his own toast, going out of his way to name Langston Hughes as an inspiration on both his poetry and his conceptualization of Black pride. Just then, as Hughes extended his widest smile, he remembered seeing Kennedy scan the table "just to see which poet I might be."[8]

THE WEDDING

Nine days before she was scheduled to fly overseas for the first time, Nina Simone married Andrew Stroud in a small ceremony held in New York at her 103rd Street apartment, number 15-D, at 415 Central Park West. The bride and groom certainly calculated in the fact that a trip abroad could serve as their honeymoon. Each knew the active role Hughes played in securing the timely getaway, but neither was aware at any time that the CIA was footing the bill. Though she had been married before (for less than a year) to Don Ross, a white man she met while playing clubs in Atlantic City before signing any record deal, Simone nonetheless confidently dressed for her wedding in all white from shoes to veil.[9] With only close family and two musicians witnessing her nuptials, the most memorable fact for Simone was that her father did not attend. The generous father figure of Langston Hughes supplied a honeymoon trip when Nina needed his timely gift most.

In addition to having to overlook an absent father, Nina had an even deeper wound that she hoped might be healed by an international escapade. According to Simone, she was physically abused on the very night of celebrating her engagement. Sometime around September 1961, three months before her wedding, she remembered being hit repeatedly on the street no fewer than seven times. Her assailant next hailed a cab and pushed her in. The two then walked through her building's lobby, with Simone finally staggering into her apartment. Held at gunpoint, she was tied to a chair with her hands twisted forcefully behind her back. She was heatedly queried about her full sexual history, with unyielding demands that she spare no details. Essentially now a prisoner, Simone responded to question after question through bloodied lips. This went on for five hours. Terrified and exhausted, she was then tied to her bed frame and raped. In her autobiography, published in 1991, Nina Simone claimed to know the man who did this to her. He was drunk on rum. His name was Andrew Stroud.[10]

Nina spent the next two weeks being nursed back to health by recording producer Hecky Krasnow and his wife. Their daughter Judy remembers the chicken soup Nina ate to regain her strength. Andy Stroud consistently denied that any of this ever happened. He continued to assert his innocence as late as 2005.[11] To better understand this, it is useful to realize that both Langston Hughes and Nina Simone were closeted bisexuals. According to Patti Bown, a pianist Nina saw frequently at the Village Gate, Nina had at least one girlfriend at this time. Simone's brother Sam shared that there were other female partners as well over the years.[12] Did Andy try to end these liaisons with physical force before they married? As a police detective, did he commandeer a colleague to carry out this mission in hopes of intimidating her from being with women?

All of these scenarios are legitimate possibilities. It seems clear that someone abused Nina. Nina's memory should be considered in light of her having bipolar disorder and seeing a psychologist in 1961. Regardless of the passing of time, Nina was consistently unreliable when remembering her personal past. What we do know is that she was assaulted, under psychiatric care, and hiding her lesbian encounters. These three facts turned her upcoming honeymoon into as much of a false front about her life as the CIA's clandestine funding of AMSAC.

NIGERIA

Andy Stroud, Al Schackman (Nina's guitarist), Langston Hughes, and Nina Simone found themselves traveling together by bus. They were on their way to the airport for a flight that would take them to Nigeria by way of Rome. Tellingly, it was Al who sat directly next to Nina, with Andy and Hughes taking the two seats just behind. The singer and poet each had window views. As Andy and Nina marked the exciting occasion with another photograph at the airport, Simone and Hughes faced the lens in synch while Andy stood near, slightly back, with closed lips.[13] Without touching, Andy played the role of a working manager much better than he did a newly married man.

Then there were the drums. Nina Simone first experienced Africa accompanied by a soundtrack of drumming. Though it was nearly 2:30 a.m. when the AMSAC artists landed, a welcoming party of Tiv, Alum, and Atilogu dancers greeted them along with musicians whose hands were rapping so fast the dancers hardly knew what part of their bodies to shake first. Cloaked in feathered headdresses, the ceremonial dancers waved shields and machetes. Nina wrote, "It started the minute we got off the plane. . . . Fifty women, men, and children dancing, beating drums and singing—this in addition to a receiving line and another two hundred people standing around to greet us. Cameras flashing—everybody talking and stinking! Yes, you must get used to body odor. . . . These fools [on board] had been dancing since 10:30—we arrived at 2:30."[14]

Hands, hips, and feet vibrated as most of the thirty-three artists excitedly descended a rolling jetway whose stairs had been quickly rolled across the Ikeja airport runway.[15] Small groups were forming right out on the tarmac. Slung over her left shoulder, Simone's beige coat had been removed as December cold in America now gave way to African humidity. It neatly matched her skirt. Either tired, or determined to seem fashionable, her Ray-Ban sunglasses shielded her eyes as she looked left and listened to her traveling companion Babatunde "Michael" Olatunji hold forth. His right hand was clasping the leather strap of the camera case that hung around his neck.

Nina later wrote, "It is so fantastic—like leaving the security of a womb where you've been all your life and running head long into a volcano—about to erupt!"[16]

Occasions such as the official reception and opening dinner, city sightseeing, a special art exhibition, and a full evening of nightlife offered the new bride ample opportunities to enjoy many of the activities that make a honeymoon one of the happiest periods of a marriage. At the opening dinner at the Federal Palace Hotel on December 17, Hughes took his place of prominence at 8:30 p.m. at the head table next to Ameka Azikiwe, the son of Governor-General Nnamdi Azikiwe, and Horace Mann Bond. Only two seats removed from the governor-general himself, Hughes, Bond, and the other distinguished guests from America all wore white dinner jackets with black bow ties.

Semiformal social events, such as a dinner hosted by Solicitor General Godfrey Amachree on December 15 and then another on December 20 at the home of USIS host Dr. John Noon, gave way to more celebratory occasions. Barhopping on December 16, the group enjoyed the kind of local music that had just replaced the standard British songs as they made their way through the heart of Lagos, with stops at Kool Cats Inn, Caban Bamboo, and Papingo.[17] The first two locations had been founded by local icon Bobby Benson, and Papingo often featured the trumpet playing of Victor Obiya, who eventually earned the title "the evil genius of highlife music" as he blended "European tonal practices, Afro-Caribbean percussion, and Nigerian melodies."[18]

But anyone bumping into Simone might have mistaken dancer Geoffrey Holder or film star Brock Peters for Nina's new husband. Posing during the layover in Rome, Simone beamed standing next to Holder, a six-foot-six-inch-tall dancer. One of Simone's black leather gloves rested naturally inside Holder's elbow. Between performances in Nigeria, Nina would break out her revealing two-piece bikini and dance the twist with Peters on the sands of Tarkwa Bay Beach. Peters's six-foot-two-inch frame matched his smooth movie star looks—he had made a name for himself starring as the dangerous Crown in the 1959 film version of *Porgy and Bess* and would soon have an important role

Fig. 6.1. Nina Simone and drummer Babatunde "Michael" Olatunji (to her left) after landing at the airport in Lagos, Nigeria, about 2:30 a.m. on December 15, 1961. (James Weldon Johnson Memorial Collection in the Yale Collection of American Literature, Beinecke Rare Book and Manuscript Library, Yale University.)

in the film *To Kill a Mockingbird*. As a singer, he joined Martha Flowers (who was also on this trip) to sing Hughes's lyrics to "African Lady" on Randy Weston's seminal 1961 album *Uhuru Afrika*. A full picnic was set while the shirtless Peters entertained Nina the newlywed. She wore a large hat the size of a pot used for planting. It perfectly concealed the hair she hid onstage under a wig. But Peters's eyes were scanning lower to check out Nina's form. Nina's husband, Andy, was nowhere in the frame. In fact, despite all the stars falling neatly into place, Andy never set foot in Nigeria. Once the bus arrived at the airport in New York, he bid Nina, Al, and Langston farewell and took a lonely cab ride back to his home. Had Hughes's invented alter-ego Jess B. Semple written one of his weekly headlines in the *Chicago Defender*, it would have read "Bride Honeymoons Alone."

Nina wrote Andy from Lagos, Nigeria, by air mail. She praised the modern hotel: "It is huge and beautiful—must have at least 700 rooms." After a shopping trip to the local open markets to secure gifts for Andy, she also showed her naive innocence: "In many ways, what we have seen in the movies about Africa is true—the women carrying children on their backs as much as 75 to 100 pounds on their heads and everybody is busy trading at the market place." As to personality, Nina felt at home despite the "uninhibited" display of nudity by many of the locals: "They are bashful and shy at times—in this category I feel quite at home—the southern Negro is very much like that." After three days on the continent, Nina was finding the joy she had lost in her homeland. She was in grand spirits: "I've started exercising again and hope I have a chance to ride a bicycle tomorrow." But as she reveled in the luxury, she also longed for her groom as she described her accommodations inside the lavish Federal Palace Hotel: "Air conditioning that works, huge bathrooms, fountains and terraces where we eat and watch the boats and fisherman go by—Baby, it's like a dream—I wish for you so much! I don't know if I'll rest until you've come here with me."[19]

Hughes knew as early as 1959 that the money sustaining AMSAC was likely flowing from the US government. Walking in Nigeria would have provided further reflection as he likely would have noted just how close the AMSAC offices were to the US consulate. As both a novelist and Communist Party member (since 1929) Lloyd Brown remembers speaking to Hughes in New York at the Hudson's hotel bar. After Brown noted that the AMSAC writers' 1959 conference had been "very well-funded," Hughes replied, "Yes, by somebody with a whole lot of dough." Lloyd went further in hinting that the "somebody" Hughes was referring to was Uncle Sam: "And he can print all the money he needs." Hughes responded with a knowing but silent shrug.[20] Furthermore, Hughes knew that AMSAC wanted middle-of-the-road political stances at this moment and thus went out of his way to retune a dial set by default to radical. Speaking at the organization's conference on March 28, 1959, Hughes had made the uncharacteristic choice of downplaying race when he admonished the next generation of writers to "be a writer first. Like an egg: first egg, then an Easter egg, the color applied." However, at his next large public appearance, far from the ever-watchful eyes of John A. Davis and the perked ears of Horace Mann Bond, Hughes returned to declaring the very foundations of his career: "There is so much richness in Negro humor, so much beauty in Black dreams."[21] What accounts for this change? Hughes's desire at this precise cultural moment to play ball reveals the desire to reenergize his public image. He needed to find a middle ground so that he would not be remembered as the subversive radical McCarthy had framed on TV sets across the nation.

Although it does not appear that the known CIA agent James "Ted" Harris went to Nigeria on this trip, at least one lesser agent who knew that AMSAC was a front did attend. Yvonne O. Walker enjoyed both the entertainment and her accommodation in room 403 of the Federal Palace Hotel. In a meeting with John A. Davis and two male CIA officers, Walker had been asked to "swear a secrecy oath" before each man disclosed their association with AMSAC.[22] Because Hughes was so involved in every aspect of presenting the AMSAC program in Nigeria, he received regular updates and provided feedback on sessions and their participants. One handwritten note from Walker to Hughes documents how these two partners worked in silence, ignoring the truth they each knew: "Langston—John [Davis] asked me to send you this Yvonne."[23] By the summer of 1969, AMSAC had effectively run its course, but its covert association with the CIA was not revealed to the public until February 1976.[24]

Whereas Hughes clearly knew that the US government was backing AMSAC, Nina Simone remained forever in the dark. This was a topic a father sometimes avoids telling his daughter about.

While this was Simone's first trip overseas, Hughes had been to Nigeria the year before for the inauguration of the country's first native leader, Governor-General Benjamin Nnamdi Azikiwe. The two men had first met as college students in Pennsylvania at Lincoln University more than thirty-five years earlier. "Zik" sent Hughes a personal invitation, and he himself read Langston's poem "Youth" to close out the ceremony. The poem looks forward to days ahead that shine bright as a flaming sun and ends by declaring that such light is a "Broad arch above the road we came, / We march!" Hughes was the perfect choice for the celebration; his poems had been featured all across Nigeria in newspapers for years. Among an American inaugural contingent that included Nobel Prize winner Ralph Bunche, W. E. B. Du Bois, and even Martin Luther King Jr., it was Langston Hughes who stood out after the speech among all the "throngs of admirers."[25] Yes, contrary to what readers would expect today, Nigerians held Hughes in "far higher regard than King in 1960."[26] This is why he was such a valuable cultural asset to the CIA.

THE FESTIVAL: A NINE-DAY HONEYMOON

AMSAC's cultural exchange trip to Nigeria in 1961 allowed the US government to put Langston Hughes into the field fighting its battles on multiple cultural fronts, including talks, presentations, and photo ops. But with this trip serving as her lonely honeymoon, Nina did not accompany Hughes to any of these sessions. After all, who would want to skip the warm sand and lovely social company of other Black musicians her own age? Instead, Nina experienced the thrill of a lifetime. She wrote Andy: "Can you imagine me humbly bowing before a 'King'? Yes, I got lucky enough and had someone take me just this afternoon to meet one . . . donned in expensive robes, with five wives and expensive cars. . . . He is a King, has a special room that is his 'palace,' with women waiting on him hand and foot, and people, bowing before him—and make no mistake—he lets you know he's a King! Goddam, I tell you, I ain't never seen nothing like it."[27]

The first evening session must have given Simone a sense of déjà vu as Hughes was again presenting musicians just as he had at the Newport Jazz Festival in 1960. Dancers Al Minns and Leon James wore the same matching plaid jackets and snake-thin ties that they had in Newport. Hughes alternated with a man known locally in Nigeria as "pocket size" Bobby Benson, an actor and musician who welcomed African artists to the stage like a "bearded goon."[28] By contrast, the elderly Hughes introduced American singers Odetta and Brock Peters, and then dancers Al Minns and Leon James, with what the local press termed "sincerity and warmth and friendship."[29] Some regarded Odetta as the "nightingale" of the evening as she closed with "He's Got the Whole World in His Hands." Peters sang "The Railroad Worker" and "Chokombe-Chokombe" with such force that he was asked to repeat the songs the second evening.[30] Filled with expectant nerves and anxiety about her own upcoming set, Simone surely would have felt a sense of growing admiration for Hughes. Here was a man who claimed to be a poet but kept appearing onstage as a cultural ambassador with immense musical clout.

The proposed list of performer appearances featured an agenda that would have left everyone in Nigeria, as well as each of the thirty-three passengers from the United States, in the thrall of the inimitable skill of Miss Nina Simone. After collaborating with Davis, Mann, and Hughes, the tentative schedule for December 5 that Hughes reviewed had Nina taking the stage for the two nights on no less than five occasions. It was originally thought that Simone would close out the Monday session before staying on for a large finale. The idea of a large free-for-all finale sounded very similar to what Hughes had executed with Little Jimmy Rushing the year before at Newport.

The second evening had Simone penciled in to perform in the unenviable spot soon after festival headliner Lionel Hampton finished. The compensation? Simone would have her own set and then share the stage with drummer Babatunde "Michael" Olatunji before coming back for another finale. This would have worked the new bride into a stunning five onstage appearances, with all five being nothing less than the show-closing final sets of each night that led directly into group finales where she would also be included. Either Hughes had tremendous leeway in suggesting the schedule or his co-organizers respected Simone's music to the same high degree. No doubt the basis for

Hughes's instance would have been his high regard for the way she galvanized an audience when he watched her perform live.

However, when the final program appeared in print, Randy Weston took Nina's slot in the final program by closing out night one. He also accompanied Hampton twice on the second evening.[31] Hughes and Weston knew each other well. After meeting at the Village Gate on May 3, 1959, they began collaborating on songs such as "African Lady," for which Hughes provided these lyrics:

> Dark Africa of my dreams
> You're my Queen
> My Queen of Dreams.

Weston's musical composition is so complex that it earned the title "Second Movement" within the sequence *Uhuru Afrika*. Yes, having collaborated with Odetta on multiple occasions, Hughes literally knew every American performer personally (except for concert pianist Natalie Hinderas) before the contingent even boarded the plane to Nigeria.

Why the change from Nina to Weston? A capitalistic democracy such as the United States believed wholeheartedly that jazz music was "universally adaptable to all cultures of the world."[32] The CIA-backed AMSAC agreed. In this definition of "jazz," both the United States and AMSAC privileged the kind without any words. Though Simone was clearly a fully engaging performer who projected greater star power than Randy Weston, her lyrics were a diplomatic distraction. Hence, Weston's wordless riffs closed night one without any finale or jam session reminiscent of the Newport Jazz Festival. Instrumentals were the weapons of choice in this Cold War setting.

The proposed program of December 5 bears the heavy-handed influence of Langston Hughes. This is the lineup he would have both created and approved. After all, who among the group had more knowledge of these musicians than Hughes? The revision displays AMSAC's internal agenda and goals. The crowd would get the kind of content that the CIA believed moved most easily across borders. Thus, Nigerians saw not the best that America's Black performers had to offer but rather the kind of "Negro" artists the US information and intelligence agencies thought Nigerians wanted to admire. Given its ultimate array of insensitive or even racist choices of costumes and dances, the final program contained not only a visible record of how the US government believed it could win Nigerians over to democracy but ultimately a representation of what it naively imagined was true of Nigeria itself.

Had the originally proposed program been presented, there would have been no more consistent and beloved American presence onstage at the

AMSAC festival in Nigeria than that of Langston Hughes and Nina Simone. Before playwright William B. Branch took Hughes's place, the agenda of December 5 also featured Hughes presenting every US artist, making him the sole American narrator for both nights of the festival.[33] Hughes's fingerprints are everywhere on both the original schedule and the subsequent lineup that in effect tried to present Simone as America's star musical ambassador.

Sometime after 11:00 p.m. on Monday, December 18, Nina Simone took her place before four thousand people in Lagos's King George V Stadium. She was elegantly seated behind a silver microphone stand. Footlights ran the length of the stage. Langston Hughes passed her as he walked briskly offstage, having just finished the fifth of his six introductions. Nina sat with the perfect posture of a classically trained pianist. She was wearing a full-length satin dress with sleeves that ended just above her elbows. With a jewel in her barrette and her pageboy wig held tightly in place, she looked far too tame to have earned her current nickname, "Afro-Simone." With the crowd to her right, Nina started with the light and childlike piano notes that introduced "Zungo," a song she had learned to sing in its original Yoruba language from Babatunde "Michael" Olatunji when the two met in Greenwich Village. They had just performed "Zungo" together at the Village Gate on September 9; now these two were in front of a Nigerian audience who heard a Black American woman calling the Zungo area of Nigeria her home. The coordination between Hughes's opening comments (or was it a wedding toast?) and Nina's performance (like her first dance) suggests remarkable collaboration. Hughes had opened the session testifying to the audience that we have come "in all humbleness with love and sincerity. In a sense, we feel we are coming home, to our ancestral home, back to the roots of our culture."[34] Now the bride was underlining those sentiments with an ink as bold and black as her piano keys.

Olatunji was a native Nigerian who had made a name for himself in the United States with the release of two albums released on the prestigious Columbia label. "Zungo" was from his recent album, and inauspiciously, Olatunji would in the end prove to be the most visible performer of the entire festival as he opened solo and then closed each session with Randy Weston both nights. His five total performances (the number Simone was originally slated to take) resulted in universal condemnation by the Nigerian press, where his playing was critiqued as being at the tenth-grade level.[35] Regarding the antics he invoked in his personal set, in which he pretended to warm the skin of his drum by a bright light so that it would tune just right, newspaper accounts angrily asked, "Who gives a damn about Olatunji here?"[36]

Now onstage with her guitarist, Nina looked to her right and found the only white man among the thirty-three artists to make the trip from the United States. Having asked him at one point how that felt, Al Schackman smiled, fully cognizant of what Nina was implying.[37] Now, even more on his own, Schackman sat down, unable to hide that he was just as white as the governor-general's agbada robe. He prepared his lanky fingers to shape his staccato chords so he could match whatever rhythm Nina and Olatunji would land on. The strap hung unused from an acoustic six-string complete with a black custom pick up fitted above the open sound hole. He had to be ready for anything: Nina often set opening rhythms that were sometimes unexpected and often unrehearsed. Abdul Malik's oversized upright bass joined Nina's piano to create a samba beat, and Nina's own instrumental song "African Mailman" showed that she already had a repertoire of songs that conjured her conceptions of African rhythm. Though no recording of this performance has survived, it is tempting to picture Nina hitting this song from the first bar as fast and reckless as her tense version from the Montreux Jazz Festival of 1976. There Nina screamed one minute and forty seconds into a track that not only propelled listeners to clap faster but also seemingly wore out the legs of the song's imagined subject. The fast pace captures the breathlessness of a man who is not so much late as being chased by a wild animal. With this second song, her six short minutes of allotted time onstage in Nigeria were up, and Nina exited the stage to her right without having sung a single word in English. Just as compliant as she had been all through her high school years in Asheville, North Carolina, she was following the AMSAC company line in privileging wordless jazz over English lyrics.

Night two found Nina as upset as the Nigerian press. Though she immediately followed Nigerian Francesca Pereira and the Bob Fowler Combo onstage, Lionel Hampton had clowned so much earlier in the evening's session that Nina visibly displayed the same reaction as the locals. Hampton clearly felt he had earned special privileges as the headliner, which sent Nina over the edge. Having been flown over separately to accommodate an earlier concert commitment, the bandmaster and his famous vibraphone now felt inclined to show his peers that strict time constraints simply did not apply to him. Nina was not alone in her disdain. Weston well remembers his experience accompanying Hampton for this set: "He rehearsed a lot of good music, but once the show started, he went into his 'show biz' routine, with a lot of clowning around. I guess the Africans felt like he was insulting them."[38] Hampton literally acted like a juggler when he tossed both his xylophone mallets to Governor-General Azikiwe, who "skillfully" secured each of the soft blue ends into his palms.[39]

Nina's anger was unmistakable when she took the stage. She told her audience: "This number is a fast one, and we should all be exhausted at the end of it. It is all about sinners, which we all are."[40] With that terse introduction, Nina started into one of her epic versions of "Sinnerman." Was Nina thinking of Hampton as her chords beat behind an accusatory "Oh Sinnerman, where you gonna run to?" or was she perhaps projecting a deeper anger at Andy's abuse into a song where there is no place to hide? Replacing Olatunji this evening, Clarence Stroman had the challenge of keeping time on percussion. Hughes had heard this tune before—Nina regularly used it to close her sets at the Village Gate—but the pacing of the interlude here, which includes hand clapping, clearly suggested that the song had an African tempo and rhythm. In her first set the night before, the "African Mailman" she sang of sounded as if he was trying to escape a deadly attack; tonight, the very intensity of the Second Coming and its condemnation of the damned were centered by a frustrated artist.

Nina's final cadenza of "Sinnerman" featured her moving right to left down the full length of the keyboard with her flying hands crossing over one another. The effect was of hearing a piano being thrown down a flight of stairs. Hughes might have turned a suggestive glance at Davis and Bond, perhaps wondering if the final decision to bring Hampton up again to close the festival should have been avoided. With her music "rumbling like low thunder," the crowd wanted Nina to perform an encore.[41] Nina's versions of this song always came as her final song, as if there was nothing else to pour once the glass was full. Even though it approached ten minutes in length, the nearly six thousand in attendance had been treated to just one song by the amazing Nina Simone. What kind of accusation against Hampton would the song leave if Nina stayed longer? She could move this crowd to a higher appreciation than Hampton ever received in less than half the total time. She left the stage "in an undisguised huff."[42]

THE OFFICIAL LUNCHEON

Photographers were stationed everywhere. Intent on capturing every moment that showed Nigerians appreciative of Americans, so many US government cameramen were at festival sessions that two or more photographers often appear in the background of the developed images. At the governor-general's official luncheon, Hughes found himself sitting four seats away from Azikiwe. Simone would have noted that Hughes was the most prominently placed guest of those without official ranks and titles within AMSAC. As American entertainers arrived on December 19, a camera clicked when Nina Simone and Zik made eye contact just before being seated for the meal. Shaking hands as he welcomed guests, Zik extended both hands to Nina's smile as she revealed how ecstatic she was to have landed on the African continent. Simone's two performances had clearly made quite an impression on Zik. When it was time for the group photo at the statehouse, Simone found herself prominently placed immediately right of the Nigerian leader. She had met both a real king earlier and now the country's most powerful leader. Hughes might have arrived as Zik's closest connection within AMSAC, but Simone was leaving as the governor-general's favorite performer.

THE AFTERMATH

Although Lionel Hampton was by far the biggest target, with his behavior during one set and his subsequent finale derided by every media outlet, few Americans escaped ridicule in the Nigerian press. One article headline said it all: "Stop Faking African Culture." Brock Peters was singled out for insulting his band, drummer Babatunde "Michael" Olatunji was characterized as "the less said, the better," and one writer claimed that he was "beaten hollow to hear singers at the top of their voices" presenting Italian arias from *Madame Butterfly*.[43] Critics wondered why the accomplished Odetta flew all the way across the Atlantic to only sing three short songs. Words of praise were reserved exclusively for only two people: dancer Geoffrey Holder and Langston Hughes.[44] Holder had performed barefoot with black makeup darkening his eyes into the shapes of Egyptian hieroglyphics, and his traditional costume featured beads wrapped around his neck, elbows, and wrists.[45] Interestingly, no comments on Nina's appearances note anything but her visible disgust with Lionel Hampton's antics for holding forth too long. Despite a legion of photographers trying to frame audiences supposedly enjoying the concert and performances, the AMSAC concert in Nigeria was a flop for US diplomacy, and no assemblage of similar American talent was ever sent to Africa again to play the role of cultural ambassadors.

But a failure for the US government was also an opportunity for many of the participants. Randy Weston, who had collaborated with Hughes on the album *Uhuru Afrika*, returned from his visit to Nigeria obviously animated about the idea of bringing even more African rhythms to his music. As editor of the recently published *African Treasury* and *The First Book of Africa*, Hughes himself now had deeper connections to both distribute and ground his recent work on the continent. Simone herself would return to Liberia in September 1974 and then spend the rest of her life abroad, including in France. Traveling to Nigeria in 1961 on a trip paid for by the CIA was her introduction to the world. This is all to say that these artists were using this fully funded trip by "accepting it on one set of terms, then actually spending it accordingly to another, turning it to the limited advantage of their own race. They were, in other words, 'putting on'—a skill that perhaps helps explain why they were so much better than other front groups at maintaining the appearance of being 'unwitting.'"[46]

Hughes took the idea of cultural exchange seriously. He was one of the few participants who cared enough to complete an AMSAC questionnaire when he returned to Harlem. The two-page document was carefully typed and included nearly a full page of feedback under a heading so often left blank: "Other Comments." Hughes suggested three ways the morning educational sessions might have been better attended. He called for avoiding the Christmas holiday in the future, providing better publicity, and moving the entire endeavor to the country's intellectual center, the city of Ibadan, where a Nigerian "university committee" could work out advertising and programming details. Calling this first endeavor an "excellent initial project," the fourth full paragraph of his comments was both earnest and specific. Hughes understood that no future music should include songs that were white or European. He also imagined continental representation from places such as South Africa, Ghana, and Sierra Leone, believing that "there should be a next time—many of them if they can be worked out." Perhaps somewhat selfishly, he underlined the idea of a "LONGER time-period" so that travelers would stay three weeks or a full month in the future.[47] Though he did not say it, perhaps this would have enticed actor Sidney Poitier and South African–born singer Miriam Makeba to accept a future invitation.[48]

In many ways, Hughes's underlining also spoke to the wishes of Nina Simone. She, too, wished she could have stayed longer in Nigeria to truly experience even more of Africa. However, her manager and husband, Andy Stroud, booked her into a showcase that was too good to miss. On New Year's Eve, "The Amazing Nina Simone" played Carnegie Hall for the first time as an "added attraction," joining fellow North Carolinians John Coltrane and Thelonious Monk as concert headliners.

Nina would not be replaced by Randy Weston in the United States. On December 22, Nina Simone left Africa behind, taking the expected flight back to New York reserved for AMSAC's performers. She packed up the photo she had of Andy and left room 316. He learned by letter that it had served its purposes while they were apart: "I have your picture with me, so I think I'll make love to myself and go to asleep—see how discreet I'm getting? (smiles)."[49] Hughes stayed in Nigeria an additional seventeen days. He joined American ambassador to Nigeria Joseph Palmer and his wife for a night of singing Christmas carols. Perhaps wishing he had someone like Simone to share his trip with, Hughes traveled back to the United States only after having stayed more than a week in Paris. But before he left Lagos, just in case he had wondered how it truly felt to be a father of the bride, Hughes found himself trying to check out of room 203 of the Federal Palace Hotel owing more than five hundred dollars.[50] The sum, accrued from various charges not covered by AMSAC, forced him to wire home and wait through an excruciating series of telegrams and transfers.[51] In the end, Hughes was stuck with the bill, a father facing demanding creditors after the party had gone over budget.

7

Carnegie Hall

On February 18, 1964, Langston Hughes received a pair of guest tickets from Andy Stroud "to see the amazing NINA SIMONE at Carnegie Hall March 21, 1964."[1] The language was by now habitual for Stroud, as posters all around the iconic building advertised the event as a chance to see and hear "The Amazing Nina Simone." Simone was represented as a caricature, wearing a full-length black dress and arm-length gloves that matched her pink lips.

Signing his Western Union telegram merely "Langston," Hughes wrote the following well wishes to Nina on the very day she was about to take the stage for a historic concert at Carnegie Hall: "HERE IS WISHING YOU THE BEST / AND ALL THE REST TONIGHT."[2] Hughes needed to be there. After all, his 1960 endorsement declaring "She is Unique" accompanied formal advertising in the newspaper ads that promoted the show.

Hughes likely arrived early for the 8:30 p.m. curtain and entered Carnegie Hall unaware that he was about to hear two new Nina Simone songs. One would become such an essential tune in her repertoire that she would sing it for the next thirty-six years. The other would define a new direction in her career. Though Hughes could not have realized it yet, by embracing political topics in her music, Simone was reactivating the types of artistic protest he had engaged in more than forty years earlier. With this new trajectory, she was now becoming the ideal vehicle for performing the kinds of verses he had been writing for decades.

LIVE IN CONCERT: MARCH 21, 1964

The house lights went out, and Nina Simone took her place at the piano seated on a padded black stool. She wore a pageboy wig that left her bangs hanging straight down her forehead and both ears covered. Her painted-gold eyes flashed above a full-length white dress; Dorothea Towles's makeup ensured that Miss Simone was ready for her close-up. The Steinway grand piano had its lid completely removed so that the microphone could amplify *and* record the full resonance from the strings. The band stood stationed directly behind her. To address the audience, Miss Simone looked over her right shoulder. No one would mistake who was the star attraction.[3]

As Hughes settled into his seat, it is tempting to wonder if he felt a bit sentimental thinking of everything that had led Simone to this shining moment. We might imagine that, sitting quietly in the dark concert hall, Langston allowed time for some memories to begin flooding back and how he may have pondered their friendship, collaborations, and support of one another on this night in March 1964 at Carnegie Hall.

"I LOVES YOU PORGY"

The words "I loves you Porgy" followed four short notes on the Steinway, and Hughes might have revisited his earlier experiences with this song as performed by Billie Holiday. It was 1935 when he first saw the original Broadway production of *Porgy and Bess*. Now it was being performed at Carnegie Hall by Nina Simone, someone he forecast for stardom first when he wrote "To Be Somebody" in 1949 and then later when he named her in his 1961 poem "Horn of Plenty." One of the first cards Hughes received from Simone arrived three years earlier when that later poem was published. On her card, musical notes fluttered straight off the staff, curling madly across the air. Nina had written to thank Hughes for sending an autographed copy of his book of poems *Ask Your Mama*, saying: "It still makes me want to laugh and cry at the same time."[4]

If the line "Don't let him handle me with his hot hands" seeped into his consciousness, Hughes might have sensed that Simone could not take the same risks made at the 1960 Newport Jazz Festival in singing "I Loves You Porgy."

October 20, 1961

Dear Langston,

I received your copy of "Ask your Mama", which you know is so very beautiful. It still makes me want to laugh and cry at the same time.

I still hope to get together with you and have a long chat.

Affectionately,
Nina

Fig. 7.1a–b. Nina Simone's card acknowledging her receipt of Hughes's autographed book of poems *Ask Your Mama*, October 20, 1961. (James Weldon Johnson Memorial Collection in the Yale Collection of American Literature, Beinecke Rare Book and Manuscript Library, Yale University.)

Instead of singing lyrics written by Dorothy Fields and Jimmy McHugh, Simone tactfully took the context of the white privileged space of tonight's hall to play the expected Gershwin hit that was as important to her career as the poem "The Negro Speaks of Rivers" was to Hughes.

"PLAIN GOLD RING"

Indiscernible sounds might have reminded Hughes of listening to Ella Fitgerald scat. The woman onstage—was she moaning, chanting, or simply crying in an unknown language? "Plain gold ring on his finger he wore" finally unscrambled themselves from untuned frequencies and found shapes that again resembled words the audience knew. Hughes had sent his first birthday card to Simone last year while she was away from the studio relaxing on Chicago's South Shore. Onstage, Nina was now slurring her words so that it was clear that her opening indiscernible cries of sadness were in fact meant to be a mix of wine and tears. Nina was inhabiting the soul of a woman who loved a man who was already married. As to wine, Simone would eventually write in her autobiography: "I was guided by Langston, who sometimes gave me books he thought I should read, but more often simply sat me down and told me what I should know. I'd go over to his place in Harlem and over dinner—southern style—we'd talk, recite songs and poems and drink wine until the sun came up. Then I'd catch a cab home, high on wine, music, and laughter."[5]

A color photo remains from one of the first evening's Hughes had returned the favor by visiting Simone's home north of Harlem in Mount Vernon. Nina is smiling broadly as she sits on a couch shared with Hughes. Hughes has already loosened his thin black tie, and the collar of his cream shirt stretches wide, resting on both shoulders. For some reason he is staring right past Simone as if something has just moved and caught his eye. Relaxed but not provocative, Nina is wearing a striking blue shirt with the two top buttons undone, and her bright taupe pants are tightest where her knees cross. Her hair is ruler straight. The glass of red wine in her right hand reveals just how much fun (or wine?) they were having.

But now, as she sang, the woman onstage was slurring her words as he had sometimes heard in person just before settling Nina or himself into a cab.

As Simone extended the ends of the rhyming words "see" and "me" until they conjured a redundancy of the pronoun "he hehe hehe hehe," Hughes could have thought about another important "he" who had helped him launch his own career—Harlem photographer Carl Van Vechten. Just before Hughes set off to Paris in the summer of 1963 to keep tabs on his play *Black Nativity*, Hughes contacted the photographer to try and keep Simone squarely in the public eye on two fronts. Van Vechten had "photographed practically everybody in the Theatre from Tullulah Bankhead to Harry Belafonte."[6] As he continued in a written letter to Nina, Hughes had already called her husband, Andy, and "took the liberty" of giving Van Vechten her address. Hughes had direct access to two lines where the New York City police detective could be reached. Both phone numbers for Andy, MU 7-3071 and -3072, were written on a memo sheet and were always within reach on Hughes's desk.[7]

Hughes had long trusted and relied on Van Vechten, who was white, and thought that connecting him with Nina would yield similar fruit to his own relationship with the photographer. It was Van Vechten who first championed Hughes's poetry in 1925 and thereby secured a careful reading by his friend Blanche Knopf, who immediately published his first volume, *The Weary Blues*. Hughes had reminded Simone that although he would be in France during the summer Newport Jazz Festival of 1963, he was still intentionally showcasing her upcoming appearance on the program. He wrote: "I want to see you-all and your baby sometime when I get back. Mentioning you in my POST column about Newport Jazz Festival coming out next week."[8]

The song "Plain Gold Ring" neared its conclusion with the words, "I left a note on his dresser / and my old wedding ring." By January 1964, Nina Simone and Langston Hughes were the closest of friends. Thick as thieves, they now saw or communicated with each other every month of 1964. Her song ended "Goodbye old sleepy head."

"PIRATE JENNY"

Hughes and the audience around him had come to Carnegie Hall to hear a concert, but the woman up onstage was now in full costume. Simone was wearing a flower-print apron with a red polka-dot bow tied high around her waist. She even had a matching head rag tied around her hair. Who was playing piano behind her now while she wagged her finger back and forth? The white-robed Simone had transformed into a vengeful maid. Simone twice laughed sinisterly about halfway through the performance of her next song, "Pirate Jenny." Simone was now channeling the anger of Low-Dive Jenny (who is both a maid and a prostitute) in Kurt Weill's and Bertolt Brecht's *Threepenny Opera* (1928). Though it is uncertain, Simone may have heard the song "Pirate Jenny" if she attended *Brecht on Brecht* at the Theatre de Lys in Greenwich Village in 1962. If not, Columbia had released a full live cast album of the show in 1963.

Right now, seated in Carnegie Hall, Langston likely was recognizing a persona waiting to be expanded. What role would further extend Nina's uncommon force and capture her power to mesmerize? And what role would he play?

After once again exchanging Christmas cards with Hughes in December 1963, Nina and Andy hosted him the following month. It was the end of January at their home in Mount Vernon. Their address, 406 Nuber, had come up earlier in one of Hughes's letters: "I'm wondering if you ever met my biographer (doing a book about me) and your neighbor, James Emanuel (and wife and son) just across the street from you."[9] Remarkably, the first of Hughes's seven biographers lived right across the street from Simone. Over time, Emanuel's penchant for living near Simone continued. In fact, like Simone, he spent his last years in France (though never again as her neighbor).

Simone opened her mail on that Saturday in 1964 to find Hughes had written to her the very next day after their get-together. Hughes typed: "The evening at your house was a lot of fun . . . THANKS! And I do think we are helping to make a new star. In case your recording session for next week is not set as yet, you might look over these two songs. I think SEE-LINE WOMAN is particularly suited for you . . . custom-made."[10] Hughes was revealing his goals and aspirations. He was her professional mentor. Simone could become an even bigger attraction than even she knew. That is why he was now so specific in his directives. Rather than supplying mere encouragement or kind words, after visiting with her and Andy, he thought of how he might continue to buoy her career.

"SEE-LINE WOMAN"

The audience responded to a Congo drum beating out an intoxicating rhythm. Nina had recently been playing this new song at smaller shows, but this was the first time Hughes heard Simone perform "See-Line Woman." The enduring confusion over the spelling of the title was in play from the first instance Hughes sent the song off for her upcoming recording session. Having originally typed "SEE-LINE WOMAN," he poetically gestured to its ambiguity by referring to the song at the bottom of the same letter as "SEA LION WOMAN." When the song was released in mid-July, the outside of the sleeve even continued in this vein and titled the song "SEA-LION WOMAN" even though the 45 RPM record inside spelled the song "SEE-LINE WOMAN."

"Sea-Line Woman" fits best, since towns along the sea line were the kinds of places most applicable to the sexual activities outlined in this song. It is along sea lines where women historically wore specific-colored clothing to advertise which sexual favors they were selling. If "Sea-Lion" suggested the women who lure men to their shore, then "Sea-Line" points listeners toward historic ports such as Charleston or Barcelona.

Simone had now left her piano to go shimmering in her full-length dress before an excited audience. *Careful.* She had carefully selected a color not mentioned in the song. She sang about women wearing green with golden seams. Red and black dresses that made men lose their heads or pay a thousand dollars for these women to wail or moan. Even though the actual lyrics indicated that she was merely narrating the lives of these sex workers, many in the crowd might have simultaneously imagined that Nina was embodying what the era termed a "prostitute." But she was also sultry (even if she was not actually purring like one woman she described). The lyrics conjured images of a snake charmer serenading something from a wicker basket. Hughes sat and watched Nina Sea-moan.

While Hughes would soon propel Simone to an even more political trajectory that attached her singing to histories of creation in the face of oppression, his suggestion to use prostitution as a vehicle complicates our sense of each of their gender politics. On the one hand, Hughes's song suggestion was tempting Simone to integrate the exotic allure of Black women into her strategy for artistic success. Yet this is a role the powerful antiestablishment figure of Nina Simone was now willingly accepting. As a man, did Hughes really consider a song about providing sexual favors to somehow be empowering? More importantly, did Nina unconsciously internalize male valuations of female worth? In many ways, sex workers are the ultimate outsiders. Simone seems to be trying to find a unique way to both embody and appropriate them to offer a startling social commentary. She was only getting started.

Following the lyrics precisely, the pronoun "she" is invoked consistently so that the song never makes any direct connection between Nina and the song's characters. As the song's narrator, Simone was only observing, not testifying. Nonetheless, once the audience saw Simone start dancing provocatively, swaying her hips, and singing about purring, such rhetorical distance was at best collapsed if not fully erased. In the song, what happens to these men? The women are paid. Hughes sat among a capacity crowd hearing the lasting effect repeated twice at the end of the song: "Empty his pockets / and wreck his days." Although real sex workers face the horrific effects of being trafficked and often abused, listeners can momentarily allow themselves to consider that the men suffer differently (in this specific presentation). It may be just a fantasy or an illusion women tell themselves to continue in the profession, yet "Sea-Line Woman" was portraying women in control who leave male victims in their wake. Not objects longing for agency, these "Sea-Lions" are applauded by the audience for being man eaters. At least in the short term, they end up with sparkling clothes, while it is the men who lose their heads. The crowd cheered the new song Hughes suggested for Simone.

Hughes could never have thought at this moment that his song suggestion would become a mainstay in Simone's live repertoire for the rest of her long career. One reason for this may be nothing more complex than its infectious beat. Nina would often find this both a relief from sitting at the keys and a way to invoke audience participation. Rudy Stevenson not only played flute on the track but helped arrange the song. Crowds often chanted "See-Line," clapped, or at the very least tapped their toes to its pounding rhythm when Simone performed it live. When she performed it at the Montreux Jazz Festival in 1987, a new more direct verse opened the song. Listeners are immediately introduced to a woman "Dressed in white / sleep all day / ball all night." At Montreal in 1992, another figure was also now

> Dressed in blue
> watch out fellas
> gonna' steal you.

Besides sleeping all day (on her back if she wore black), listeners learn that this temptress is inclined now to save her soul (linked in a strange rhyme with "gold"). The idea that the act of love could mean so little emotionally to a woman who drank coffee or tea (or even champagne in one version) before going home suddenly adds up to something that contrasts sharply to men who lose their minds, cash, and hour after hour of "their days." Though many other complications come to mind today, Simone's repeated (and varied) renditions of "See-Line Woman" provoked many of her contemporary listeners to arrive at an unexpected conclusion and ask, "Who really has the power here?"

As Simone continued to sing "See-Line Woman" later and later in her career, was it really the story or the alluring dancing that endured? Her white dress concealed only a few hip swivels when she sang it during a key early media appearance on *The Steve Allen Show* on September 16, 1964. The song was a staple throughout her European tour in 1968, which took her to Montreux, and she revived it there again when she returned nineteen years later. She was singing it in Amsterdam in 1971 and in Montreal on July 18, 1980, where she withheld praise for the audience until the timing of their clapping was "ex-actement."[11] After reviving it in Montreal one more time on July 2, 1992, Simone played "See-Line Woman" in Miami as late as November 2000. One little prompt from the mind of Hughes had informed Simone's music for the next thirty-six years. This was only the beginning of their collaboration.

"MISSISSIPPI GODDAM"

Mirroring his own humorous sensibilities, the poignant yet funny song "Go Limp" now slowly gave way to a tune the audience sensed might be another satire. The crowd around Hughes was in high spirits. When Simone stated, "The name of this tune is 'Mississippi Goddam,'" many near him in the audience laughed, believing she was continuing in the previous vein of the rollicking song about a woman getting pregnant after marching with the NAACP. Noting the chuckles, Simone made an important turn by adding an alternative tone: "And I mean every word of it." Fewer laughs.

Most in this audience had never heard Nina perform "Mississippi Goddam." As she was saying, it was indeed a Broadway tune without a show. Hughes was listening as Nina named three states.

"Alabama"—Simone sounded upset because everybody knew that four little Black girls had just been killed the previous September while attending Sunday school in Birmingham. Hughes had recently written two poems about their deaths. "Birmingham Sunday" accused the KKK members who planted the bomb of being worse than Communist China, which never used the very dynamite invented there to enact such murder on Americans. In "Bombings in Dixie," Hughes tried to be even more direct. He noted that prayer was useless in an America where living conditions were so bad for Black people that they are "burned to death—*and bless the fire.*" Thinking of the repercussions of attending church—or the lack of results from highly visible reverends who preached nonviolence?—the songstress at the piano was now intoning: "I've even stopped believing in prayer."

"Tennessee"—Had Simone lost sleep when the sit-in movement in Nashville targeted the Wilson-Quick Pharmacy, B & W Cafeteria, and a local YMCA in 1963? John Lewis had carried signs imploring others to "Join the Freedom March." Or perhaps Simone had seen the photo of Martin Luther King Jr. hung in effigy outside the city's police headquarters on April 13, 1963. Was there something eerily prophetic about the inclusion of a state that currently did not seem equivalent to Alabama and Mississippi? Would someone end up being assassinated in Memphis? Hughes heard Simone now addressing the audience as if she were unexpectedly speaking over the music of German lieder: "I bet you thought I was kiddin', didn't ya?"

"Mississippi"—Hughes knew better than most about this state's history of lynchings, but now something in the tone here may have turned him to thinking instead about the murder of Medgar Evers in June of 1963. If his mind went further, perhaps it conjured the bravery of James Meredith, the Black man who decided to attend college at segregated Ole Miss in the fall of 1962. Simone would tell late-night TV host Steve Allen that her song was new, but it was "conceived, though, during the time when James Meredith was finally getting into the University of Mississippi."[12] Hughes had devoted an entire *New York*

Post column at the time declaring that Meredith (and *not* Mississippi author William Faulkner) should had received the Nobel Prize for dodging bullets, rocks, and bombs upon entering the University of Mississippi as its first Black student. As Hughes sat there in Carnegie Hall, he may have felt his prose wish finally being heard. Hughes's column had included a remarkably relevant final plea for Meredith: "I hope some of these cool jazz men will write a cool piece and dedicate it to a cool cat you."[13] Simone was the cool jazz *wo*man who had written a red-hot piece.

Like "Pirate Jenny," the song's vengeance echoes yet another song written from composer Kurt Weill's time working with Bertolt Brecht in the 1920s. The music of Simone's "Mississippi Goddam" resembles Kurt Weill's jerky musical composition for "Alabama Song," included in *Rise and Fall of the City of Mahagonny* (1930).[14] The avant-garde opera portrays the events of what happens in the imagined American city of Mahagonny to offer a commentary on the effects of unchecked capitalism.

Simone's choice to use the word "die" in "Mississippi Goddam" echoes the repeated lyrics sung by Weill's wife, Lotte Lenya, in "Alabama Song." Lotte sang: "I tell you we must die." Simone was reactivating the rhythm of that musical passage. She was now singing: "Where are we going / What are we doing? / I don't know." The word "tell" appears in "Alabama Song" as much as "die," and Nina's "Don't tell me / I'll tell you" also blurs with Lotte's

> I tell you we must die
> I tell you
> I tell you.

Just as the children in "Alabama Song" were preparing to leave that state and pondering where to go after their mother died in *Mahagonny*, Simone was now indirectly asserting that Alabama's children in the 1960s now have nowhere to go if both enrolling in public college *and* attending church are deadly and off-limits. Bertolt Brecht had his "Alabama Song," and now Nina was debuting her own Mississippi song right in front of Hughes, the man who first called for it to be performed.

Simone's song was scathing, but this was hardly the first time her music had been political. Her recorded version of Oscar Brown Jr.'s "Brown Baby" was a quiet plea for the future, and a tune she had performed earlier this evening, "Old Jim Crow," was a polite request for the very embodiment of prejudice itself to step aside. Simone's vinyl version of "Work Song" ends with the pick striking not the rocks but instead the chain itself to send the convicted off to enjoy their new freedom. Simone had been mirroring the beliefs of Hughes's friend and her neighbor Ruby Dee, who saw "art and the Struggle as inseparable bedmates."[15] Now Simone was assertively testifying right before him about the amplified role she was now going to take in the civil rights movement in joining the likes of Dee, Lorraine Hansberry, and himself: "Just trying to do my very best / Stand up and be counted with all the rest." In memorializing the cause, Simone was reenergizing the strategies of resistance Hughes had pioneered during the Harlem Renaissance.

As for Hughes, he had recently let Simple speak even more directly in a *New York Post* column. His imagined Jim Crow had "writ a letter to Hitler during the War and said, 'You are alright with me because you do not like Negroes, either.'" By the time Hughes ended the column, Simple was instead speaking directly to Jim Crow: "You did not know a Negro / Was going to preach your funeral, Jim Crow!" The final lines end the eulogy: "All I can say is, Jim Crow / GO TO HELL!"[16] Simple understood Nina's anger. This is why Nina kept saying "Goddam." Simple was hardly done. He asserted, in a satirical logic that was at once humorous *and* condemning, "Hell has more towns in it named after America than any other country in the world. . . . There is a Birmingham, Hell. There is Oxford, Hell."[17] Simone may have sounded radical to some ears not used to hearing anything political in this hallowed place, but Hughes's words had long been going much further. They were placing the same eternal damnation on earth now captured in Nina's cursing. There was little wonder that only one of them had been called to testify before Joseph McCarthy for writing "Goodbye Christ," a poem delivered from the perspective of a person willing to insinuate that Lenin should be more esteemed than Jesus.

Simone was engaging in some very complicated rhetoric in this new song. She was moving beyond nonviolence and a "repressed female sexuality" to challenge liberalism's ideas of gender itself.[18] When she sang "You all gonna die and die like flies," Simone was briefly reprising something from her earlier role this evening as Low-Dive Jenny.

Hughes likely could not fully absorb what he had just heard in "Mississippi Goddam." Nina was now accepting her deserved applause. Marking this song as a signpost for just how far Nina had come on her musical journey, her band played her off the stage to Miles Davis's "Milestones."

THE AFTER-PARTY

As he double-checked his invitation to be sure he had the right address for the reception, Hughes was ending the eventful month of March 1964 on a high note. After a young boxer took out heavyweight champion Sonny Liston to shock the world, Hughes sent Cassius Clay a copy of his newly revised book *A*

Pictorial History of the Negro in America (1963). Hughes's missive not only drew the new champ's attention to a section on the Black Muslims but also pointed Clay to a poster featuring one of the earliest rallies in Harlem headlined by Malcolm X. Hughes could not resist encouraging the poetic and political Clay by writing:

> I HEAR YOU ARE INTERESTED IN HISTORY.
> WELL, HISTORY IS NO MYSTERY.
> WHY, OUT OF THE FACT
> THAT SOME MEN ARE BLACK,
> OTHERS TRY TO MAKE A TWISTERY
> IS THE ONLY MYSTERY.
> TAKE IT FROM ME —[19]

In addition to mentoring boxers about history, Hughes had also been regularly engaging in overtly political appearances. The day before Simone's iconic Carnegie Hall concert, he appeared at Columbia University for an event sponsored by the Congress on Racial Equality. The stunning poster for his appearance communicated the revolutionary nature of this event. A Black working-class man is portrayed in a sharp, one-dimensional outline. His hands, just out of

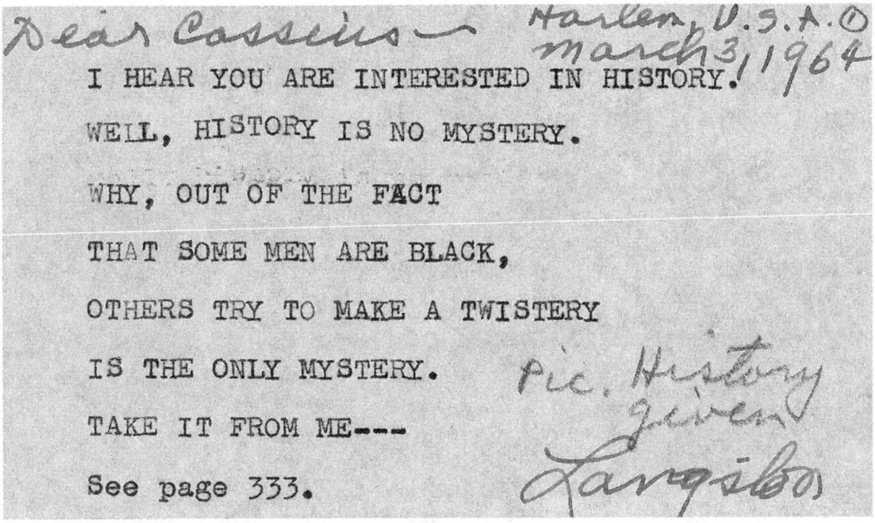
Dear Cassius — Harlem, U.S.A. ① March 3, 1964
I HEAR YOU ARE INTERESTED IN HISTORY.
WELL, HISTORY IS NO MYSTERY.
WHY, OUT OF THE FACT
THAT SOME MEN ARE BLACK,
OTHERS TRY TO MAKE A TWISTERY
IS THE ONLY MYSTERY.
TAKE IT FROM ME---
See page 333.
Pic. History given
Langston

Fig. 7.2. Langston Hughes inserted this poem in the copy of his book *A Pictorial History of the Negro in America* (1963) that he sent to Cassius Clay (Muhammad Ali) on March 3, 1964. (James Weldon Johnson Memorial Collection in the Yale Collection of American Literature, Beinecke Rare Book and Manuscript Library, Yale University.)

frame, might be followed to reveal that they could be in chains. The face is both determined and strained. Across the figure's open collar, the name of Langston Hughes appears. It is in orange spray paint, filling the gaps left by stencil-lifted letters. The name holds—a tag of graffiti. The political rather than capitalist venture is clear to everyone as the "no admission charged" in the lower right-hand corner signals for a crowd in place of a paying audience. In the upper right-hand corner, something is nearly dripping, looking so wet that it would stain your hand should you try and touch it: "CORE presents an evening of readings by the world-famous Negro writer."

Moreover, the multimodal nature of Hughes reveals that he would also be appearing at this CORE event with the lead actor in his current Off-Broadway production *Jerico-Jim Crow*. Gilbert Price would sing Hughes's lyrics in a musical about the civil rights struggle. Hughes's poetry and song lyrics were interwoven in the most warmly received play of his distinguished career. Protest was a common setting for Hughes this year. In another eight weeks he would headline an event for the Association of Artists for Freedom with his forward-leaning friends Ossie Davis and Ruby Dee. The advertisement for that event read: "The long crucial summer of 1964 has already begun in Jacksonville, Florida! What is the responsibility of the American Artist to the Negro Revolt? We believe that a cultural revolution is needed to unbrainwash the thinking of the entire nation." Those interested were encouraged to come hear "an evening with Langston Hughes—a dramatic presentation of some of the monumental works of the dean of Negro Letters."[20]

Unlike Simone's performance of April 12, 1963 (which Hughes did not attend), this standout concert at Carnegie Hall on March 21, 1964, was not an occasion to skip. Hughes knew it once he reread the limited invitation, printed on a plain white background:

Stroud Productions
and
Mr. Felix G. Gerstman
request the honor of your company at a
RECEPTION
for Miss NINA SIMONE[21]

Andy Stroud had risked a substantial amount of his personal savings to secure the promotion power of Felix Gerstman, and it had paid off with a sold-out show and the subsequent recording of what would become one of the seminal live albums of Nina's career. After the concert ended, Hughes arrived at the

Fig. 7.3. CORE promotional poster for the Langston Hughes event at Columbia University featuring Gilbert Price singing songs from Hughes's musical about the burgeoning civil rights movement, March 20, 1964. (James Weldon Johnson Memorial Collection in the Yale Collection of American Literature, Beinecke Rare Book and Manuscript Library, Yale University.)

Park Sheraton Hotel on Fifty-Sixth Street and Seventh Avenue still wearing his full suit and patterned tie. A simple white shirt highlighted the most important visual fashion statement: He had shaved off his trademark mustache. He stood for a time at the after-party just below the entrance to the hotel's Skyline Suite, where the reception was located. Comedian Godfrey Cambridge was there, someone both Hughes and Simone knew from his sets at the Village Gate (as well as his role in Hughes's 1960 stage production *Shakespeare in Harlem*). Cambridge clowned by giving Simone the side-eye. He spent an eternal moment hunched down to her height while placing his right arm over her shoulder. Whatever Godfrey was drinking was now concealed behind his back with his other hand. Hughes carefully folded his black-rimmed glasses into his right hand. Balancing a glass now empty of its gin, he thoughtfully removed the lit cigarette from his lips.

Nina's dress was elegantly tied at the waist. The pattern on the belt is either blooms or sparkles. In this beautiful moment, her right arm crossed over Hughes's, the guide and the traveler were clearly linked and forever identified, silently bound by what was or wasn't whispered. At this moment, Hughes was listening to Simone speak. Her eyes painted with unusually long black liner. Her wig holding straight, gently curled at the bangs and edges. It covered both ears and formed a silent parenthesis that ended at the neck. Unlike on her concert poster, Simone's high-heeled shoes were—in real life—a perfect white. They seemed thin as slippers at the all-important toes—needed for dampening the Steinway with precision. They were also a practical choice for dancing to "See-Line Woman."

Flanked on her left, Simone turned to her right. Hughes was there to save her. Through all the noise and confusion, only Simone and Hughes knew what was spoken. In her first interview about "Mississippi Goddam," Nina asserted that she had started to "conceive" of the song in late 1962 after Black student James Meredith enrolled at the University of Mississippi.[22] (This is one of the reasons why "Mississippi" and not "Alabama" is the state named in her title.) As for the word "conceive," Nina was pregnant with her daughter, Lisa, at this same time. This was important. Was Nina focused on Lisa's future education when she said she "conceived" the song "Mississippi Goddam"? Did the four little girls killed in a church bombing in Birmingham, Alabama, remind Nina of just how vulnerable Lisa was, even in attending Sunday school? The photo accepts our gaze, but never it speaks.

Fig. 7.4. Langston Hughes, Nina Simone, and Godfrey Cambridge at the Park Sheraton Hotel after her Carnegie Hall concert on March 21, 1964. (Collection of the Smithsonian National Museum of African American Culture and History.)

1964 (CONTINUED)

The weekend over, Hughes turned back to the daily work of being a writer. Still firmly committed to social justice, Hughes now chose to align his vision for freedom with one of his oldest supporters. He had published in the NAACP's journal the *Crisis* since 1921, but the more conservative civil rights group was neither as progressive as the Association of Artists for Freedom nor as youth-centered as CORE. However, Hughes launched his civil rights offensive on all fronts, often coming within orbit of numerous political groups—yet still staying independent enough to maintain his own circuit. After he published "Dream of Freedom" in the April 1964 issue of the NAACP's *Freedom Journal,* he passed a copy of the poem along to Andy and Nina, where they read, "There is a dream in the land / With its back against the wall."

Ever the advocate, Hughes was not only informing Nina and Andy in his letter that he would soon be reading the poem on TV but also asking Andy if he knew anyone who might want to sign Gilbert Price to a recording contract. Accompanying the letter were numerous glowing newsprint reviews of Price's performance in *Jerico-Jim Crow*. Hughes once again took it upon himself to try and guide another musician through the gates that concealed show-business fortune. Hughes always displayed an unwavering drive to support the next generation of Black performers. Hughes felt that they were far more than entertainers: He knew they were major artists with political capital.

With Simone now taking song recommendations from Hughes, correspondence between the two increased in frequency and intimacy. In June 1964, Hughes received a postcard of two sailboats heeling in a stiff breeze. Simone had sent along an image of a single woman standing deftly on the edge of a twenty-five-foot boat as it turned left toward shore. Perhaps neither Hughes nor Simone herself thought of the image of a "Sea-Line Woman" when it was selected, but the image of the lone woman suggests the same impression of allure. Simone wrote: "We're thinking of you up here in Cape Cod where we've been for almost 3 wks. We had the XXX children for a little while—Have you been here? It's such a change from N.Y. I wish we could stay all summer. Returning home the 31 of July. Andy sends Love."[23] In one of her more revealing moments, Simone employs her own poetic vocabulary. The word written beneath the crossed-out scribbling that precedes "children" is "dear." Although she would have wanted to celebrate Lisa as well as Andy's two surviving children from a previous marriage (Andy Jr. and Renaldo), the horrors of the Sixteenth Street Baptist Church bombing in Birmingham cannot blot out Simone's seeming inability to suggest that her real time as a mother is as rewarding as she might have idealized.

Nina, Andy, and Langston were now talking so frequently that phone calls and personal visits were commonplace. As she had earnestly suggested in her summer postcard, the three convened again soon after Simone's return from Cape Cod. One topic must have been: "How else could Hughes support her forthcoming album?" He had already suggested the song "See-Line Woman," which would be one of the record's features. What other songs might he suggest next?

As 1964 ended, two more items addressed from Nina and Andy arrived in Harlem at 20 East 127th Street. In addition to another Christmas card, Hughes received a complimentary copy of the new album *Broadway-Blues-Ballads* a few days before Thanksgiving. Andy wrote, "I thought you'd enjoy having it for your collection."[24] However, Andy's letterhead had changed. No longer working from their home in Mount Vernon, Andy had now positioned Stroud Productions and Enterprises farther south owing to Nina's newest success. The new headquarters were now at New York City's unmistakably visible Fifth Avenue. This prestigious move meant that correspondence to Hughes now came on Weston's Merit Bonded paper. The company logo was a spotlight—mirroring the title and key image from Hughes's original 1960 endorsement in "Spotlight on Nina Simone." It was now shining even brighter. The company name was radiant in a fluorescent blue. It was of course Nina's tireless recording and performances that truly watermarked his paper, not Andy's management or even Hughes's mentoring.

Nina had worked relentlessly to achieve such success for herself and Andy. To so many young women her age, a piece of her now belonged to everyone. Only combining every jagged shape could present a whole picture of Nina. After her iconic Carnegie Hall concert, she returned to the studio to record alternative versions of both "See-Line Woman" and "Mississippi Goddam." Those who bought the new single were informed that these two tracks were released "FROM THE ALBUM 'NINA SIMONE IN CONCERT.'" The sleeve continued, "This single has been issued for DJ's in answer to your many requests. It has been specially edited for air play, featuring the 'BEEP-BEEP' in place of @*?!!??. 'NINA SIMONE IN CONCERT' is proving to be a big exciting album. **MISSISSIPPI** @*?!!?? is receiving tremendous recognition. It may be the most topical selection in years. This outstanding message song, with the great 'SIMONE' feel and rhythm, makes this a @*?!!?? hot disc." Contrary to what we read, this "damn" hot disc does not actually include live songs from Nina's famous March 21, 1964, concert at Carnegie Hall. Philips was trying to use these two songs to promote sales of that album. As for side B, the sleeve spells the song "SEA-LION WOMAN," while the green record labels inside that same sleeve read: "SEE-LINE WOMAN."

More importantly, once the needle drops, there isn't a "BEEP-BEEP" sound like the one television programs used to make to edit out unwanted material. Instead, a two-syllable whistle tone comes in to replace Nina singing the word "Goddam." It mimics the sound of a bird chirping "WHIT-woo," with the emphasis on the first syllable. Imagine a cheap handheld recorder pressed against the lips. At the end of the song, Nina sings her final "Goddam" so long each of the individual bits of tweeting had to be added nine consecutive times. Without being seen or heard (hidden behind both the obscure typographical symbols and the sounds of bird whistles), some listeners had to guess exactly how Nina felt when she chose to sing the word "Goddam!"

Although we may now find it quaint and outdated to learn that the word "Goddam" was not allowed on the radio or TV in 1964, it is critical to remember that many Black citizens were privately angry with Nina for invoking the word in such a public way. Many Black Americans were interested in embodying respectability in every way possible. This included the way they dressed, their cleanliness, and especially the words they spoke. For many, Nina's profanity connoted unwelcome levels of anger and incivility. Plus, the actual word Nina chose was blasphemous. God-fearing churchgoers had always formed the foundation of the civil rights movement, and many Black ministers and their parishioners felt that Simone had gone one step too far. She was not only using the word but also placing it front and center in the title of her most visible song.

In seeing Simone's release of "See-Line Woman" as a B-side to her vindictive "Mississippi Goddam," Hughes sensed how insightful his advice was to an artist who would soon be taking her music in a new, more assertive direction. Simone was both singing the songs he suggested and seemingly answering his calls to write in response to events surrounding political figures such as James Meredith. Together, they were heading step in step down a path that was leading them to unconsciously shape the soundtrack of the civil rights movement.

8

I Put a Spell on You

By late 1964, Langston Hughes had realized that Nina Simone was the best vehicle for singing his original lyrics and landing him a hit record. Hughes felt a sincere impulse to mentor Simone for the betterment of her career while simultaneously hoping to hear her sing one of his original songs to fulfill a decades-old ambition. One of the most direct pieces of evidence for Hughes's personal motivation occurs as an aside in a piece of correspondence with his longtime friend pianist and composer Margaret Bonds. Not only had Hughes been collaborating with Bonds since 1940, with Bonds writing and performing the musical compositions for his lyrics, but the two were so close that he had even introduced her to her future husband, Lawrence Richardson.

The familial tone of Bonds's letter is announced as their dear mutual friend Toy Harper is playfully named and teased: "First, how good of you to come to

Town Hall and bring Aunt Toy. (I really LOVE that little witch DESPARATELY [*sic*]."[1] By as early as March 1962, Bonds and Hughes had identified the woman they most hoped would sing one of their compositions. At the end of her typed letter, Bonds signed her name in blue ink and then punctuated her closing by drawing a full musical staff and notes. Under the two bars of music, she paired her handwritten notes to these printed words just as one would do on a piece of sheet music: "Ni-na's gon-na have a lit-tle ba-by." In cursive, the wish below this imagined line of verse speaks to Hughes's deep aspiration as much as to Bonds's: "but I hope she records Mary's baby first!" Bonds is referring to the nativity song the two had just finished collaborating on called "Mary Had a Little Baby." It is not hard to imagine Bonds and Hughes having already left a discussion with a hope that left their fingers tightly crossed. Although Nina Simone never recorded this song, the tune is one more example of how Hughes prompted the singer with his lyrics in hopes that Simone's star power might turn his words into a song so popular he could finally claim to have successfully crossed over from poetry to music.

Even though Langston Hughes did not persuade the pregnant Nina Simone to record "Mary Had a Little Baby," he did prompt her to record a different song that soon opened up a whole new persona Simone would portray through an overlapping coalescence of song, performance, and fashion. Revealed here for

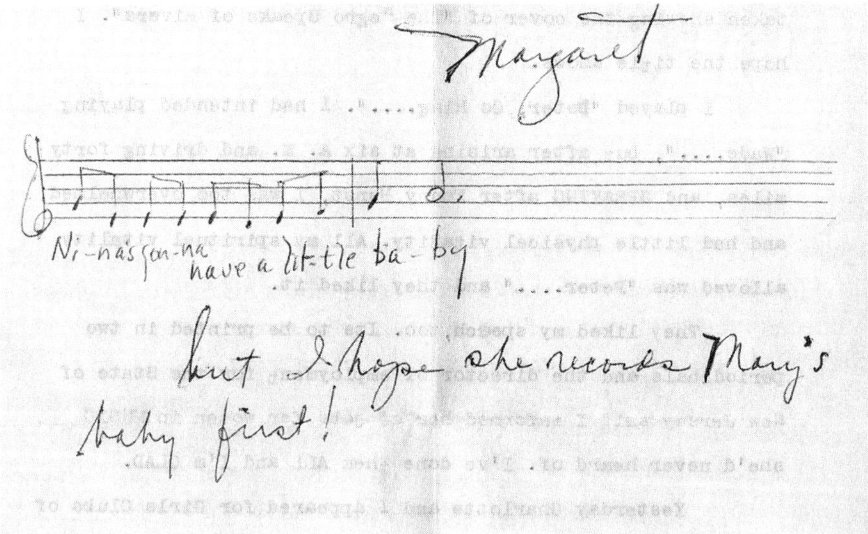

Fig. 8.1. Detail of the musical staff and lyrics created by Margaret Bonds for the song "Mary's Baby" in her letter to Langston Hughes, March 27, 1962. (Margaret Bonds Papers, Booth Family Center for Special Collections, Georgetown University.)

the first time, Langston Hughes gave Nina Simone the idea for her iconic song "I Put a Spell on You." This song became so inextricably linked to Simone that her autobiography is titled *I Put a Spell on You*. More importantly, her hypnotic portrayal of a bewitching sorceress, the essential directive Hughes gave her, became the first critical step to Nina Simone earning the title she still holds today: the High Priestess of Soul.

"PIRATE JENNY": THE PRECURSOR

By 1964, Nina's unrelentingly intense performances of "Pirate Jenny" had made this the song Hughes most revered in her set lists. Some combination of the song's social commentary, his personal connection to Kurt Weill, his theatrical roots, and Nina's unmistakable indignation left Hughes wondering what other persona might enable Nina to tap into a performative power that left audiences unable to blink, let alone look away.

Composer Kurt Weill began his operatic collaboration with fellow German lyricist Bertolt Brecht in 1927 by setting five of the writer's poems to music. Two of Weill's songs successfully crossed over into popular music to become well-known hits of their time. In 1956, Billboard named his "September Song" the fourteenth most popular song of all time, and "Mack the Knife" would stay at number one on the charts for nine weeks in 1959, eventually earning record sales of over $10 million.[2]

Nina invoked two of Weill's less popular songs. "Pirate Jenny" was a show-stopping stunner. With bassist Lyle Atkinson moving over to play piano, Nina commanded the full stage by directly challenging her audiences to imagine the fantasies of poor Black workers. Rather than achieving equality, freedom, or integration, in her fantasy this woman enacted revenge on her oppressors in no uncertain terms. The tune from Brecht and Weill's *Threepenny Opera* originally dated to 1928. It was an experimental piece that set the action of the famous character Mack the Knife in London. As Daphne A. Brooks has documented in her exceptional research, Simone was "undoubtedly the most prominent African American interpreter of Brecht and Weill's dense and disruptive songbook."[3] Artists as varied as Bobby Darin and Louis Armstrong covered this track, and Bob Dylan would point to the scaffolding of "Pirate Jenny" as a foundational principle for the types of lyrics he would go on to apply in such songs as "When the Ship Comes In."[4]

In Nina's rendering, she appropriated a history that now applied to Black workers. When Nina sang it, she added one word so that the hotel she was scrubbing and cleaning was located in a "crummy Southern town."[5] With the addition of "Southern," white audience members were left thinking of tips they gave to Black hotel staff who seemed happy to serve them. Nina also did something else to make this song her own. To deliver the lyric that decides the moment of execution, "Right now!" Nina was known to jump straight into the audience and point at a white man seated near the front.[6]

"MISSISSIPPI GODDAM" AND "ALABAMA SONG"

As detailed earlier, in chapter 8, Simone was enamored of another tune by Brecht and Weill known as "Alabama Song" (or "Moon of Alabama"). It was originally written as a poem by Brecht, and its pidgin English came directly from Brecht's assistant, Elisabeth Hauptmann. Before making its way to the stage in Germany, Weill's musical arrangement was first published on August 4, 1927, as "Alabama Song (Blues)," with the "blues" designation suggesting a bit of Weill's fascination with what little exposure he had to the idiom of American jazz and blues. Three years later, it was taken to the German stage, featuring in the opera *Rise and Fall of the City of Mahagonny* (1930). Nina's engagement with the tune reveals how easily an altered arrangement and performance setting swiftly blurs traditional lines between the genres of classical and popular music.[7]

Like Nina herself, Weill moved seamlessly between these two worlds—a classical composer who defied easy categories, he mastered the formal compositions required for opera while also being hailed as an innovator of popular music. In all likelihood, Nina saw a performance of *The Threepenny Opera* (1928) sometime between the years 1954 and 1961, when it appeared in revival during its historic run of 2,611 consecutive shows at the Theater de Lys in Greenwich Village. When her own label, Philips, released Brecht and Weill's companion work *Rise and Fall of the City of Mahagonny* on vinyl in 1962 (with Columbia following in 1963), Simone could have not only heard but even studied "Alabama Song." Alternatively, any of Simone's classical piano teachers might have also shared it with her during any stage of her formal training, as the works of Brecht and Weill hold a seminal place in the development of classical music.[8] Though far less likely, Hughes himself could have alerted Nina about this music any time after he collaborated with Weill for months writing lyrics for *Street Scene*. Before "the most important step toward significantly American opera" ran for 148 shows in 1947, Hughes gave Weill a personal tour of Harlem cabarets so that he could "absorb the atmosphere and idioms."[9]

Nina eventually gestured directly to the music of this song from *Mahagonny* serving as the source material for "Mississippi Goddam" when she performed the two songs live together as a medley at Ronnie Scott's in 1984. Revisiting the two songs, the connection between them is more striking than first appears, given that the German pronunciation for the imagined American city of

Mahagonny (Mah-ha-GON-e) mirrors the Alabama city of "Montgomery." How do the musical signposts in "Alabama Song" alter our understanding of "Mississippi Goddam"?[10]

It is no small thing that "Mississippi Goddam" was featured at Carnegie Hall in 1964. Simone considered her earlier April 12, 1963, solo show at the musical mecca a chance for her to realize her childhood dream of presenting herself to the world as a Black classical pianist. This informed both her dress and musical selections. Wearing a stunning white dress (with a matching cape she cherished so much that she kept it her whole life), she opened the evening with "The Black Swan." As the signature song from Gian Carlo Menotti's opera *The Medium* (1946), this dark lullaby forecasts Simone's future persona as a priestess who can communicate with spirits. The name here also activates the memory of Black Swan records, the first US record label owned by African Americans to reach a large market. Founded in 1921 by W. C. Handy and Harry Pace, the label featured blues artists such as Ethel Waters and Alberta Hunter as well as classical singers such as Revella Hughes and Florence Cole Talbert.

Most importantly, the very title of Simone's musical choice also allowed this song to serve as an imaginative way for her to begin her show by conjuring Elizabeth Taylor Greenfield. Known as the Black Swan, Greenfield became the first Black woman to publicly perform the scores of Handel and Mozart to great acclaim as both a tenor and a soprano. Her nickname was a response to European artists from her era such as the Swedish Nightingale (Jenny Lind) and the Irish Swan (Catherine Hayes). Greenfield miraculously rose to stardom after having been born enslaved in Mississippi. Relevant to the moment, she played a famous concert in New York in 1853. A crowd of four thousand white patrons took in her performance amid rumors of rioting or arson by those protesting a Black artist holding forth in Metropolitan Hall. In this symbolic way, Nina's version of "The Black Swan" both paid homage to Greenfield and presented Nina as a Black female artist who was also adding to the often-overlooked, though rich, history of Black classical music.

Simone delivered two more instrumentals during her April 12, 1963, concert at Carnegie Hall. The theme from Camille Saint-Saëns's *Samson and Delilah* is best known as "Mon coeur s'ouvre à ta voix," appearing in the opera when Delilah seduces Samson in hopes that he will reveal the source of his strength. Once again, the song anticipates Nina's eventual choice to inhabit the role of someone who is using every tool to acquire access to power. Her second instrumental was Irving Berlin's theme from the film *Sayonara* (1957), a Japanese song of goodbye. This ended the first section of the program before the intermission. The formality of the music in this prestigious setting allowed Simone to fulfill a lifelong aspiration.

For her return to Carnegie Hall on March 21, 1964, she took a different approach: Nina slyly nodded to her desire to play classical music by performing songs with roots in opera. "Pirate Jenny" (in full) and "Alabama Song" (coded within "Mississippi Goddam") provided a new strategy in which lyrics would make the classical roots of her music feel that it belonged on this stage. As this date at Carnegie Hall approached, Nina Simone was on the verge of secretly popularizing classical music by embedding it within a protest song intended for the general public.

"Mississippi Goddam" is cut from the same musical fabric as "Alabama Song." Weill's DNA can be heard in the "um PA, um PA" rhythm of each, perhaps sped up in "Mississippi Goddam" only because Nina has so many more lyrics to deliver. Where "Alabama Song" shifts from duples to triples when it moves into the words "Oh, moon of Alabama," Nina's musical acumen inserts something different. She initiates an offbeat rhythm that disrupts the logic and tempo of both the music and the words that lead into the line: "Everybody knows about Mississippi, Goddam!" A significant reference point for this unusual rhythmic disruption is the famous Leonard Bernstein (music) and Stephen Sondheim (lyrics) collaboration "I Want to Live in America." Featured in the Broadway hit *West Side Story* (1957), with the film version of the song sung by Rita Moreno, the tune becomes a dialogue where differing Latin perspectives on immigration are set against each other. At one point we hear that everything goes well "if you are white in America." Given this connection to *West Side Story*, "Mississippi Goddam" forces listeners to face the difficult question of whether it's better to live in America as an immigrant or as the descendant of slaves.

By playing duples immediately followed by triplets, Nina's piano produces a huapango rhythm. Nina's music of disruption leading up to her empathic delivery of "Goddam" is coding this song in a way that forces a new Black perspective on race relations within the United States. The musical cadence that captured the spirit of the immigrant triumphantly declaring "I want to live in America" is being ironically juxtaposed and simultaneously extended beyond New York City. Nina's song is activating the meaning of "live"—not just a place to immigrate to and find a home in, it is a form of existence where people are allowed to exist, not die. The music suggests that Black people want to live (not die) in an America that includes Alabama, Tennessee, and Mississippi.

But as early as 1962, Miss Simone wondered how she might include an element of "Alabama Song" as she had done with "Pirate Jenny" so that it would have the same racial overtones. For that, she would need new lyrics. Conceived when James Meredith enrolled in the University of Mississippi in the fall of 1962, rekindled by the murder of Medgar Evers in the summer of 1963, and finally set to paper after the bombing of the Birmingham church on September

14, 1963, Simone found a way to address her anger with all these events by quickening Brecht's music with her original lyrics. It is critical to remember that Mississippi, *not* Alabama, is the state named in her title: This song has its origins in James Meredith's 1962 enrollment at the University of Mississippi, not the following year's Sixteenth Street Baptist Church bombing in Alabama, as is so often cited. Weill had written his "Alabama Song"; with "Mississippi Goddam," Nina had her own Mississippi tune.

As we have already seen, Nina's renditions of "Pirate Jenny" fired Hughes's imagination. The song's original foregrounding is especially helpful for understanding why. Audiences were initially informed when reading the liner notes from the original version in *The Threepenny Opera* (1928) that Low-Dive Jenny "gazes out at the fog from Macheath's favorite bordello. Jenny is different from the other girls. She has bitter dreams."[11] "Pirate Jenny" is the secret revenge fantasy of a maid who wants to see the guests she serves executed for their pompous ignorance of her economic plight. Low-Dive Jenny also wants to see every similar building in town completely leveled. When Simone portrayed Low-Dive Jenny, her bitter dream mesmerized audiences who were both unsure of how the plot would end and just how far the singer would go in accomplishing such a revenge. In the end, Low-Dive Jenny is given the power to decide when and where her oppressors will be executed. Her answer is that all of them should be killed "NOW." Only her empty hotel building remains standing. Her pirate ship has come in.

"YOU CAST A SPELL ON ME"

With his musical ambitions, it's not surprising that Hughes invested more energy in musicians and stage performers than he did with fellow writers during the 1960s. In addition to his friendship with musician Margaret Bonds, Hughes worked with pianist Randy Weston (and his arranger Melba Liston) so often that Westen ended up performing at Hughes's funeral in 1967. The poet's social circle included dancer, actress, and singer Eartha Kitt, blues singer Ada "Bricktop" Smith, and dancer Josephine Baker. Langston was a guest at Baker's chateau near Bordeaux in the Dordogne two summers in a row (1962 and 1963), and the two made sure to meet again on four occasions when Baker traveled to New York in March and April 1964.[12] Most relevant to Hughes's mentoring of the much-younger Nina Simone, Hughes knew Odetta so well that she asked him to counsel her on which of her recorded songs she should sing for an important Easter concert in 1965. In fact, Black entertainment was so in vogue at this time that Hughes noted to another fellow songwriter, "The music, jazz bands, and dancers are getting the big budgets. We ought to learn to *also* play trumpet."[13]

Hughes's time mentoring entertainers had its deepest impact on Simone. Sometime between November 11, 1964, and early January 1965, Langston Hughes offered her direct counsel on her music, a step further than he had gone with Odetta. He used Cicely Tyson's record player to listen to Odetta's old records, but performer and songwriter Jimmy Davis knew that Hughes had bigger dreams for collaborating with Nina. Hughes wrote to Davis in early 1965, "I wish she'd do one of your yours—or mine!"[14] To this end, Langston Hughes conjured a new mystical persona intended specifically for Nina.

He began typing up a list of new songs, each focusing on her ability to captivate audiences in a more direct way. He titled this list "Incantations for Nina Simone." The very top of the page makes the incantatory goal too clear to miss: These are "Songs of Enticement, Bewitchment, Voodoo, Hoodoo, Conjuration, Bedevilment, Spell Casting, and Incantation."[15] The list of twenty-two songs includes suggestive titles such as "Ulrica's Brew," "Mojo Blues," "I Wanna Be Evil," "Old Black Magic," and "Bewitched, Bewildered, and Bothered." As the last two of these titles suggests, Hughes was conceiving ways in which the lightheartedness of two well-known Ella Fitzgerald songs could be reembodied by Nina's irrepressible intensity.

In regard to Nina Simone, merely listing song titles was not all Hughes had in mind. His list of "incantations" was just a cover sheet for seven full pages of Hughes's original lyrics. "Mojo Blues" was a song he had written years before it was finally recorded by Big Miller in 1959. A verse from one of these newer tunes spoke of a "brew" of "sweet passion" wielded by a woman who claimed, "I've got him hoodooed." It was clear what would happen in the song once "she puts her spell on him." The forward nature of Hughes unabashedly suggesting songs for Simone's upcoming studio session in January 1965 reminds us that despite the very real and very deep friendships Simone had with Lorraine Hansberry and James Baldwin, only Hughes provided her with professional guidance and source material.[16] Not only did she accept Hughes's new direction, but embracing this new persona would eventually come to define Nina Simone's career.

The most interesting lyric Hughes suggested of his twenty-two songs was originally titled "You Cast a Spell on Me." Featuring an all-too-familiar concept of Simone's repertoire that is now impossible to miss, Hughes wrote lyrics that did not fulfill the power of the persona he was aiming for:

> I will ride you on my broomstick
> I will fly you through the sky
> I'm a witch to end all witches
> So give me a try.

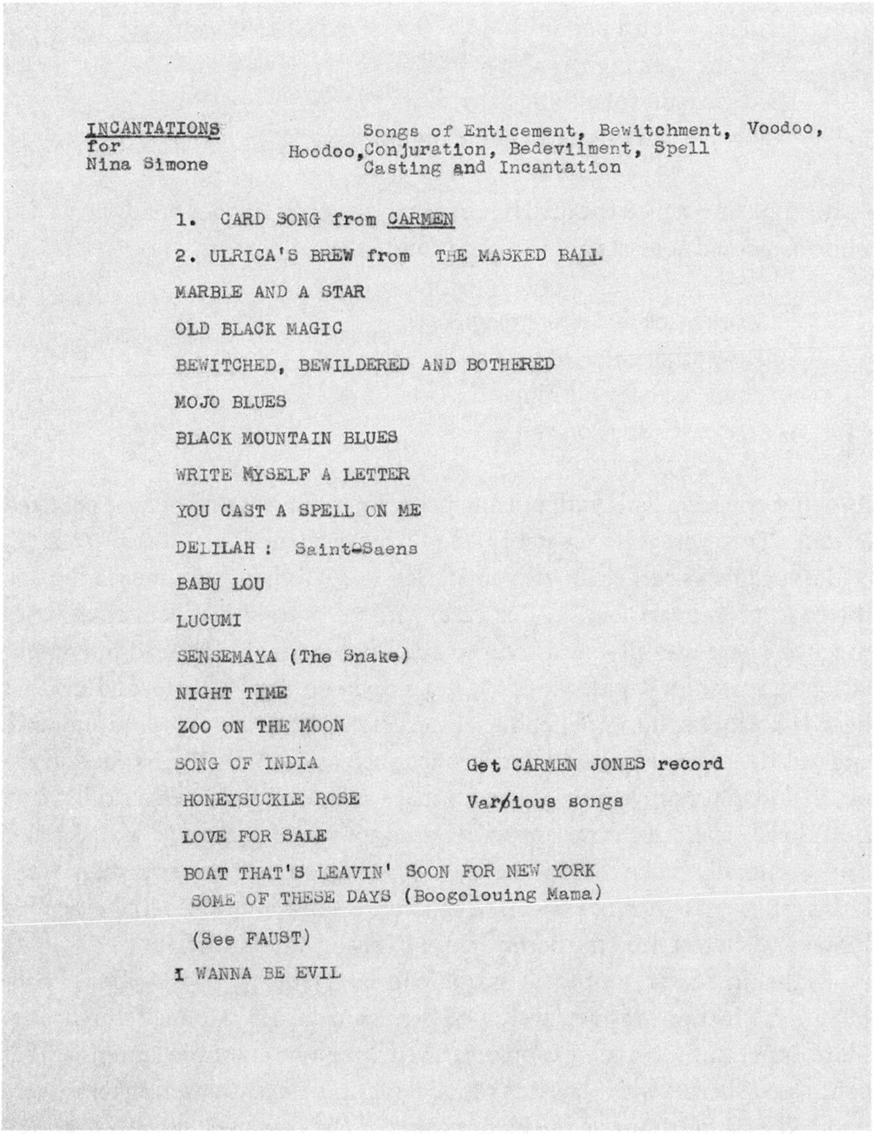

INCANTATIONS
for
Nina Simone

Songs of Enticement, Bewitchment, Voodoo, Hoodoo, Conjuration, Bedevilment, Spell Casting and Incantation

1. CARD SONG from CARMEN

2. ULRICA'S BREW from THE MASKED BALL

MARBLE AND A STAR

OLD BLACK MAGIC

BEWITCHED, BEWILDERED AND BOTHERED

MOJO BLUES

BLACK MOUNTAIN BLUES

WRITE MYSELF A LETTER

YOU CAST A SPELL ON ME

DELILAH : Saint-Saens

BABU LOU

LUCUMI

SENSEMAYA (The Snake)

NIGHT TIME

ZOO ON THE MOON

SONG OF INDIA — Get CARMEN JONES record

HONEYSUCKLE ROSE — Various songs

LOVE FOR SALE

BOAT THAT'S LEAVIN' SOON FOR NEW YORK

SOME OF THESE DAYS (Boogolouing Mama)

(See FAUST)

I WANNA BE EVIL

Fig. 8.2. Langston Hughes's song suggestions of "Incantations for Nina Simone." (James Weldon Johnson Memorial Collection in the Yale Collection of American Literature, Beinecke Rare Book and Manuscript Library, Yale University.)

Even if these lines were accompanied by music, they would still sound too trite, nearing the edge of doggerel:

> I will brew you a potion
> Will make you high as a kite
> I will give you something baby
> Will make you pass dead out at night.

By the time he reached the final line of his third verse, Hughes finally arrived at a line that could at least pass as a good song title:

> I'll work black and white magic
> and any other color, too,
> So come on, baby bunting,
> Let me cast a spell on you.

And then the song ends with unconvincing lines that would not have spooked anyone: "I'm a witch! I'm a witch! / And I'll bedevil you."[17]

Like Hughes's earlier suggestion of "See-Line Woman," Simone gladly took the concept to heart, but, in this case, without putting his ineffectual lyrics to vinyl. There was already a song so similar that Simone instead fully reenvisioned Screamin' Jay Hawkins's "I Put a Spell on You," of 1956, and made it hers. Hawkins's song amplified racial stereotypes for a largely white audience and was denounced by civil rights groups such as the NAACP. His voodoo antics included primitive jungle skirts, a mace spiked with a human skull, and a ridiculously oversized nose ring with horns approaching the size of tusks. The song eventually broke through because it was more shouted than sung. Hawkins performed it during a televised Christmas show in 1956 where he, against his own wishes, started the performance by rising out of a coffin.

By the time Nina recorded it in studio in early January 1965, Hawkins's babbling introduction was replaced with strings from Hal Mooney's orchestra. More importantly, Nina's version portrayed a genuine emotional intensity that contrasted sharply with Hawkins's vaudeville approach. Chattering teeth were updated with light taps on the high register of Nina's piano keys, and her voice announced an assertiveness that masked anger. Listeners were being invited into the place where a private ceremony had just concluded, and the priestess was confessing to the rite she had performed. When Simone began to scat after her opening line, it was filled with a touch of melancholy, not pandering.

Clearly Hawkins's tambourine, costume, and antics had been outdistanced by a tone of convincing menace. Instead of a key shift to increase the tension, the stuttering saxophone here brought out a deep revelation from her voice so that her repeated "I love you, I love you, I love you, I love you, anyhow" held as much desperation as threat. By the time Simone testified that "I don't care if you don't want me / I'm yours right now," it was clear that this particular iteration of spell casting was actually an act of desperation. A contract was being violated, and this running around was being put to a stop. This singer would do anything to keep her lover, and hoodoo was merely the next available option. There is a sadness to this performance, suggesting that every other alternative has been exhausted. Hawkins's ended his theatrical live performances with a white-eyed snorting; Simone's final scat interjects the distance between the words "because" and "your mine" with a trace of the very voodoo it took to cast a spell that was as much incantatory as it was brewed. As it trails off into her unpronounceable scat, "because" is actually enunciated only to the point where it sounds like "becoming," as if we are also privy to the final results; this man will "be comin'" back to her soon as the final proof that the powers of her spells work.

It may be significant that Hughes heard "I Put a Spell on You" when Simone played it live for the first time at Carnegie Hall on January 15, 1965. On the day of the concert, Hughes offered Simone yet another song title. Having just visited Jimmy Davis in Paris, Hughes wondered if the composer of "Lover Man" was right in identifying "Why Is a Good Man So Hard to Find?" as a possible song for her to record.[18] But Hughes's and Simone's mutual friend Lorraine Hansberry had died from cancer at age thirty-four mere days before the concert, so Davis's song suggestion was never earnestly even considered. Hughes then thoughtfully waited a full two weeks before providing a professional assessment of Nina's performance: "Your Carnegie Hall concert was terrific! Except that you don't need an orchestra. You YOURSELF are enough for anybody's money."[19] The songs for the album *I Put a Spell on You* had already been recorded earlier in January with Hal Mooney's strings; however, Nina's next studio venture, *Let It All Out*, stripped back her ensemble just as Hughes suggested. Even beyond his personal support and song suggestions, Hughes's professional instincts were ones Simone deeply valued.

In her performance of "I Put a Spell on You" in England, the TV broadcast on September 14, 1968, reveals two additions that engage with both Hawkins's original and Hughes's more recent suggestions. Having completed her first set, Simone leaves the stage wearing a black net top and matching pants that counter the more recognizable white outfit she wore at the Newport Jazz Festival the year before. When she returns, the camera finds her seated at the piano in a moment of unbroken concentration. She is staring down in such a way as to communicate self-hypnosis. Her hands play the keys as if of their own volition.

She does not blink. A full twelve seconds goes by. The piano rolls below her like a storm's approaching thunder. Most importantly, she has undergone a deliberate costume change for this precise moment. She is now wearing an outfit that reads more as a sophisticated African robe rather than an American dress. Her hair is covered with a matching headwrap. The dangling earrings are now replaced with pearl studs. Welcome to Madame Simone's, where tea leaves are read and fortunes told. Where Hawkins's dime store costumes were outlandish and kitsch, Simone outfitted herself to perform a more enchanting version of bewitchment.

The low rumble of Nina's piano gave way to the crowd's lightning recognition of applause once Nina introduced the first six words of a song that was unidentifiable to the audience until then. As Simone ends the song with a scat that is so extraordinary it defines the concept, she growls out the final "because" a capella to finally let the simmer of her concealed rage boil over into anger. Just before this, she injects a more direct nod to the "Conjuration, Bedevilment, Spell Casting" that Hughes originally envisioned: "So I went to Alabama and got me some mojo dust / and I put a spell on you." This nod to the mojo root is the newly resurfaced trace of Hughes's direct influence. In less than two minutes, Simone has embodied the essence of this song and taken it deeper into the realm of the supernatural than it had ever been before. Many artists would eventually cover this song, but none would so earnestly consider and present the actual power ascribed to voodoo in the kind of convincing way that communicated that the singer seemed to sincerely believe in it herself.

HUGHES AND VOODOO

Langston Hughes had at least three reasons to suggest that Nina sing "Songs of Enticement, Bewitchment, Voodoo, Hoodoo, Conjuration, Bedevilment, Spell Casting, and Incantation." He had experience with voodoo traditions from a famous trip he took to Haiti in 1931. Staying from April to July, Hughes used this trip as a means to recenter his own ambitions as a writer. Having recently been separated from a white benefactor named Charlotte Mason, Hughes traveled to the country where his distinguished grandfather James Mercer Langston had served as US ambassador from 1877 to 1885. When Hughes returned, he wrote the play *Emperor of Haiti*, using the story of the Western Hemisphere's first successful Black slave revolt as both a source for personal inspiration and an analogue for what he hoped might happen (in some degree) in the United States. Thus Hughes knew the names assigned to voodoo priests and at least seven loa gods.[20] He needed to know the traditions of sorcery for an important scene in the first act of the play in which a voodoo ceremony initiates the slaves' uprising against their French colonizers.[21]

Not merely drawing from his own past, Hughes had more recently invoked the names of five voodoo gods, cult leaders, and priests when writing an uncharacteristically autobiographical poem titled "Gospel Cha-Cha" (1961). Papa Legba, Ogoun, Damballa, Erzulie, and Alexander Bedward are referenced as the speaker in Hughes's poem seeks an alternative means to access a long-sought spirituality. Despite an earnest quest to travel the natives' pathway to experience genuine spirituality and authenticity, the speaker symbolically climbs up to Haiti's famous citadel only to find it that does not provide the solace he seeks. Not only had Hughes himself made the physically demanding journey to the top of Bonnet à L'Evêque three times in 1931, but this quest mirrors Hughes own failed attempt to formally make his spirit whole. At age thirteen, he hoped to see Jesus at the altar of his aunt Reed's St. Luke's African American Episcopal (AMA) Church but felt rejected when the promised savior did not arrive to provide salvation. Hughes felt unforgettable guilt when he lied about seeing Jesus appear so that he might be allowed to leave the altar where family and friends were patiently awaiting his moment of salvation.

9

The High Priestess of Soul

By the summer of 1965, Langston Hughes had become the most important sounding board in Nina Simone's life. Four months after recoding "I Put a Spell on You," and still wired after performing a concert in England, Nina took out a blue ballpoint pen and stationery from her hotel on Park Lane in London and began to write her thoughts to her poet mentor. With the recent painful death of Lorraine Hansberry from cancer earlier in January and the assassination of Malcolm X just five weeks later, in February, on Simone's thirty-second birthday, Simone sought Hughes's friendship and guidance more than ever.

One can hardly say enough about the significance of the most important letter Simone ever wrote to Hughes. At the height of a hard-won stardom, Nina directed her time and energy toward the person she regarded as her closest friend in the world. She told Langston she had recently been annotating his autobiography *The Big Sea* in pencil, and on Sunday night July 6, 1965, at the very height of her celebrity, she declared directly to its author: "If I want to get downright mean and violent I go straight to this book and there is also material for that. Amazing." Though she feels "sorta' tongue-tied now for there's so much I'd like to say to you," Nina declares: "Brother, you got a fan now! I'm going out and buy every book you've written."[1]

Simone was now experiencing new levels of international stardom and currently on her first-ever European tour. Though she was anxious, Nina and her music had been well received so far, in no small part due to the unveiling of a new enchanting persona conveyed in her song "I Put a Spell on You." The concept of the song had been suggested six months earlier by Hughes himself, and the mutual levels of artistic understanding between Hughes and Simone enable us to begin to understand 1965 as the height of the deep and abiding friendship shared by these two American icons.

Hughes's urging Nina to perform the incantations he suggested gave birth to the moniker Nina is still known by today, the High Priestess of Soul. The history of the title itself offers a fascinating story into mystic overtones that are often too quickly overlooked.

The year 1904 introduced New York City to Margaret Gladstone Stuart. Hailing from a distinct line of sorceresses in England, this "Grandniece of Gladstone" was known as "the high priestess of soul." It was claimed that as "the high priestess of the soul" Stuart could "see the aura surrounding anyone."[2] Accusations against a different "high priestess" made national news that spread all the way from Rhode Island to Alaska beginning in 1922. Minnie Englehardt accused her husband, Rev. Dr. Adolph Englehardt, of being aided by both "phantoms" and a "High Priestess" as he set up shop claiming to help women improve their health through his unique practices. When Minnie filed for divorce as his "Love Patient," she listed 122 women by name who had also been subject to wearing "Soul Colored Kimonos" as they endured something labeled with unmistakable transparency as his "'Touch System' of 'Divine Healing.'"[3]

Even as late as 1974, the time when Simone was not only openly embracing the moniker but exploring and pushing its boundaries, Ouija boards, black magic, and rubbing blood on initiates was still associated with occult groups who learned their practices under female priestesses. Testifying anonymously about her teenage experiences, "Sharon" explained that "power can be wielded over people" in its witchcraft. She referred to her leader as "an Egyptian princess whose magic is more powerful than any witches." In this coven, no less than thirteen girls between the ages of fourteen and fifteen reported to none

(1)

London, Sunday night
July

Dear Langston—

I've owed you this letter 6? for some time now—so I'm finally doing it.

Thank you—thank you for the books (your autobiographies) you gave us—I'm reading "~~[illegible]~~ The Big Sea", right now and it gives me such pleasure—you have no idea! It is so funny—I read chapters over & over again—'cause certain ones paint complete pictures for me and I get completely absorbed!

Then too, if I'm in a negative mood and want to get more negative (about the racial problem, I mean) if I want to get downright mean and violent I go straight to this book and there is <u>also</u> material for that. Amazing—

I use the book—what I mean is I underline all meaningful sentences to me—I make comments in pencil

TWENTY HERTFORD STREET
PARK LANE, LONDON, W.1
GROSVENOR 8881-2-3

(2) 13

about certain paragraphs etc. And as I said there is a wealth of knowledge concerning the negro problem, especially if one wants to <u>trace</u> the many many areas that we've had it rough in all these years—sometimes when I'm with white "liberals" who want to know why we're so bitter—I forget (I don't forget—I just get tongue-tied) how <u>complete</u> has been the white races' rejection of us all these years and then when this happens I go get your book. I'm looking forward to using it more & more in this way as times go on.

As a matter of fact, Langston, I feel sorta' tongue-tied now for there's so much I'd like to say to you and I can't possibly write as fast as I think and even if I did I'd be here all night writing this letter.

(3) 14

I know one thing—I've always admired you and been proud of you—respected you and felt honored to know you—but brother, you got a fan now! I'm going out and buy every book you've written—I had no idea I could enjoy you so. You see, reading isn't easy for me—but "The Big Sea" is so varied and so simply written that I don't have to force myself to concentrate—It grips my imagination <u>immediately</u> <u>plus</u> everything in it I identify with, even your going to sea—and I've never been to sea—

Enough of this! . . .

I enjoy it immensely—okey? 'Nough said.

Andrew, Lisa & I are in London—have been for two wks. working at a club—The job is finished; we remain here another week for promotion & T.V. and then move on to France, Belgium,

(4)

Spain for another two wks. Then home. No pleasure—just work. <u>Please let us see you sometime.</u>

We get back home August 6th or 7th—

Love,

Nina

You know who Nina is, don't you? I mean I didn't sign my last name!!? (Joke)

Andy sends love

TWENTY HERTFORD STREET
PARK LANE, LONDON, W.1
GROSVENOR 8881-2-3

other than a "high priestess" whom each considered their "soul sister." She taught the indoctrinated how to get in touch with an alternative spiritual realm to tap its hidden power.[4]

Unnamed music executives at Philips Records had multiple aims when they released the album *High Priestess of Soul* in early 1967. With Nina having recently moved on to record with RCA, Philips culled leftover material from its vaults in an attempt to cash in one last time on Simone's stardom. This coincided with Billboard's recent creation of the "soul chart," which meant that an album in this new genre could be advertised as making "the chart" to enhance future sales and spark concert promotion. Using the term "soul" in the album title signaled to bean counters that this album should be ranked there rather than on the standard pop chart. The sobriquet also created an intrigue that channeled her recent incandescent performance of "I Put a Spell on You."

The album's unsigned artwork depicts Simone with an oversized Nefertiti-slanted headpiece, consisting of a cubist representation of assorted instruments, including lute, flute, pan flute, cymbals, and saxophone. A miniature piano somehow also hangs impossibly from this crown. Nina is also adorned with a piano-keyed necklace while holding some type of pipe in her hand. Its smoke forms a background featuring a kaleidoscopic mix of cerulean, opal, and carnelian.

There is not one solitary indication that this title had ever been bestowed upon her (or self-invoked by Simone herself) before this album release. Nonetheless, Nina soon realized its potential. In some ways, it was soon used like the term "diva" to quietly mask her true emotional vulnerability. Even quicker to mine the new moniker, music reviewers and columnists could not contain themselves as they immediately began activating metaphors to expand upon the ready-made theme of sorcery. Critic Leonard Feather opened his review by calling her "one of the most hypnotic performers on any stage," continuing that she is "a spellbinder who can hold audiences captive whether with ballad, folk song, or social message."[5] Was he truly watching her perform or simply studying her latest album cover? One article in England used the moniker "High Priestess of Soul" for its title in 1968 after her TV special aired.[6] In March of the same year advertisers promoted Nina's upcoming concert in Los Angeles by again invoking the title. By the time Nina was once again proclaimed the highlight of opening night at the fifteenth annual Newport Jazz Festival in July 1968, she would forever be known as the High Priestess of Soul.[7]

Fig. 9.1a–d. Nina Simone's four-page letter to Langston Hughes, July 6, 1965. (James Weldon Johnson Memorial Collection in the Yale Collection of American Literature, Beinecke Rare Book and Manuscript Library, Yale University.)

Fig. 9.2. Nina Simone's final album with Philips Records (*High Priestess of Soul*, 1967) included previously unreleased songs, and its title and artwork set in motion the title she is still known by today.

However, this was anything but a certain inevitability, even with so many musicians being assigned such promotional monikers. There was Bessie Smith (Empress of the Blues), B. B. King (King of the Blues), Robert Johnson (King of the Delta Blues), Ma Rainey (Mama of the Blues), and of course, Elvis Presley (King of Rock 'n' Roll). In 1968, Dinah Washington was considered the Queen.[8] Surprisingly, at the time of Washington's reign, the title High Priestess of Soul was actually most consistently applied to Aretha Franklin.

Although Franklin is known categorically today as the Queen of Soul, that title had not yet even come close to being codified in the late 1960s. From 1968 to 1978, Aretha was not regarded as royalty but rather known to the world as a "Soul Sister."[9] In a review of Phyl Garland's book *The Sound of Soul* (1969), the public learned that the author labeled Nina Simone "the high priestess of soul" and Aretha Franklin "Sister Soul."[10] Garland revealed in an interview with

Franklin that Aretha "was not eager to project herself as a new queen of the blues and . . . asserted, 'The queen of the blues was and still is Dinah Washington.'"[11] Far less reserved, the title "Queen" also was being applied concurrently to Carla Thomas, who was often either the Queen of Memphis Soul or simply the Queen of Soul.[12]

In the end, Nina lost a head-to-head Grammy nomination to Aretha in 1970 and painfully watched Franklin claim another in 1972 for album of the year for *Young, Gifted, and Black*, the very song Nina had first recorded three years before. However, Simone eventually won sole possession of the title High Priestess of Soul.

The moniker was well earned: Simone embodied an undeniable focus of spirit that defined soul not as a musical genre but rather as a reflection of intensity. With this emerging persona, Nina as priestess replaced the siren call of Nina narrating the empowerment of sex workers evidenced in such songs as "See-Line Woman." Nina embraced the name until it eventually came to be an alter-ego for her stage presence in much the same way that Jess B. Semple's excited rants balanced out the level-headed, always reserved Hughes. What Nina found in the persona was the very power she was denied in American society as a Black woman. Her embodiment of Black power grew in reach and audience until it started to do more than model individual behavior: It soon became inseparable from the very calls being issued first by the Student Nonviolent Coordinating Committee (SNCC) and eventually by its West Coast extension, the Black Panthers.

TRYING ON THE MASK

Experimenting musically with this newfound persona, Nina Simone's 1965 concert performance of "Mean and Evil Blues" in Antibes, France, varies dramatically from either Dinah Washington's earlier versions (1946–49) or the related (and much older) "Evil Gal Blues" by Tampa Red (1928). The novelty of this new song in her repertoire emerges instantly as she immediately teaches her band on the fly that this blues will be played in "A flat." In fact, Nina would miss delivering her own lyric to end the third verse, subtly covering up her infelicity by emphatically demanding that Rudy Stevenson step up to add a flute solo. Outfitted in sparkling pearls and a natural hairdo, Nina was clearly enjoying herself, despite her conspicuous high heels. As she sat on her piano stool, Simone seemed to be dancing to the twelve-bar blues without so much as even moving her feet. Physical movement and a bodily acceptance of the sinister groove seemed more prescient here than bass notes. She boastfully intoned: "I'm so mean and evil / I'll mess you up with a dozen sticks of dynamite."

The unchanging attitude bound in the line "I'm gonna stay that way" had already come across sonically so that the words themselves were now echoes that reinforced what the piano had been saying. Something deep and uncontainable wanted to refuse the inevitable bars of the sheet music that were asking the groove to move and change. Nina soon moved, going much further. She was leaving the song's most potent idea until the very end. Here the lyric entangled reckless sexuality with an indifferent morality that not only acted but *shouted* its endeavors without shame to anyone close enough to listen: "I'm so mean and evil / I don't know my husband from my cousin." Startling, unhinged, and unconcerned, this statement was of course more drunken bravado than heartfelt testimony. Soon the sheer defiance of social norms and an embrace of violence would fade from her set list so that being evil slowly gave way to performances where power itself, and an ecstatic spirituality, more directly encompassed the essence of what it meant to be the High Priestess of Soul.

PURE VOODOO

In her conclusion to "Aint Got No / I Got Life" at Berkeley in 1973, Nina offered a supernatural identity that defied the boundaries of human frailty. As she asserted her desire to stay on earth "until my work is done," she extended the song's long list of items she possessed so that it eventually also included a soul with an expansive cosmic disposition: "I've got my soul. It's kept me alive for about five thousand years now. Every day I get younger, younger, and younger. So of course right now I'm only about two hundred years old. [*Nina pauses to laugh and clap once.*] And as long as I want to stay here, I'm gone stay here 'cause I know how to come back and back and back and back inside my womb [*laughter*]." Although both Walt Whitman and Rainer Marie Rilke considered the infinite nature of their own souls in their poetry, Nina's assertion of her own regeneration seems to be a mix of cosmology and sorcery not easily defined. Whether this ever represented her true conviction or was merely a practice in which her persona could model its power became muddled by the fact that Nina simultaneously asserted it as a belief all the while laughing at the impossibility. Much later in life, she declared in a sit-down interview: "Who am I? I'm the reincarnation of an Egyptian queen."[13]

Nina's haunting live performance of "Dambala" at the Lincoln Center's Philharmonic Hall in 1974 is less a song than a beguiling prayer uttered before a spellbound audience.[14] For nearly seven unblinking minutes, the crowd watches Nina summon the Haitian god Dambala with a solemnity informed by a combination of lived experience and past mourning for mistreated relatives and loved ones. Al Schackman's work on the sitar buoys the song's palpable element of enchantment, producing an atmosphere where incense and potions seem to intermingle in the very air being breathed. The hall fills with a collective hallucination sought in a hookah bar.

As she begins to sing, Nina does what she always did: She inhabits the role the song asks her to play with a fierce intensity that collapses the distance between Nina herself and her persona as the High Priestess of Soul.

The High Priestess performs a prayer that a final judgment be enacted against all slave owners. This prayer takes the form of a song originally sung by Exuma on his self-titled album (1970), extending the Bahamian native's plea all the way to the shores of the United States.[15] The spirits of the islands inform the song's solemn introduction. Nina is praying to the Haitian god Dambala, a loa spirit most often associated with a figure of a serpent in Haitian iterations of voodoo practices. The song is quiet, both as a prayer but also to capture the soft hissing sounds associated with portrayals of Dambala.

In this song, Dambala coexists with God and Satan in a synthesized cosmology. Listeners are presented with a bridge spanning between voodoo and Christianity, where slave owners receive eternal condemnation for enslaving people. From the soul of Nina Simone, such judgments need not be confined to the Caribbean: They are equally necessary throughout the Americas. Ushering in the final judgment by reversing Genesis's weeklong structure, God appears here on the seventh day, followed by Satan's arrival on the seventh night. Dambala seems to be the spiritual entity assigned the special task of persecuting the oppressors at the end of days, not the beginnings of creation.

In the end, this chant is as much a curse as it is a prayer. If Dambala consents, Haitian slave owners will neither rise to heaven nor sink to hell. To truly know what it is to be treated inhumanely, one must be reduced to a mere body without a soul. "You'll remain in your graves," she sings, "with the stench and the smell." Nina, the expert on all things that address the soul, reminds us that the enslaved were made to feel subhuman. They were made to work the earth as animals who lacked spirit. This final judgment is the only way for the enslavers to suffer the condemnation Dante wrote of where the punishment fits the crime. Nina's plea is an open invitation for this judgment to come now—before the end-times.

Like "Dambala," "Obeah Woman" came to Nina's attention through Exuma's self-titled record of 1970. His "Obeah Man" becomes Nina's personalized "Obeah Woman" in what results in her most autobiographical song.[16] As with Hughes's poem "Gospel Cha-Cha" (1961), something about voodoo's symbols, African origins, and priesthood enabled each artist to explore significant aspects of their inner lives. With "Obeah Woman" paired with the song "Nina" from this same show (in which she intones her own name over and over with infinite variety), Simone was finally ready in 1974 to explain the joys and burdens of her career. "Obeah Woman" becomes a song in which the subject is herself. References to her upbringing in the Holy Roller Church, asides about her daughter, Lisa, and finally the mix of affirmations and confessions about her persona as the High Priestess of Soul engage sermon, testimony, and confession in one unforgettable brew. In less than seven minutes, Nina covers the entire subject of her evolving spirituality. Rightly read, "Obeah Woman" is one of Nina Simone's most iconic songs, standing out with distinction among the entirety of her resplendent discography.

The Caribbean tradition of obeah is the perfect match for Nina's persona as the High Priestess of Soul. Derived from practices used throughout the West African diaspora, the obeah tradition encompasses a wide range of spell-casting and healing traditions in which the leader's sorcery is the seat of unquestioned powers. To begin, Nina conjures a combination of muses and spirits to help her as words such as "soul," "body," and "Bible" seem to coalesce in only a partially recognizable chant that elevates scat to the level of sacred dance. She is in no hurry, patiently waiting for the spirits to move. She announces, "Gonna take my time getting this one together." It is her final song of this concert, the place where she often slotted a tune that revisited her church roots. When Nina inquires whether her audience has heard of the Holy Roller Church, she emphatically asserts that this is simultaneously where she came from and where she has now moved beyond. Unusually candid, she is equally proud of both.

Just shy of three minutes into a pulsing rhythm, she is standing far from the piano. The crowd claps to the beat. Primed for a full vision of the High Priestess of Soul, Nina instead announces that she is a goddess called the Obeah Woman: "I can eat thunder and drink the rain." The autobiographical angle of the song is undeniable once she declares "Yeah they call me Nina and Pisces, too." Limitless in action and coequal to Pisces, Nina enthusiastically presents a version of her persona that is old as Greece and as exotic as Africa. The Zodiac sign is more apt than we might realize. Not only does Nina's birthday fall in the astrological window for a Pisces, but its visual representation as two fish swimming in opposite directions is meant to portray the constant division of Pisces's attention between the two spheres of reality and fantasy. What could be a more apt symbol for capturing the song's internal digressions from Nina the actual woman to the High Priestess of Soul, her invented persona?

But is she merely being playful in this song or unmasking a force hidden too long? Indignant at an audience either perpetually suspicious or momentarily unconvinced, Nina asks the crowd if they hear her with an intense conviction that displays either her private imagination or her performative ability to fully inhabit whatever role she is currently projecting onstage. Then the facade breaks back toward reality for a moment, and something of the challenges of being a Black female musician in this era suggest that this metaphor has been remarkably empowering. In musing aloud how she has lasted this long in the music business, Nina is testifying to the veil she put up. Langston's original concept has simultaneously protected her and become a useful marketing strategy. By the end of the song, something of its potency has been drained, exhausted, or perhaps oversaturated. Or, as a true artist, is Nina confessing that now portraying herself as a goddess who stands as a gatekeeper to the other world has pushed to the very furthest reach of where this persona can go in both life and song?

To end the song, Nina calls the burden of having to be a goddess a heavy one. She even asserts that it is a title she never put on herself. Nina's final line of the song both ends the original vinyl album and serves as its title. She simply says, "It is finished." Then the song ends. The biblical echo to Christ's final words on the cross animates the idea that Nina is now publicly declaring she is forever letting go of the crucifying weight of her goddess status, just as Christ let go of his earthly life. This phrase, recorded in John 19:30, is one Nina certainly knew given her extensive church background, and it gives deeper meaning to her intentional references to the Holy Roller Church used to introduce the song. With this precise declaration, Nina complicates our sense of prophecy. Her recording career would never really be the same again. Like her once-high demand, the persona, too, could go no further.

10

No Hidin' Place

Iconic guitarist and singer Richie Havens believed that Nina was the single biggest influence on his remarkable musical career. He recalled his first time playing on the road in March 1959: "We were at the Howard Theater in Washington, D.C., doing three shows a day. Every time Nina went on, I'd watch her from the side of the stage. I listened to jazz a lot. The singer who most influenced me was Nina Simone, mostly through the suggestion of how she sang, [and] taking other people's songs and singing them the only way you can." Havens soon found himself performing other people's songs by making them uniquely his own: "If it wasn't for her, I would have always respected the songwriter's way of doing it," he said. It is clear that "while Simone's presence, powerful voice and dynamic delivery were a major influence on Havens, it was ultimately her process of reinvention that inspired him to re-work traditional numbers like 'Run Shaker Life,' as well as Dylan's 'Just Like a Woman,' and George Harrison's 'Here Comes the Sun,' which climbed the charts to #16 in 1971."[1]

But on the second night of that unforgettable engagement in Washington, in 1959, Havens got the biggest surprise of his professional life. Nina's assistant set up a meeting. Simone met with Richie and asked if he knew how to play her song “Sinnerman.” Havens explained in an interview that nothing happened right away:

> “For whatever reason, she didn't say a word to me for the next six shows. Not one word. We had three more gigs to go,” Havens recalled. Then, on March 16, 1959, Nina's assistant suddenly reappeared, this time in a panic: “‘Richie, she's calling you! She's up there playing. Get the hell up there.’ I walked over to the curtain and she's playing Bach—deedle deedle, deedle da da da, singing ‘Richie, Richie come to the stage and bring your guitar . . . ’ I almost fainted. The minute I hit that stool, we just took off with ‘Sinner Man.’ When she hit that thing [the piano], you'd better be there. We blew it up. It was the first write up [music review] I ever had. It was so far out. That lady was magic!”[2]

While Havens's memories of playing “Sinnerman” with Simone were indelible, the song itself is so malleable that it has no definitive version—the variety of versions means that it is loaned to someone to accomplish something different each night it is performed. In essence, it belongs to everyone. But one thing is clear: “Sinnerman” is Nina Simone's most enduring contribution to the soundtrack of the civil rights movement. “Sinnerman” is sampled by contemporary musicians today in ways that have relegated the once-iconic “Mississippi Goddam” to a song now belonging only to a bygone era.

To understand exactly what led Simone to reenvision this song, we have to track the song's long development, beginning as a revival piece sung by Eunice Waymon when she was just a child. As we shall see, “Sinnerman” moves easily from tent revivals to Greenwich Village night clubs and eventually to stages where, on one night, Simone's unexpected tone of personal testimony surprised even her bandmates. Once again, Langston Hughes's professional mentoring was responsible for Nina Simone deciding to record the most iconic version of the track in 1965.

“SINNERMAN,” 1961

Before recording her definitive studio version of “Sinnerman” in 1965, Nina had played the song as part of the second set of her concert in Carnegie Hall on April 12, 1963, as well as earlier during her AMSAC concert in Lagos in 1961. The first known recording of Nina's version of “Sinnerman” dates from an April 1961 live set at the Village Gate in Greenwich Village, but the song was not released on the album *Nina Simone—At the Village Gate*. Very often, the final songs she played at the end of these sets at Art D'Lugoff's famous club were long pieces she could extend and stretch. Nina was a perfect fit for the Village

Gate after D'Lugoff took special note of "the blacklisted or barely working folk singers who needed a place to perform."[3] These long pieces were ones Nina often associated with her childhood. For example, with the scriptural tune "Children Go Where I Send You," Nina asked her listeners, "You ever been to revival meetings?" When a band member quietly replied, "They don't know nothing 'bout that," Nina amplified the sentiment to those not onstage: "I'll bet you don't even know what I'm talking about. Well, you in one right now."

Nina ended this show in April 1961 with a very different childhood song. Though it seemed similar, it did not present an ecstatic celebration of discipleship or missionary zeal. Introducing the tune, Nina told the audience that she remembered first hearing the song when she was a very young girl. Nina's left hand rolled through the notes that make a very low B minor as drummer Bobby Hamilton's brushes moved quickly across his snare. Speaking very softly, as if playing such a spiritual in a club was sacrosanct, she let them know in a solemn tone what they were about to experience: "This is a song I learned when I was a little bitty girl, in Bible meetings. It happened when my mother, and lots more like her, were trying to save souls."

On its surface, the song opens with the unredeemed seeking shelter from the Lord's wrath on Judgment Day. "Oh, sinnerman, where you gonna run to?" Looking for anything to save him, the speaker addresses places such as a "rock" or a "river" where he might try to hide from God's judgment. When the sinnerman eventually runs to the Lord himself, Nina repeats the most famous word of the entire song. Nina sings "Power" seven times, all while "Power, Lord" is the response from the rest of her band. This simple repetition serves as a trellis for the whole song, allowing all the other verses the space to grow or stop wherever they want. In some ways, it seems as if the word "power" here is the final remainder from an ecstatic cry lifted from the final lines of the Lord's Prayer: "For thine is the kingdom, and the power, and the glory, forever and ever."

On a surface level, the only answer for the unredeemed is prayer. About four minutes and twenty seconds in, Nina can be heard scatting in tongues before verbally shifting the song to a higher key. She calls out, "Let's go up," and the verses about seeking out the rock, the river, and the Lord eventually achieve a critical change signaled by the timely shift in key: The sinnerman reaches the Devil to find him praying as well. Absent drums, bass, and guitar, this quest for salvation reaches its quiet conclusion when Nina softly concludes, "There's nowhere to run to." The helplessness of these dead-end signals appears to be a spiritual defeat. But rather than leaving her audience despondent at the end of the show, Nina returns the music back to the central feature of the song so that everyone instead leaves hearing the shouts of the converted as she repeats, "Power!"

THE ICONIC VERSION, 1965

Nothing truly prepared listeners for experiencing Nina Simone's studio version of "Sinnerman." It is the rare song that earns the title "masterpiece." Nina's definitive version of "Sinnerman," included on *Pastel Blues*, was *not* recorded live. This remarkable energy and communication between musicians were recorded in the studio in May 1965 and released in October. Coming in at a full ten minutes and fifteen seconds, the song was actually recorded *before* Bob Dylan's mythically long "Like a Rolling Stone." When Dylan released his song as a single on July 20, 1965, Columbia Records falsely listed the running time as 5 min., 59 sec., to try to fool disc jockeys to play a song that actually clocked in at 6 min., 6 sec. A full four minutes and nine seconds longer that Dylan's hit, "Sinnerman" could never have been released as a single: It literally would not have fit on one side of a 45 RPM record.

Nina's 1961 plea for power had now become a demand. The 1965 studio version of "Sinnerman" opens with Nina playing five notes that could be accomplished only by someone with true classical training. Using only her right hand, Simone forms a triad in the key of B minor and somehow reaches all the way down to A major by way of quickly linking the two with an E.[4] The physical dexterity of this technique is remarkable. She creates this fast pendulum without shifting her fingers to different piano keys. The song starts to sizzle as Bobby Hamilton joins in with sixteenth notes on his closed hi-hat before Lyle Atkinson's upright bass opens with double stops combining B and F-sharp before he settles into a pulsing rhythm of quarter notes. As the song continues, it loosely follows a sixteen-bar blues structure employing the chords of B minor, A, and E minor and then uses F-sharp as the turnaround reminiscent in many blues patterns. The song reaches its furious apex in a mere three minutes, a musical sprint to a mountain's summit.

After this heated tempo, Nina's stunning two-minute-and-twenty-five-second interlude is a cool study in musical control and unedited studio recording. Rudy Stevenson sets a rhythm on his guitar moving back and forth between B minor and A major as Al Schackman adds a few licks from his own fretboard playing lead to maintain the overall tension of the moment. Chords of F-sharp alternate with E minor until we hear a final thematic turn comparable to the way Nina reinterprets "Tomorrow Is My Turn" and concludes both "Go to Hell" and the epic medley "My Sweet Lord / Today Is a Killer." Then we hear: "I want." She pauses, then repeats, "I want." Nina's signature cadenza travels the full course of only the black keys on the piano as she hits notes that comprise the chord of F-sharp. The highly sampled final demand is complete only when she asserts a personal desire for something that does not yet exist: "Power, Lord!" The music ends when thundering drums combine with guitars, bass, and piano so that the final cymbal crashes are at once a frustration and a demand for power that is nowhere present in any other of her live or studio recordings. "Sinnerman" simply had to be her last song—at both concerts and on the vinyl of *Pastel Blues*—because it is impossible to imagine what song Nina Simone could have played next.

IN CONCERT

As pressed to vinyl in 1965, Nina Simone's concert versions of "Sinnerman" showed just how malleable the tune was in context of time and place. Instead of letting listeners feel that they had been targeted for conversion at a tent revival meeting in rural North Carolina, on one occasion in 1965 at the Cellar Door in Washington, DC, Nina personalized the song so that it suddenly became a way for the High Priestess of Soul to witness to her congregation on the current state of her own soul. This personal approach was completely unexpected on this night. Even her bandmates were caught off guard. As the musicians prepared for an up-tempo declaration, hand claps and a tambourine opened the song by setting a pace that Nina immediately countered with soft piano notes followed by an unmistakable "shhh" three lines into the first verse. She was addressing the band, not the already-silent audience. Tonight, the river and sea that are sometimes portrayed as "flowin'" do not receive this realistic description. Instead, they are "boilin'." When she announces, "Goin' home with this one," she is signaling to the audience that this is her final song of the show.

Muting her typical loud cries of "Power," Nina instead speaks the entire first section when her musicians were expecting shouts. She signals as much with "Said power, Lord," forcing her bandmates to repeat her words in subdued tones they are wholly unprepared to echo. Instead of the song landing crescendos here, Nina is nearly whispering "power," and she soon stops speaking completely. For her famous piano interlude, she plays a few quiet phrases on the keyboard with her right hand and then finally finds a mood that is a heighted plea yet still not a demand. Listening feels like walking in on someone who is praying out loud.

"I said power" brings the song's revivalist energy up until she finally starts to call out combinations of "Bring Down now now now / Throw Down." Each of these is followed by the backup singers now forcefully delivering the "Power" they expected when the song began. As Nina counts time, "One, two, three, yeah" (to triumphantly halt the rising music), the crowd mistakenly thinks the song is over after a mere four minutes and thirty seconds. She responds by immediately pounding the keys hand over hand in what signals true frenzy. A pregnant mood then emerges as Nina's piano telegraphs the feelings of a person on the run and hiding from the law. The bass and drum mimic the tension of the search party who know their suspect is close at hand. The loud heartbeat they amplify suggests the physical anxiety of a freight car stowaway about to have the flashlight turned toward his face as he huddles in a corner.

Anguished and forlorn, Nina testifies as if she is recalling actual past sins she has yet to atone for. It sounds almost too personal for a public song when she states that the Devil was waiting "to do me in again." The pain here feels real as the distance between performer and persona collapses. She continues: "I said, Devil, I don't like you / but the Lord won't have me." Nina is now someplace very private and personal. She states: "The Lord won't have me / until I get some clothes." Is Nina recalling the guilt associated with waking up naked some morning after having spent an intimate night with a person who is not her spouse? For the next eight seconds, Nina stretches one word: "Poooooower." It hangs in the ear nearly as long as Nina's stunning downward slur of "leaves" in the final verse of her version of "Strange Fruit." After twelve and a half minutes, this plea now sounds physically exhausted and emotionally desperate. The song ends with Nina stretching an extended vocal cry: "I want Power, Lord!!" Put simply, this stunning version of "Sinnerman" is the most emotional song in her discography. It is little wonder that it has continued assertively to hold a place of privilege among other musicians.

More than any other song by Simone, the accessible studio recording of "Sinnerman" from 1965 has resurfaced on multiple occasions to leave various indelible impressions throughout popular culture. Talib Kweli's "Get By" (2003) samples the song; Nina's two calls for power open a track that also builds a piano riff based on Nina's bridge. Salamishah Tillet, an expert on how Simone's work is used in modern hip-hop, notes, "Instead of pulling from the chord progression of the eight-bar blues that is repeated throughout 'Sinnerman,' [Kanye] West samples a single, nonrepeated line from her piano solo."[5] This same bridge, complete with hand clapping, opens the song "Oh Timbaland" (2007) before Nina's voice is modified from the original chorus of "Oh, Sinnerman" so that she is made to sing "Oh, Timbaland, where you gonna run to." The move is salient as the artist Timbaland answers Nina by declaring "Nowhere" in a response that asserts his defiant lack of fear. Taking an even more direct approach, Nina's song stood as a very symbol of the civil rights movement to a musician hailing from Ireland. In a concert in 2018, Hozier brought in Mavis Staples to sing a version of "Nina Cried Power" with music emphasizing the spiritual roots of Simone's arrangement and a long list of cultural activists symbolizing the song's uncontested connection to political activism. With "Nina Cried Power," all civil rights singers before and after Nina assemble under the iconic status of Simone's mantra.

"NO HIDIN' PLACE"

Although the origins of any folk song do not account for what alternate verses might have evolved or what has been lost to memory, one very early version of "No Hidin' Place" by Newman I. White was recorded in Durham, North Carolina, in July 1922.[6] The song appears to have migrated south from Richmond, Virginia, via Lucius Chapin. Some versions integrate passages from the tune "Mary Wore Three Links of Chain," a song with imagery that may code the hidden cover sought by a runaway slave. The one-hundred-year-old wax cylinder of White's voice sounds as if it was recorded in the midst of woodsmen sanding rough-cut boards. In the fifty-four seconds of White's entire 1922 performance, we can barely hear:

> Oh, Sinnaman sittin' on the gates of hell
> The gates flew open and in he fell
> There's no hidin' place down there.[7]

Transcribing from original audio reveals the initial and persistent tension over how to type "Sinnerman." Although it often appears as two words—"Sinner Man"—these earliest renditions verbally ran the sound together to form what is best transposed as "Sinnaman." Hence, standardized English first moved to amend the dialect to prescriptive spelling, leaving the word still singular but now standardized. Confusion continues to surface as to whether this should be one word or two. Simone's earliest record presents "Sinnerman" as all one word.

Nina also uses the word "Sinnerman" in one other song. It surfaces in the song "He's Got the Whole World in His Hands" when she sings:

> He's got the gamblin' man
> in His hands,
> He's got the Sinnerman
> In his hands.

While no other known version that precedes Nina's contains the iconic cries for "Power," it just may be that this is precisely how Black congregations in Western North Carolina performed the song at tent revivals in the late 1930s when Simone was a child.

"POWER"

Among the twenty-two titles Langston Hughes suggested for Simone to sing in late 1964 as "Songs of Enticement, Bewitchment, Voodoo, Hoodoo, Conjuration, Bedevilment, Spell Casting, and Incantation," he included a lyric he wrote especially for her. Because it was created for Nina, this lyric deserves extended discussion. In writing a song titled "Power," Langston Hughes was the first to recognize the word's potential for expanding Nina's burgeoning political appeal. Imagining no one other than Nina singing, Hughes begins his song "Power":

> Power! Ha—aa!
> Hypnotized by Power!
> What I would do if I had Power!
> Um! Um! UM UM!
> I would be a—something—yes, with Power!
> First I'd have me
> Peace of mind with Power.
> Then I'd have,
> "Leave me be,"
> With Power.
> I would be my own "sweet" self with Power,
> I'd own my each and every hour, me, with Power.
> I'd say, "Come kiss me, Sweet," I've Power.
> I'd say I love you, baby, with Power!
> I'd would walk, dance, prance, yes, dance, with Power.
> It's me, Miss Nina, Yes, I've got Power.[8]

Hughes would have had at least two experiences to prompt him to write Nina Simone a song centered on the idea of her declaring "Power." First, he had heard Nina's stunning eight-minute (and sometimes ten-minute) performances of "Sinnerman" at the Village Gate as early as April 1961. He had also watched Nina on the second night of the AMSAC Festival in Lagos when she played it through a scowl aimed at Lionel Hampton. In those stirring renditions, it is hard for anyone to ignore the force with which she calls out "Power" throughout several unforgettable passages in both the rising middle and the climactic end of the song. In fact, these repeated calls for "Power!" are the most representative sections of the entire song. The numerous examples of sampling this song combine to make Nina Simone's iconic version of "Sinnerman" her most representative contribution to contemporary music today.

It is also important to note that Howard A. Roberts's arrangement of "Sinnerman" debuted within Alvin Ailey's iconic dance *Revelation* on January 31, 1960. Less than six minutes in length, it more closely resembled straightforward calls for spiritual repentance as recorded by Les Baxter (1956), the Swan Silvertones (1957), Guy Carawan (1958), and the Weavers (1959). In one early iteration, the groundbreaking Ailey used this song to choreograph three shirtless dancers beginning on a blue stage framed by a red sky. Urgently pursued by a force that never arrives, one man remains alone onstage pirouetting in black pants as he seeks a shelter he never finds. Lyrics for "Sinnerman" are heard where the rock is "meltin'" and the sea is "boilin'." In the spiritual context of Ailey's work, traditional associations resonate. The rock echoes the one Moses struck at Mount Horeb in Exodus 17:6; the bleeding sea conjures the Red Sea; and the boiling waters activate images of the Leviathan described throughout Job 41. After two key changes take the music's energy and tempo to an even higher pitch, "Satan" appears at last as something inescapable. This turning point in the full dance production signals a revelatory return to God signaled by the show's remaining scenes, each set to redemptive spiritual and gospel songs.

Hughes attended Ailey dance performances on three occasions—February 10, 1961, January 21, 1962, and August 21, 1962.[9] It's fair to wonder whether hearing this version of the song stuck with him, serving as a reminder that Nina's version was more profound, determined, and assertive. If so, did his repetition of the capitalized word "Power," located at the end of so many of his lines, seek to pluck from the essence of Nina's own effective use and refacet it into a new song so that it could shine on its own as a demand rather than a prayer? With nearly every line ending with this word, the lines to Hughes's song continue:

> Milk and honey would be mine with Power—
> Here on earth, <u>I mean</u>, with Power.
> But I would share my milk and honey,
> (You could have some) with Power.
> <u>Everybody</u>, "Eat!" if I had Power.
> Stop that fighting, I would say, if I had Power.
> Turn the moon into a park for kids, if I had Power.[10]

Unlike "Sinnerman," Hughes's lyrics gave the singer tangible ways to use her power. As a Black man in America, how might Hughes have responded to President John F. Kennedy's repeated calls to set a man on the moon? Kennedy, in the searing heat before a nearly all-white audience at Rice University on September 12, 1962, said, "We choose to go to the moon in this decade and do the other things, not because they are easy, but because they are hard." As listeners wiped sweat from their brows, he continued. The moon could be a place to go "without repeating the mistakes that man has made in extending his writ across this globe of ours."[11]

Here, in his song, Hughes imagined Simone doing more than correcting the racial mistakes on earth. She was flipping who had control:

> Make a nice zoo up there, if I had Power,
> Zoo—Moon—if I had Power,
> And put in it—oh, well, you know who.[12]

Hughes's handwritten notes mark that at exactly this place in the song the "strain of 'Swanee River'" should be a musical reference.[13] Dating to 1851 and debuting on the big screen in the film *Mississippi* (1935), this minstrel song offensively posited that an enslaved man would long for his "old plantation." After roaming up and down "de whole creation," he wanted to return to that place that was "far, far away" because "oh, darkies, how my heart grows weary / far from the old folks at home." In reductively symbolic terms, "Swanee River" idealizes the search for a safe place. The embarrassing product of racist fantasies of white beneficence, "Swanee River" remained the official state song of Florida until 2007, long after Hughes had his fun with it in 1964. Wouldn't it be nice to hear a contrasting Black fantasy instead, one being sung by Nina Simone to match her intensity in "Pirate Jenny"?

In Hughes's song, white people were condemned to enjoy equivalent treatment to slavery at the hands of Black people. This would occur once the United States colonized the moon:

> If I had Power—a human zoo, if I had Power.
> No charge for admission, if I had Power.
> Open Sundays, too, if I had Power,
> To see the <u>monsters</u> we have got on earth,
> If I had Power.

Hughes's original title to this song was "My Zoo on the Moon." After first crossing out the first word "My" in lead pencil, he took another green pencil to the whole line and simply wrote "<u>Power</u>" as the new title above his typed letters. He had first written the lyrics by hand in pencil, then made a typed copy that he marked with revisions, before retyping the third and final copy.

Comedian and activist Dick Gregory had a joke in his set where he told audiences that Blacks were safer on the moon than in Alabama, and these lines have the kind of sarcasm that Gregory would have appreciated. White racists in 1966 brandished painted signs that read: "The Zoo Wants You" to intimidate Black residents who wished to move into segregated neighborhoods in Chicago. At this more precise time, the zoo was a means for cautiously addressing race in Dr. Seuss's latest book, *Put Me in the Zoo* (1964). Unlike the beloved leopard who actually could change his spots, the "monsters" noted earlier in Hughes's song are whites held captive:

> Oh, what a lovely zoo I'd make up there on the moon,
> If I had Power—and I'd put you in it, too,
> If I had Power.

In underlining both "monsters" and "you" in green pencil, Hughes shows us exactly the kind of a song he wrote for Nina. Like us, Simone would have made this startling realization: *A zoo for humans is called a jail.* If the Americans beat the Soviets in the space race and claimed the moon as their own, Hughes was re-animating a very different idea of "race" by imagining Nina as superintendent.

As he retyped his revision to the first marked draft, Hughes envisioned Nina as the song's sole performer. In his strained metaphor, she is now less of a songstress and more of a zookeeper:

> In my zoo on the moon, if I had Power.
> Don't worry, I'd be there, too
> In my zoo
> My zoo, my zoo, my zoo on the moon, if I had Power.
> We'd beat everybody there, you and me,
> And have a receiving line
> For that opening reception for that zoo on the moon.
> Good evening, Mister
> So-and-so, you!
> Come on in my zoo.
> On the moon, you,
> On the moon, me,
> On the moon, if I had Power,
> Power, baby,
> Power!
> What I wouldn't do, if I had Power!
> Me, Miss Nina, uh! with power![14]

But in this original song suggestion, instead of annihilating all her oppressors when the black freighter arrives in "Pirate Jenny," the protagonist in Hughes's alternative fantasy reaches one step less toward vengeance but a full leap further in revenge as caged white prisoners are allowed to live. They are allowed to live on the moon only under conditions where they are subject to a total lack of freedom and human dignity, as was being felt at the time by many Black Americans. In many ways, eschewing their executions has a more sinister appeal: It makes them suffer and endure a life of humiliation without the emotional escape afforded by death.

Just as he did when suggesting "You Cast a Spell on Me," Hughes was hoping Simone would reprise a role equal to the force he saw her embody as she performed "Pirate Jenny." And, once again, she took his concept ("Power") and arrived at another existing song that was already far better. Soon after Hughes wrote the song "Power," Nina Simone recorded her definitive studio version of "Sinnerman" calling for the kind of "Power!" she really wanted: one that could be enjoyed here on earth. And in contrast to the versions of "Sinnerman" recorded by white singers such as Les Baxter, Simone's version also captured how race criminalizes Black people's struggles for justice as it renders them immoral. Langston Hughes and Nina Simone were defining the way the civil rights movement would be reactivated by contemporary musicians.

11

From a Whisper to a Shout

Seeing its use in the modern television and cinema—notably in the Benedict Cumberbatch-starring *Sherlock Holmes* BBC show and in 1999's remake of *The Thomas Crown Affair*—"Sinnerman," perhaps Nina's most political song, offers a foundational question about her worldview and her artistic outlook: Could the choice made by a fully politically engaged Nina Simone to finally record this song in 1965 have its own historical characters that time has forgotten?[1] Is this due at least in part to song lyrics not receiving the depth of scholarly interpretation and analysis we readily assign other forms of literature? In other words, what historical considerations are we forced to grapple with when we ask: Who would have been assigned the role of "Sinnerman" in the Black community when the song was definitively recorded by Nina Simone in May 1965?

Given her politically literate audience, what civil rights figures of this era would have been assigned the roles of the Devil, the Lord, the Sinnerman, and the embodied voice who actualizes the unforgettable final demand, "I want Power!"? Nina Simone took a prayer that was whispered and turned it into a shout. She also gave an old song new meaning. She was doing this concurrently with other songs. In 1965, during the same summer she recorded "Sinnerman," Simone added a new verse at the end of "Go to Hell" (to make the song about the present day rather than the future) and even inserted a spoken introduction to live performances of "Tomorrow Is My Turn" to reframe the song as a claim of what she deserved as a Black woman in America.[2] We have already started to trace the deep roots of "Sinnerman" and a malleability that allows it to resonate both at tent revivals and as a vehicle for Nina Simone to publicly share vague aspects of her personal testimony. What other significant aspects of this song have been overlooked?

Today, rightly heard, with the attentiveness we bring only to the most profound forms of art, Nina Simone's studio recording of "Sinnerman" in 1965 ranks among the most accessible histories of the civil rights movement. It turns out that music contains as much history as any classroom textbook.

Tracking "Sinnerman" from its earliest known recording through multiple iterations reveals how Nina Simone offered up to the world the emotional power of Black music, music that became a political tool in her arsenal and connected her with civil rights leaders of the era. One such leader was Stokely Carmichael, the man immediately associated with the first invocations of the phrase "Black Power" in June 1966. Though it is through language that we can establish the connection between Carmichael and Simone, ultimately the precise words themselves are not as substantial as the emotion that produced them. Nina's calls for power registered complaint in a new tone, one fueled by an anger that could no longer be suppressed. They were an emotional demand made to the highest authority she could imagine. From Stokely Carmichael and SNCC, these same demands for agency were made in the new emotional register only Nina Simone had opened to clear a path forward. The emerging leader of the civil rights movement of 1966 issued his cries against the most powerful authority in America. In short, if power could be demanded of God, it should also be asserted toward white men. This emotional relationship among language, advocacy, and music reminds us how blurred the lines really are in the roles of poet, singer, and civil rights activist. We need not remove the pencil-drawn boxes that frame these three individual professional identities; rather, we can rub an eraser across staggered sections of their perpendicular lines to show how easily ideas move freely back and forth across these permeable categories.

"SINNERMAN" AND "BLACK POWER"

Nina Simone's 1965 recorded version of "Sinnerman" established a new emotional register that paved the way for Stokely Carmichael's unbridled calls for Black Power. In that song, Simone's full range of emotions about civil rights came to the surface in an unrestrained performance that injected the old song with new political meaning. Here's what we don't know: Did the leaders of SNCC create their calls for Black Power as a direct result of listening to Nina's repeated calls for "Power!" in her song "Sinnerman"?

Here's what we do know: The Simone-Hughes collaboration resulted in a fresh realization that such demands could be shouted without constraint. The conclusion of "Sinnerman" expresses an unapologetic desire to replace prayer with demands. It casts aside nonviolent submission in favor of an attitude of assertion. If the Black Arts Movement was an idea rather than an era, then its best idea resulted in an art that gave citizens a determined belief in the self. Unrestrained emotion and aggressive demands shifted the entire tone of the civil rights movement in the mid-1960s. If the question was, "Is it possible for the civil rights movement of 1965 to find an alternative way forward that does not harness the collective energy of either Christian religion or Muslim faith?" then "Sinnerman" offers the first definitive answer: "Yes!" Rather than wait for divinity to intervene, power could be demanded by anyone courageous enough to scream for it.

In asserting control rather than submitting pleas, "Sinnerman" and calls for "Black Power" ultimately became mutually reinforcing. To be clear, Philips Records released "Sinnerman" eight months before Carmichael called for Black Power in June 1966. Nina's recording preceded Stokely's protest. Simone's calls for power have experienced an unfortunate twist where the late now seems early and the early feels late. The real-life figures from 1965—the ones who had even more charisma and appeal than Thomas Crown, Sherlock Holmes, and James Moriarty—have real names and even more impressive biographies. Martin Luther King Jr., Malcolm X, Annie Lee Cooper, and Jimmie Lee Jackson held the undivided attention of Americans in 1965. Each was often on the wrong side of the law, with no place to run to and nowhere to hide. Following Sterling Brown's unpublished poetry collection *No Hiding Place* (1938) and contemporaneous with Martha and the Vandellas singing "Nowhere to Run" (1965), Nina Simone's epic ten-minute-and-fifteen-second version of "Sinnerman" rekindles our capacity to revisit a precise moment in the nation's history when the struggle for civil rights involved complex historical figures who not only served as martyrs but also fell short of achieving their aspirations. Eventually, patience is the virtue cast aside by the undeniable will for power. In this historical, musical, and literary reading of Nina's arrangement from 1965, the

"Sinnerman" most resembles an often-overlooked hero: the Black activist seeking a leader who will finally secure real political power for their people.

JIMMIE LEE JACKSON

It is little wonder Nina Simone was so uniquely revered by civil rights groups like SNCC. Civil rights activist Jimmie Lee Jackson came into the national consciousness in February 1965 when he joined a march led by C. T. Vivian in Marion, Alabama. James Orange was being held in a nearby jail, and the reaction to the peaceful protest calling for his release turned a night of collective hymns into a national atrocity. A collection of Alabama state troopers, sheriff deputies, and Marion policemen had assembled near the post office, located between the start of the peaceful march at Zion United Methodist Church, and its destination, the Perry County jail. After authorities either turned off—or perhaps simply shot out—streetlights, protesters were assaulted with billy clubs. After running into a location behind the church known as Mack's Café, Jackson was clubbed and beaten on the kitchen floor. The twenty-six-year-old Jackson was then shot twice after being thrown against a cigarette machine. Jackson somehow staggered away from the café before collapsing near the bus station. Hospitalized, he lived an additional eight days. Fifteen years later, presiding physician Dr. William Dinkins believed that Jackson died only because of an overdose of anesthesia when a white attending surgeon conducted a second surgery.[3]

Martin Luther King Jr. delivered Jackson's eulogy on March 5, 1965. Jackson was first inspired to serve after King—the leader of the Southern Christian Leadership Conference—came to Selma, Alabama, to energize local voter registration campaigns. However, in circumstances such as these, competing civil rights groups sometimes balked, believing that King serendipitously arrived just in time for the cameras and press coverage. Few Black theologians held a PhD at the time, and King was silently referred to at the grassroots level in a somewhat derogatory way as "De Lawd."[4] In other words, he came in to impose his presence on the work they had already been doing by themselves. King's arrival—both haughty and essential as it was—resonated with them as both overshadowing their own efforts and being undeniably important. They were mere disciples; he was the savior.

Following the trajectory of blues music, the white man has long been associated with occupying the figurative role of a devil. Thinking literally, one of Malcolm X's most repeated statements may be representative of how some Black Americans looked at the world in 1965. Here's just one famous exchange he had, with reporter Louis Lomax in November 1963:

> MALCOLM X: Why would any black man want to marry a *devil* . . . for that's just what the white man is.
>
> LOMAX: I have heard you say that a thousand times, but it always jolts me. Why do you call the white man a devil?
>
> MALCOLM X: Because that's what he is. What do you want me to call him, a saint? Anybody who rapes, and plunders, and enslaves, and steals, and drops hell bombs on people . . . anybody who does these things is nothing but a devil.[5]

The Nation of Islam minister not only declared this stance on numerous occasions (repeated a "thousand times") but established it early on in his conversion to Islam as one of his core foundational beliefs.[6]

Jimmie Lee Jackson had no place to hide after he went to "De Lawd" and confronted the white devils; thus, he animates the indirect political implications Simone activates in "Sinnerman." Like James Moriarty and Thomas Crown, he, too, is being pursued by policemen even while being cheered by everyday people. He had run at "De Lawd's" calling, and yet his life was not spared. By the time the song was released in 1966, activists might also think of James Meredith and his March Against Fear. The same James Meredith that Simone responded to by conceiving of "Mississippi Goddam" in 1962 was shot and then hospitalized in June 1966 for walking across Mississippi to draw attention to his freedom to go anywhere he wished.

Put simply, the cultural reputation of Martin Luther King Jr., belief of Malcolm X, and impact of Jimmie Lee Jackson's murder could not have been more timely or appropriate for Simone's song. Malcolm X had been assassinated less than two months earlier, on Simone's own birthday, and she had seen the other, Martin Luther King Jr., in person herself less than six weeks before. In the wake of the three ensuing marches to Selma, all sparked by Jimmie Lee Jackson's death earlier in February, both white pastor James Reeb and Viola Liuzzo had also been murdered in March. In late April, Hughes was still using his newspaper columns to highlight the shocking TV footage from Selma showing Annie Lee Cooper knocking Sheriff Jim Clark to the ground.[7] Having arrived with Langston to perform "Mississippi Goddam" in Montgomery on March 24, 1965, Simone knew of these deaths and aggressions on an intimate level. In Simone's mind, these types of murder and harassment suggested that a potent poison still endured at America's core fear of integration's menace. There was nowhere to hide from police officers and the white supremacists they either enabled or tolerated from their positions of power. In such a world, Nina Simone wanted power here on earth, not in a zoo on Langston's imagined moon.

THE ORIGINS OF "BLACK POWER"

Tracing the full evolution of the phrase "Black Power" reveals just how timely Nina Simone's calls for power were in her song "Sinnerman." While the phrase "Black Power" had been used incidentally in 1954 as the title of Richard Wright's book on African politics and was later invoked by performer and activist Paul Robeson, Adam Clayton Powell Jr. almost accidently used the phrase as he spelled out his actual conceptualization of "audacious power." Speaking during a commencement address to the graduates of Howard University on May 29, 1966, the longtime Harlem congressman declared five rights everyone deserved:

> Our life must be purposed to implement human rights: The right to be secure in one's person from the excessive abuses of the state and its law enforcement officials. The right to freedom of choice of a job to feed one's family. The right to freedom of mobility of residence. The right to the finest education social order can provide. And most importantly the right to share fully the governing councils of the State as equal members of the body politic. To demand these God-given rights is to seek Black power, what I call audacious power, the power to build Black institutions of splendid achievement.[8]

Although the concepts it stood for have long and deep roots, none of these invocations of the phrase "Black Power" took hold in the consciousness of America. Instead, it took the Student Nonviolent Coordinating Committee to bring the phrase into the place of prominence it still holds today.

Formed in April 1960 at Shaw University in Raleigh, North Carolina, Ella Baker's project would soon relocate to Atlanta and produce some of the nation's greatest leaders. Julian Bond, Marion Barry, and John Lewis represent just a few of its luminaries. Unlike Wright, Robeson, and Powell, SNCC had taken a very methodical path to making power a cornerstone of its core beliefs. In 1963, Jack Minnis first published an eight-page booklet for SNCC titled *The Care and Feeding of Power Structures*. Remarkably focused, the tract aimed to educate politically engaged college students to recognize the true nature of economic forces that needed to be dismantled. Polemic in the extreme, it concluded, "Informing the people about the nature of power in the community strikes a very real blow at the power structure; mobilizing the people to united action toward specific objectives will unstructure the power structure."[9] Directives against this power structure continued to inform SNCC policy as late as April 2, 1966, when John Hulett informed listeners who were about to form their own political party in Lowndes County, Alabama, "We have to form our own power structure. If we stay within the Democratic Party, the same people, will still be in control."[10] Eight weeks before Black Power was about to emerge as its new slogan, SNCC saw voting and political representation at both the local and national levels as focal points for deconstructing such foundations. So how *exactly* did SNCC arrive at the slogan "Black Power"? Because SNCC's documents are so accessible, we can pinpoint the emergence of this slogan with remarkable accuracy. After all these years have passed, we turn to these documents in search of a concept that may have arisen unconsciously.

Throughout the years leading up to 1966, SNCC continued to keep the ideological issue of power as one of its essential planks while also highlighting more visible goals. Its carefully vetted concepts were often chosen as a result of SNCC leader James Forman's creative savvy for seeking and then promoting recognizable slogans based on his own poetic interests. SNCC slogans such as "Freedom Now!" and "One Man One Vote" fulfilled his criteria for an idea whose compressed agenda would resonate profoundly with listeners whose lives the organization earnestly worked to improve. SNCC even titled its Freedom Summer 1964 film about poverty, voting rights, and domestic terrorism after Langston Hughes's poem, calling it *A Dream Deferred*. The organization sought slogans with the most resonant cultural capital when it came to advertising their political campaigns. In contemporary terms, branding defined SNCC more than any of its peer organizations, such as the Southern Christian Leadership Conference (SCLC), the NAACP, CORE, and the Urban League.

When staff assembled for a two-day conference in Atlanta on November 24, 1965, field secretary Courtland Cox began speaking about the "Alabama Plan." After Cox's assignment in "Bloody" Lowndes County, SNCC leader James Forman recalled Cox saying, "The people want power, power to control the courthouse, power to control their lives." Walking to the blackboard, Cox then wrote three words: "Power. Education. Organization." Cox was determined that his fellow SNCC members finally realize their ultimate goal, "enabling the people to establish 'basic organizations in order to achieve power.'" Moving forward from this precise moment, a new and ultimately unwavering agenda for SNCC was now set in motion. Foreman asserted, "From that time on, SNCC began to talk more and more about power for Black people."[11]

To keep the timeline straight, when Langston Hughes wrote and delivered his song for Nina Simone entitled "Power," this SNCC meeting had not yet taken place. "Sinnerman" was released in October 1965. With these calendars documented so clearly, Nina first externalized the soulful depths of an idea that had yet to be declared by the voices of SNCC. As simple as it may seem, we may never know the full implication of the answer to this question: Was anyone in SNCC listening to Nina's demands for "power" in "Sinnerman"?

Although Stokely Carmichael seems to have left no formal written record behind of his deep affection for Nina, we know that Simone herself considered the chairman of SNCC to be on her same wavelength politically. Fortunately, Martin Luther King Jr.'s close confidant the future ambassador Andrew Young and Carmichael lived in the same dormitory at Howard University. Young remembered his roommate's early and sincere love for Nina Simone's music, dating back to before she started cocreating the soundtrack of the civil rights movement with Hughes. After Young went to the record store and bought an album for the first time—a copy of *Nina Simone at Town Hall*—"Carmichael played the Simone album repeatedly throughout their freshman year" of 1960–61. Years later, when Young traveled on official business to meet with advisers, donors, or potential converts to the civil rights cause, he noted the records he saw: "Every home I went to had Nina Simone—I mean, every one."[12]

Young went even further in underlining just how essential Simone's music was not only to SNCC but even to conservative groups such as his own Southern Christian Leadership Conference: "There were two things that people in the movement would fight over. One was if you took their books. The other was if you took their Nina Simone albums."[13] Echoing Stokely Carmichael's praise of Nina, Young concluded, "She was so present—she was everywhere in our projects, in all our work. . . . Nothing was so cogent of the frailty, and the humiliation and the sadness and the joy of what we did than her music. . . . Her music always seemed to be on top of our situation."[14] In between his firsthand reflection, the words "anger" and "frustration" might also be written with invisible ink. If the question is, who inside the civil rights movement was listening to Nina Simone in 1965, the definitive and unequivocal answer was *everyone!*

Members of SNCC openly declared their love of Nina's music. When they gathered, "The music of Otis Redding, Sam Cooke, B. B. King, Nina Simone, the Temptations and the Four Tops, Martha and the Vandellas—all were included in a kind of soundtrack that got SNCC folk through the rough times. Singing and dancing together helped balance out the tension and dangers they faced much of the time. It also helped strengthen the bonds that united them."[15] It is important to remember that among all the musicians listed above, Nina Simone had developed a unique relationship with SNCC by 1966. After declining to sing for them (and thereby trying to avoid seeming overtly political in 1963), Simone soon started receiving more money than any other musician who appeared on their benefit programs once she performed at a SNCC benefit event in April 1964. After this, Simone received an "effusive thank you note" and return invitations to perform that she accepted, and she soon felt "the most at home with SNCC."[16] The struggle for inclusion is rarely waged alone. As part of those excluded from America's central premise of equality, Nina and SNCC collectively sought to secure invitations.

Moreover, SNCC's creative process with similar critical strategies for branding is illuminating. According to SNCC field agent Willie Ricks, he was with a group of people in Lowndes County, Alabama, when an unexpected moment of levity suddenly inspired one of the most recognizable and enduring symbols of the civil rights movement: "Miss Moore was one of the people, after we had to come up with a name . . . we needed a symbol. She was a big, big, Black, beautiful Black woman. And, somebody joked, let's name it 'Black Panther.' Miss Moore looks like a big black panther."[17] Eventually SNCC's Jennifer Lawson went back to SNCC headquarters in Atlanta and created the original Black Panther logo in 1966, apparently based on the mascot for Atlanta University.

If Ricks's account is accurate, that the origins of one of the most iconic political symbols in US history was the result of playful banter, the possibilities for a similar group of staff gathered together while spinning Simone's latest cries for "power" throughout "Sinnerman" would fit the bill for the way key creative ideas were generated throughout SNCC. Not concerned with its rhetorical origins, people within SNCC instead wanted real power to define a new mode of being in their everyday existence.

In a substantive article published early in June 1966, only weeks before he would first emphatically incite a crowd in Greenwood, Mississippi, with chants of "Black Power," Carmichael's thesis had not yet asserted or defined Black Power—it focused squarely on merely power, not "Black Power." In the SNCC newsletter *The Movement*, a summary quote was pulled directly from Carmichael's article and placed in bold: "Integration is completely irrelevant to us: what we want is power for people who don't have it."[18] Creating an unmistakable distinction between SNCC's aims and Dr. King's goals of integration, Carmichael continued through the piece without once combining the words "black" and "power." Mentioning power itself in more half a dozen instances, his statement in fact distanced his ideology from any definitive distinctions about race: "We want power, that's all we want. After we get power, we can talk about whether we want all Black of [*sic*] not."[19] In other words, in this document, the very same demand for power was indeed being asserted by both Stokely Carmichael and Nina Simone.

We have to travel to Tennessee to locate the origins of SNCC's invocation of the phrase "Black Power." Though the phrase was officially embargoed for the next five weeks, the logic of "power for the people" unintentionally became the shortened slogan of "Black Power" during the days when the organization met at Kingston Springs, Tennessee, beginning on May 8, 1966. SNCC emerged from the three-day retreat at this posh resort location with Stokely Carmichael replacing veteran John Lewis as chair. About ten days later, SNCC's new executive secretary, Ruby Doris Robinson, was asked why desegregation was no longer the organization's priority. She responded, "We've been head-lifted and upstarted into white societies all our lives, and we're tired of that. What we need is Black power."[20] No cameras recorded her reply, and her comment predates Adam Clayton Powell's commencement address by a week.

Two weeks after Robinson's comments, Willie Ricks asked James Forman for permission to try out the phrase "Black Power" on an audience, and Forman encouraged it. So, during the March Against Fear, a continuation of a march started by the now hospitalized James Meredith, SNCC's brand-new chairman found himself facing a throng of tired marchers in Greenwood, Mississippi. On June 16, 1966, wearing the trademark bib overalls of the Mississippi fieldworkers he served, Stokely Carmichael stood on top of a flatbed truck in the middle of a field addressing a group of over six hundred people. Though Ricks asserted crowds responded fervently when he called for "Black Power," Carmichael was not fully convinced. With Ricks urging, "Hit them now. Hit them now," a surprised Carmichael lit an audience who had been primed. After asserting that his arrest earlier in the day was his twenty-seventh, he ended his speech, "All we've been doing is begging the federal government. The only thing we can do is take over." Holding up a clinched fist, he yelled for every camera to record: "What do we want?" The crowd responded with *Black Power!* He yelled the question five times. Each time, the response: *Black Power!* Carmichael later recalled, "I myself, to be honest, I didn't expect that enthusiastic response, you know. And the enthusiastic response, obviously, not only shocked me but gave me more energy to carry it on further."[21] Stokely Carmichael's calls for Black Power immediately captivated all of America. From this moment on, many would refer to him as "Starmichael."

NINA AND STOKELY

When CORE and SNCC cosponsored a Black Power rally on July 17, 1966, in Philadelphia, only four weeks after Carmichael gave audiences the new term "Black Power," the indoor auditorium at the Church of the Advocate overflowed to the point where some people simply could not get into the venue.[22] One of the star attractions was Nina Simone. However, Nina was there to speak, not sing. Nina's presence as an advocate for Black Power overshadowed that of Carmichael.[23] The front-page news coverage opened with these words: "Tears streaked the checks of singer-pianist Nina Simone." It continued, "Miss Simone was so moved before the overflow crowd of at least 1,000 . . . she was lost for words but finally said: 'I have been thinking of some of these things since

I was three years old.' A hush fell over the audience (and those who dared to speak while she hesitated were quickly warned to shut up) as Miss Simone, saying [*sic*] nothing, tears staining her cheeks."[24]

What brought Nina to tears? Was she perhaps realizing that by so forcefully enunciating her emotional desire for power in her prophetic anthem "Sinnerman" she had now summoned it into being? Or, equally profound, was she internalizing the overwhelming feeling that a song she had learned as a "little bitty girl" had now become the central tenet in the civil rights movement? Sometimes enunciating an idea this intently summons it into the world. Is this why Nina Simone was invited to speak at this precise time by Stokely Carmichael?

Like SNCC, Nina Simone cared most for the achievement of the goal. She was not interested in asserting "authorship" for an idea she herself had inherited from tent revivals she attended in the 1930s. Once again, church music had been reanimated to become a protest song. Moved to tears, Nina was standing in a church where religion and protest merged in the selves who had the spirit to achieve power for their people.

Once the rally was over, Nina and Stokely were photographed together. The image complemented another, larger image depicting the standing-room-only audience in the chapel. Although the two are staring into each other's eyes like a young couple about to leave the dance together early, the caption contextualized their glances as an example of respect rather than allure: "Mutual admiration is exhibited by Stokely Carmichael and Miss Nina Simone as they exchange remarks at the 'Black Power' Rally held at the Church of the Advocate."[25]

Only a month had passed since Stokely had become instantly famous for declaring "Black Power." Now he was sitting next to the very woman whose music he had been listening to religiously since he was a freshman in college, and one might be inclined to imagine that he could not wait to thank her privately in person. Yet there is no evidence of such an exchange. Neither Stokely Carmichael nor Nina Simone ever spoke publicly about the relationship between "Sinnerman" and "Black Power." Each concurrently enunciated a power they instead longed to live—and, in living, finally stop having to assert.

The nation's conscious connection between Simone and Stokely only grew as 1966 came to a close. Reviewing Nina's concert appearance on December 16, 1966, at the Uptown Theater in Philadelphia, Ray McCann definitively captured just how linked these two icons were heading into Christmas. The article, titled "Hail Singer Nina Simone as 'Black Power' Princess," opens with a remarkably intuitive connection: "Stokely Carmichael is single. Too bad Nina Simone is married. If they could marry, they would undoubtedly become the Prince and Princess of Black Power." The piece went on to link Nina to the movement in ways that were simply unmistakable and forever binding: “Miss Simone is obviously the darling of the Black Power set.”[26] On this occasion, the correct assertion had less to do with Nina’s songs than with the context in which she was once again appearing. This was a benefit concert for the Philadelphia chapter of CORE, and local representative William Mathis even spoke from the stage about economic control in his city during an intermission.[27] After “Sinnerman” and Carmichael’s subsequent calls for Black Power, Nina, Stokely, and the civil rights movement were simply inseparable by the end of 1966. From now on, Nina’s performances of her reimagined version of “Sinnerman” would reinforce a call for power spoken by Stokely Carmichael, tested by Willie Ricks, and conceptualized for Simone by none other than Langston Hughes. A civil rights leader, singer, and poet were each sharing ideas freely across the boxes we build to arbitrarily divide them.

12

The White Backlash

White backlash was a direct response to Stokely Carmichael's calls for Black Power in June 1966. The idea of Black Power, and what it really meant, immediately captured everyone's imagination. Suddenly joined in a spotlight he was unaccustomed to sharing, Martin Luther King Jr. was consistently forced to address both topics. He told listeners, "The so-called white backlash is caused by the slogan 'Black Power.'"[1] These two interrelated phenomena shaped America's consciousness throughout the fall of 1966. Black Power was on the minds of those who attended the Church of the First Unitarian Society in Schenectady, New York, where on October 23, John J. Waggy Jr. delivered a sermon entitled "Black Power and the Disrobing of White Liberality." As a white preacher, Waggy reminded his listeners what really scared them most about the term "Black Power": "In our own building of the systems of life we, the white community, have always kept open the alternative of violence." He asserted that the community's reaction was against, not violence itself, but the "dread of black men who might issue the kind of violence that has been historically reserved in this country for white men."[2] The topic of Black Power dominated the nation's racial discourse for four consecutive months.

References to white backlash reached their height that autumn. On October 2, Rev. Donald Szantho Harrington spoke to his congregation at the Community Church of New York, likening Black Power to the gathering forces of "a hurricane of hate" that "carries a McCarthy mood." He asked, "Why should the call for black power have evoked the furies of the white backlash?" Outlining the key issues of the moment, Harrington surmised that the crisis in the Black community centered on issues of employment, education, and housing.[3] Newspaper columnists soon conducted summative autopsies on the November elections: "Stokely Carmichael and the New Left helped elect a number of 'white backlash' governors, Congressmen, and Sheriffs." Setting back integrated neighborhoods, white backlash also led to "the defeat of the Open Housing proposals in Congress."[4]

How did Langston Hughes finally write the lyrics of what would become his most important song? To be clear, Hughes had enjoyed various levels of success with his previous lyrics. The song "African Dance" appeared in the film *Stormy Weather* (1943); both "Louisiana" and "Good Ground" rang from the silver screen in *Way Down South* (1939); "Freedom Road" was included on two radio programs during World War II; and "Going Mad with a Dime" had been heard across the country in 1951 when it featured in Duke Ellington's West Coast tour.[5]

In addition to having his lyrics recorded by Marian Anderson, Paul Robeson, Abbey Lincoln, Josh White, and Roland Hayes, the song "Moon-Faced, Starry-Eyed" featured Hughes's lyrics set to the music of Kurt Weill. Their collaboration resulted in the most commercially viable song of Hughes's career. After it debuted in the opera *Street Scene* in 1946, it was regarded as the most important song of the Broadway season. The song was recorded as an instrumental in 1946 by the Teddy Wilson Quartet and sung by Johnny Mercer when he was backed by Benny Goodman and His Orchestra, landing on the charts on May 3, 1947, as the fourteenth most-played jukebox record of the year. It would eventually become a standard of Max Roach and Betty Carter, but only after both Freddy Martin and Bing Crosby sang the tune on live radio programs. In each of these instances, excessively prudish standards forced one change in Hughes's lyrics. A true sign of the era, "You're apple pie with cheese on the side" was feared to be too sexually suggestive. Hence, with substance abuse understudied and unnamed, mixing alcohol was deemed a far lesser evil: "You're whiskey straight with beer on the side."[6]

Most of these songs by Hughes appeared in the 1940s. Hughes's close friend lawyer Loren Miller marveled at how Hughes achieved such musical success. He once asked Hughes, "How can a guy who can't carry a tune in a bucket be a member of ASCAP with more than 40 published songs to his credit?"

"All right. I know I can't carry a tune," Langston replied, "and never could. But I like music, and I really hooked up with some good musicians. . . . And I have been listening to and setting down the words of blues and other folk songs as long as I can remember."[7]

Rather than presenting double entendres about love, Hughes took the events of 1966 as a point of departure to begin what is now recognized as the definitive song of his career. In the end, both the poet Hughes and musician Simone coauthored the lyrics to "Backlash Blues." Hughes was always inspired by current events and popular culture, and the first step in his process for writing lyrics to this song involved watching journalist Mike Wallace's latest hour-long TV special, "Black Power: White Backlash," which aired on September 27, 1966.

"BLACK POWER: WHITE BACKLASH"

Opening with images of a wide-eyed Stokely Carmichael leading a crowd in chants of "Black Power," the program featured Wallace interviewing more than a dozen personalities.[8] Wallace was seeking to understand the new spirit afoot in the United States. One of the first to weigh in was Atlanta's moderate white mayor Ivan Allen: "I have never seen as strong a reaction amongst the white citizen as there is at the present time." Wallace then interviewed Carmichael, whose answers raised the intensity: "We have to move to a position where we can control the housing in our neighborhoods so that we are not exploited. So that we are not charged high rents to share apartments with rats." Wallace then queried Carmichael on Vietnam: "Do you really believe that the military polices of the United Sates are designed to exterminate the Black man?" "I most certainly do," Carmichael responded. "I look at the recent statement by racist [Robert] McNamara who says that thirty percent of the people who are going to be drafted now under his new system are going to be Black people, and that is nothing more than urban removal." With Blacks comprising only about 11 percent of America's population, these numbers were too high for any listener to ignore.

Wallace then sat down with a man Hughes knew well. In fact, they had traveled together to Nigeria in 1960. Now defensive and uncomfortable, Martin Luther King Jr. was trying to summarize the root problems beneath the summer's recent wave of violence. "A riot is the language of the unheard," he told Wallace. "What is it that America has failed to hear? It has failed to hear that the economic plight of the Negro poor has worsened over the last few years."

Filmed in his office chair, *Liberator* magazine editor Dan Watts challenged King's authority in the wake of Carmichael's current popularity: "Roy Wilkins, your Martin Luther Kings, your Whitney Youngs, they do not represent the aspirations of the brother who is standing out on 121st street and Lenox Avenue now who doesn't even have two coins to rub together." Watts corrected Wallace's terms. The "radicals" Wallace spoke of—ones who were willing to die—were better labeled "freedom fighters." Watts then explained why death itself needed to be parsed into different types: "We are dying today. The Black boy, the Black man who is shot in the back by a white policeman while he is handcuffed on the way into the station for allegedly trying to escape, that is dying. The child who is dying of malnutrition because of the oppressive economic system where the parents can't find work, that's death. What I am suggesting is if we must die, let it be a meaningful death."

The responses from whites had to be painful for Hughes to hear. Representing several white neighborhood community organizations in or near Cicero, Illinois, Walter Douglas explained his constituents' positions on any Black marchers who might dare return to demand open housing.

"Next year, there will be riots," Douglas said. "There will be bloodshed.... Our gun shops in the Southern suburbs sold out of ammunition and guns. These people are armed. One man was bragging to me that he has twenty-five pounds of dynamite in his garage. They are armed. They are ready now.... Next summer it will not be rock and bricks and bottles but actual armed rebellion against these civil right marchers coming into the area. And people are going to be hurt."

Wallace asked Daniel P. Moynihan to weigh in from his perspective as director of the Joint Center for Urban Studies at Harvard and MIT. Wallace was particularly interested in the issue of the ballot box: "How serious do you imagine the white backlash will be this November in votes?"

Wearing a brown sports jacket, the professor answered into a microphone attached to a cord hanging just outside his tie and shirt collar. "The backlash," Moynihan said, "if that's the word, has already been felt. We lost the civil rights act. We did not get the president's bill. The most powerful Democratic liberal voting majority in the history of this century did not do what it ought to have done."

The black-haired Wallace ended his reporting by moving into a series of polls. These were aimed at comparing just how much had changed in US race relations. He asked, "What about the backlash in the November elections?" Louis Harris, *Newsweek* magazine's public opinion analyst, provided this definitive response: "It could be decisive in this election. It could be decisive because it could tear the Democratic Party apart at the seams in the North.... It could have an effect in twenty of the forty-five freshman Congress seats. The white backlash issue could be the decisive issue November eighth."

FROM POEM TO SONG

After twenty-six years of trying to rekindle the lyrical success he had in working with Kurt Weill, Langston Hughes began to write the most defining song of his life soon after watching this TV special, which touched on housing, schools, economics, and Vietnam. Hughes now intended to include these political issues throughout his verses. To bridge the genre of poem and song, he had to learn a long and painful lesson. For the first time in his professional life, Hughes understood that the prior musical success he'd had occurred most often when people such as Marian Anderson and Margaret Bonds turned his existing poems into songs. Personifying the new phenomenon of white backlash as a person, Hughes first started "The Backlash Blues" as if he were composing song lyrics. He used the upper left-hand corner of each page to note in green ink that each of his first two attempts was "too long."[9] This phrase suggests that they were too long to sing, not to publish within a book.

As he typed, Hughes kept following a traditional blues structure of repeating each idea twice in his six-line verses. Hughes's drafts further confirm this was intended to be a true song when one of his verses clearly invokes the filler "yeah" he is imagining a singer will deliver "Every dog will have his day . . . Yeah! . . . Yeah!"

Hughes's song is addressed to "Mister Backlash." The title alludes to James Baldwin's play *Blues for Mister Charlie*. Though he was not impressed with Baldwin's play, Hughes clearly took away at least one idea. Hughes's first draft of the song clarifies that he has a specific type of white man in mind when he writes "Listen, Mister Congressman." We must ask ourselves, why did Hughes spell out the entire word "Mister" when the contraction "Mr." was both easier and currently acceptable? The fall of 1966 was a critical election season when white politicians across the country knew the key issue was how to counter Black Power. Headlines everywhere proclaimed, "White Backlash Threatens Black Hopefuls at the Polls." The opening sentences of one such article are representative: "WHITE BACKLASH helped Lester Maddox, an unsuccessful chicken shack owner, to become Democratic candidate for governor in Georgia. White backlash appears to be putting Ronald Reagan, a man of many, varying political moods, out front against liberal Democrat Pat Brown."[10] Reagan rode that white backlash into the governor's mansion of California in November 1966 on his way to defining the 1980s as two-term president of the United States of America.

When Hughes addressed "Mister Backlash," he was pointing his finger directly at such politicians in a way that silently signaled a much-deserved critique on the legacy of power in America.

Following James Baldwin's lead, Hughes spells out "Mister" to give life to its roots in the word "Master." When the word "Mister" emerged in the English language in the mid-1700s, it served as a substitute for "Master." In the United States, the term "Master" includes the horrific legacy of being the word demanded by white owners and overseers as a means of address from the lips of enslaved Black people. In fully exploiting this linkage, Hughes goes much further than Baldwin as he does more than connect the terms to show the surprising continuity over time between the past and the active levers of power and control in America. Unlike Baldwin's "Mister Charlie," Hughes's "Mister" is one engaged in enacting a backlash. Hughes's personified congressman resembles a master who lashes the backs of his subjects. In this way, Hughes is quietly animating the forgotten history of the most common and derogatory name for a white man. The word "cracker" does not denote a white man who is square and bland as a saltine. No. The term "cracker" has its roots in the practice of Floridian ranchers who took the whips they applied to the cattle and then turned them on the slaves they owned. A "cracker" is a white man who whips the backs of slaves who work his land. In this way, these workers were treated like animals.

In the collective language of the blues, this "master" is known as a *mistreater*. When Hughes spells out the full word "Mister" as a form of coded address for this congressman, he lays bare the infuriating reality that a lawmaker can act in the full spirit and negligence of a slave-era cracker. In this way, the expected honorific "Mr." gestures in two ways. "Mr." is the word that appears to be said and heard (as if it were an earned term of endearment); however, it is also unbound from its contraction as "Mister" to subversively undermine the man it addresses who is still acting as if he were a "master." This is a hard-earned literacy that exposes the long history of a title for what it really is. The very act of spelling accomplishes the dual purpose of simultaneous submission and rebellion continually being refined by those who oppose their oppressors.

As Hughes's drafts reveal, rather than continuing to compose lyrics for a song, he slowly shifted his address to this modern-day cracker by writing an actual poem. The "Yeah! Yeah!" was dropped, and he eventually moved the text to a tight conclusion mimicking the lines of closure provided by so many of his other poems. Addressed straight to Mister Backlash, the final lines were underlined for emphasis: "<u>You're the one'll</u> / <u>Have the Blues</u>." Hughes next did two things to "The Backlash Blues." First, he included a version of it in his forthcoming edition of poems entitled *The Panther and the Lash*. Hughes had pitched a book of poems addressing the civil rights movement to his editor, Blanche Knopf, in 1964, only to have her balk in the wake of both Hughes's insistence on printing a cheap edition and his underperforming (and very expensive) previous project, *Ask Your Mama* (1961). Now she said yes, giving the go-ahead to a new collection of poems.

Released posthumously, in June 1967 (after Hughes made all final editorial choices himself), *The Panther and the Lash* had a telling title. Although the Black Panther Party had formed in California in 1966, to date it had only thirty-one members. With Hughes's book including works that addressed Stokely Carmichael (not Huey P. Newton or Bobby Seale), the poet was likely thinking of the symbol of the Mississippi Freedom Democratic Party, which had inspired the Black Panthers to adopt a similar image. The "Lash" in the title not only connotes a whip to control this panther but more directly offers a riff on the form this control had taken as white back*lash*. It is clear how central the poem "The Backlash Blues" was to Langston Hughes's final collection of poetry. Second, and more important, Hughes was aware that Nina Simone was preparing a new album composed exclusively of blues songs. He brought the poem to her to see if she was interested in recording it as a song.

Though no biographical evidence remains of the exchange between the poet and the priestess, the textual changes to "The Backlash Blues" clearly show that significant revisions were made by none other than Nina herself. At the time he brought it to her, Hughes's poem, which he had also now prepared for publication in *The Panther and the Lash*, still included repeating verses (of six lines) where the idea of lines one and two is repeated in lines three and four. Moreover, it still had a fully unsatisfactory ending that read: "*Yes, you're the one / Will have the blues.*" (This is the version that appeared in *The Panther and the Lash.*) Given Simone's standard approach to recording, it would have been completely without precedent for her to take any lyrics and leave them unaltered.

In moving from a work written by Langston Hughes to a song that was essentially coauthored by Nina Simone, the poem lost its opening "The" to become "Backlash Blues." The song that immediately followed this collaborative version of "Backlash Blues" on *Nina Sings the Blues* (1967) perfectly epitomizes Nina's typical approach. Here, Simone took only the best images from Bessie Smith's 1931 song "I Need a Little Sugar in My Bowl" and updated it to sharpen her own shorter version of "I Want a Little Sugar in My Bowl." In amending Hughes's poem into a song, Nina took into consideration at least two things: "How do the words pair with the rhythms I need to sing?" and "Can this be tightened to a length where it might be a single that charts from this album?" By the time Simone had addressed these two questions, the song had three key alterations. First, Nina dropped the repetitions so that each verse was paired from six to four lines. Second, a short refrain was added to mimic something of a chorus: "Mister Backlash / I'm gonna leave you with the blues." Third, and

THE BACKLASH BLUES
by
Langston Hughes

Mister Backlash, Mister Backlash,
Just who do you think I am?
You raise my taxes, freeze my wages,
Send my son to Vietnam.

You give me second class houses,
Second class schools.
Do you think that colored folks
Are just second class fools?

When I try to find a job
To earn a little cash,
All you got to offer
Is a white backlash.

But the world is big,
Big and bright and round——
And it's full of folks like me who are
Black, Yellow, Beige, and Brown.

Mister Backlash, Mister Backlash,
What do you think I got to lose?
I'm gonna leave you, Mister Backlash,
Singing your mean old backlash blues.

You're the one
Will have the blues.
Not me——
Wait and see!

Fig. 12.1. Final draft of "The Backlash Blues," 1967. (James Weldon Johnson Memorial Collection in the Yale Collection of American Literature, Beinecke Rare Book and Manuscript Library, Yale University.)

finally, a line was added to an ending that still didn't quite feel finalized: "*Wait and see!*" Nina likely imagined that this song had a chance to chart in Billboard's recently created category of rhythm and blues. Equally important, because she made such alterations to lyrics all the time, at this first stage of the song's long development, she would never have considered herself coauthor of its lyrics—only the creator of its music.

To this point, *Jet* promoted their collaboration by noting it as a protest song. In a section entitled "People Are Talking About," the magazine wrote with glee about Miss Nina Simone:

> This sometimes abrasive songbird is bound to start tongue wagging over another of her latest hits. Entitled *Backlash Blues,* the tune written by Miss Simone and poet Langston Hughes on the RCA label, joins other searing social protest numbers, *Four Women* and *Mississippi Goddam!,* delineated by the great singer and is bound to sweep the country in controversy although at present, deejays are shying away from it like the plague.[11]

Hardly alone, Sid McCoy, a disc jockey out of Chicago before he became the TV announcer for *Soul Train,* wrote liner notes on the album that followed this same approach in summarizing the song: "It's a scathing, heated political comment on the socio-political times."[12]

"I'M GONNA LEAVE YOU WITH THE BLUES"

"Backlash Blues" confronts us with an intellectual dilemma far more intricate than it immediately appears. This is not surprising, considering its lyrics were written by a poet. What does it mean to leave Mister Backlash with the Blues? Or, restated with its allusive connotations included, What does it mean to leave *Master* Backlash with the Blues? The song offers four responses to this question. Put simply, each of these responses calls us to first understand the way the song is animating the importance of colors. In fact, the easiest way to understand "Backlash Blues" is to realize that it is simply a song centered around Langston's "Hues."

The poem spells out its logic for us in black and white. As the personification for all white power in America, Mister Backlash may get the blues whenever a Black candidate wins political election at any level. The final version of the poem was completed in October 1966, with national elections in November only days away. How could a politician who raised taxes, cut wages, stunted job opportunities, and provided nothing but second-rate infrastructure for living and learning expect to win every seat when all the ballots were counted? Hughes's poem imagines an actual reckoning at the polls in November where at least a few of these types of congressmen will be voted out of office.

Because the song asserts that Mister Backlash will ultimately be the one singing the "mean old backlash blues," this declaration of musical connectivity highlights the irrepressible success of Black music as represented by the color "blue." Blues music had already made its way into the ears (and out of the mouths) of whites around the world. Blues, jazz, and the roots of rock 'n' roll signify how the indignities of the past have been shaped for centuries by Black artists into a resistance and beauty that white America is still fully embracing. Reckoning with this commercial success for the first time in 1965, *Billboard* enumerated the financial success of songs it now ranked on its newly created rhythm and blues chart. "Backlash Blues" asserts the power of this wide range of music that white elites are already listening to and promoting, at home and overseas.

Third, the Simone–Hughes song is subtly—yet with urgency—predicting that Mister Backlash will have another form of the blues when America eventually recognizes the failed logic of fighting in Vietnam. In other words, the blues is a pain that ensues whenever masters are resisted by their subjects. The poem's first invocation of Vietnam signals the disproportionate numbers of Black men who were drafted. Black Americans were perhaps nearly three times as likely to be killed fighting for a freedom they had yet to experience in their own country. Opening up larger repercussions, Hughes expands this theme when he includes the color "Yellow" among the list of people who comprise the wider world. This capitalized term signals to us Hughes's anti-Vietnam position. It was an unwavering stance wholly unknown and ignored among even those who knew Hughes best.

To everyone's surprise, Hughes first spoke out publicly against the Vietnam War on February 16, 1967. For context, Langston Hughes spoke out on behalf of the Vietnamese eight weeks before Martin Luther King's infamous public address at Riverside Church in New York on April 4, 1967. Flashing a smile to try to counter the heavy mood, Hughes shared his empathetic answer to what he thought of the Viet Cong. He told the audience in Los Angeles, "I don't see how anyone in their right minds would want to be captives of the Americans." After a delayed, slow, tenuous, and then very gentle applause, he continued, "Because *we* have been captives for three hundred years and we know what it's like."[13] Subjugation and slavery were connected in Langston Hughes's imagination.

After the applause grew louder, he spent the next two minutes listing how many times images of Black people in America being beaten (or worse) by white policemen covered the front pages of international newspapers.

"Therefore," he said, "I can't *imagine* the Viet Cong passively accepting captivity. Strange things happen in the world. My poems about the war haven't yet been translated. Almost all my other poems have been translated, even into Vietnamese." One can see Langston thinking that his translated poems could offer the Viet Cong comfort as well as show them, through the translated words, that they had allies in the United States.[14]

Moreover, Hughes continued to be associated with those who stood in solidarity against the Vietnam War. One example includes a musical tribute to the fallen Martin Luther King Jr. on May 24, 1968, at Carnegie Hall. After listening to David Amram's cantata set to Hughes's poem "Let Us Remember," featuring the repeated prayer, "Let not the oppressed become oppressors," distinguished composers including Aaron Copland sat and heard Elie Siegmeister's new orchestration of Hughes's four-poem sequence "The Face of War."[15] Hughes had written of the dead on both sides of the conflict who cannot possibly see who really wins in war. He also asked:

> What color
> Is the face
> Of war?

Hughes is arguing that every brown, black, and white face who dies is claimed equally by the grave, no matter which side they fought for. Given this occasion in 1968 and his earlier address at UCLA in February 1967, "The Backlash Blues" stands as Hughes's first statement in a long line of protests against the American occupation of Vietnam.

Hughes added colors beyond black, white, yellow, and blue to the song to make obvious the unresolved tension of the moment. Mister Backlash will be the one who eventually ends up having the blues if the Marxist dream of proletariat revolution successfully unites the workers of the world. Though certainly the song's most violent idea, one that reads as "red," it is also clearly the most obvious to those really listening:

> But the world is big,
> Big and bright and round—
> And it's full of folks like me who are
> Black, Yellow, Beige, and Brown.

To suggest that "the world is / Big and bright and round" is to picture the world being overshadowed by the persistent presence of a menacing white cloud. The idea of a round world both struggling and fighting against a white power circling over them is best contextualized as a bloody war of colors. As Randal Jelks has wisely noted, "For Langston it was important for Negroes to understand their class solidarities with people in the United States and around the globe."[16] This idea is perhaps best read against another poem Hughes was writing concurrently. In "Question and Answer," Hughes asserted that the universal sense of struggle around the globe had an aim: "a world to gain." This is an assertion repeated three times before the poem ends by asking: "But suppose I don't want it, / Why take it?" The final line makes the effort clear: "To remake it." While the emphasis in "Backlash Blues" is on how blue this remaking will make Mister Backlash feel, Hughes very much had his sights on an internationalism that showed a world in desperate need of reformation.

Hughes's poem frames the attitude of the world's oppressed in clear terms. "Backlash Blues" asks, "What do you think I got to lose?" The implication is that any colored person on the earth currently being treated like a subject is now poised for red revolt against any white master who mistreats them. If Uncle Sam thinks the world is composed of only those with Nordic skin tones, Hughes's lyric forecasts a fast-approaching time of global identity where every alternative hue unites to halt Mister Backlash's capitalist agenda. The song's final "Wait and See!" issues an exclamation that is not intended for verbal emphasis as much as it is for declaring a moral certainty. "Backlash Blues" is ideally suited for Nina Simone because it is more than a protest song: It provocatively declares the redemptive dream of "Pirate Jenny" in living color as a forthcoming moment in world history.

This understanding of their song's lyrics arises directly from revisiting the cultural contexts it documents. In the political environment of late 1966, Nina Simone trimmed a Hughes poem that was "too long" into a song she could sing around the world. Knowing that Nina was working on an album of blues songs that would become *Nina Sings the Blues*, Hughes was able to correct course from a strategy that had been consistently failing him since 1940. Up until 1966, Nina had shied away from recording Hughes's song lyrics, choosing instead to gladly accept his highly intuitive concepts. But Hughes had finally found a winning formula: Instead of handing Nina song lyrics, this time he gave her a poem that would become the most important song he ever wrote. The aging Hughes needed Nina's energetic expertise at every key step in the process.

13

Crisis

While working on a written request from Harry Belafonte in May 1967, Hughes felt a sharp pain. It was not the first time. He wanted to go on ignoring it, as the pain complicated his plans to travel to Paris. Fifteen hours later, Hughes was admitted to New York Polyclinic Hospital and assigned to a urologist. He had been ignoring painful urination for the past two months. To avoid being recognized by staff, he used his birth name, "James Hughes." The two interns who examined him feared prostate cancer when a mass was discovered near his bladder. Badly infected but not cancerous, the tumor of the still-unrecognized and uninsured patient was scheduled for removal on May 12.

Surviving both the surgery and a vasectomy, Hughes also had pneumonia that required medical treatment. Penicillin was quickly prescribed. Five days after the operation, Hughes was critically ill and admitted to the hospital's intensive care unit, where he was placed on dialysis. Langston Hughes fell into a brief coma before dying of septic shock late in the evening of May 22, 1967. Only a few close friends knew he had been ill.

The stunning news of Hughes's death was featured the next day on the front page of the *New York Times*. Nina herself was neither mentally nor physically able to attend Hughes's funeral: Her taxing recent tour of England had left her "plagued by insomnia, tears, and constant exhaustion."[1] Even without Simone present, Hughes's funeral service was an unforgettable event. Randy Weston and two other musicians played a selection of old and original blues songs, ending with Duke Ellington's "Do Nothin' till You Hear from Me." During the final section of the program, people genuinely did not know whether to laugh, remain seated, or get up and leave—Hughes had deliberately requested this song to capture some of 1920s Harlem and its odd and unsettling funeral traditions.

Hughes's body was cremated, and his remains remained on the mantel of his assistant and literary executor George Houston Bass for over twenty-five years. Today, they reside beneath a marvelous design located in the floor of the Schomburg Center for Research in Black Culture in his beloved Harlem. Based on Hughes's greatest place references, the circling symbols (known as a cosmogram) feature lines from "The Negro Speaks of Rivers." The center held an event featuring poets Maya Angelou and Amiri Baraka in 1991 to formally intern Hughes's remains.

ROY WILKINS AND THE NAACP

As the leading publication of the NAACP since 1910, the *Crisis* devoted a staggering eight pages of its June 1967 issue to celebrating the life and work of Langston Hughes. Like its May issue, the journal opened with a color page advertising "Mr. Hughes' latest book." Where May used orange, June featured white letters across a green page encouraging readers to purchase *Fight for Freedom: The Story of the NAACP* because "this exciting piece of living history is yours for only 50 cents." Later in this June issue, NAACP president Roy Wilkins penned a tribute to Hughes in a tone that was a bit too eager to align the poet with his organization: "We count it a special privilege that it was the official magazine of the National Association for the Advancement of Colored People, THE CRISIS, which gave Langston his first publication anywhere in 1921 when it appeared with his poem 'The Negro Speaks of Rivers.'"[2]

Wilkins and Hughes had known each other since 1939. At that time, Hughes began sending poetry submissions to Wilkins, who served as editor at the *Crisis*. Hughes's first letter opened with a startling complaint. The first words read: "I hate to be professional quarreler, but what you guys on THE CRISIS do to poetry is a sin and a shame. You stick it off in far corners in a column next to the adds [*sic*], and put it in small type that makes it harder than it naturally is to read, and you thus hurt the poets' souls."[3] In accepting for publication the two poems that accompanied Hughes's letter, Wilkins responded playfully, saying he wanted to give poems more space and wider margins, but "most of what I receive is fit only for filler."[4] In their working relationship, Hughes delivered two original articles in 1941 in exchange for free advertising in the *Crisis* to promote his cross-country readings and lectures.[5] In 1944, the two worked together on a select committee to award the NAACP's highest honor. That year Dr. Charles Drew's pioneering work to store and collect blood plasma meant that singer Paul Robeson and Supreme Court Justice Thurgood Marshall had to wait before each eventually won the Spingarn Medal.

When Wilkins was elevated from *Crisis* editor to NAACP executive director in 1955, Hughes no longer submitted works directly to him. Though Wilkins read Hughes's Simple columns "practically every week" that year, Wilkins's role as NAACP leader left him little time for making publication decisions.[6] Instead, Wilkins had the honor of alerting Hughes by telegram that the NAACP covered all travel and lodging expenses for Hughes to return to New York when he won the Spingarn Medal in 1960. At Wilkins's request, Hughes also presented an original poem, entitled "Dream of Freedom," at a televised fundraising event for the NAACP on May 14, 1964. Broadcast live to forty-nine cities across the United States, the extravaganza at Madison Square Garden included Duke Ellington, Josh White, and Sidney Poitier.[7]

Now, with Hughes's unexpected passing in 1967, Wilkins was eager to invoke his colleague's death to bolster his organization's quickly fading relevance within the civil rights movement. The NAACP considered itself the founding father of civil rights, yet it had been slowly shadowed in the public imagination by the incandescent successes of Martin Luther King Jr. and his Southern Christian Leadership Conference. With credit and control at stake, the highest point of tension in the relationship between Wilkins and King occurred in June 1963 during the planning for the March on Washington. In 1967, the current wave of Black Power meant that the Student Nonviolent Coordinating Committee had also eclipsed Wilkins's conservative organization.

The NAACP was feeling less attuned to the current political moment than at any other time in its long and distinguished history. While attending a political fundraising event that featured leading civil rights figures from the Congress of Racial Equality, the Urban League, and the NAACP, Hughes used his playfulness to tease his dear friend Roy Wilkins. On December 22, 1966, the Taconic Foundation—founded in 1958 by Stephen Currier and his wife, Audrey (Andrew Mellon's granddaughter)—was intent on connecting their philanthropists with those who were leading voting registration initiatives across the South. In private moments alone, Hughes prodded his dear friend Roy Wilkins about recently being called out in shocking terms by poet LeRoi Jones (later Amiri Baraka) in his "Civil Rights Poem." Holding nothing back about what he perceived was too passive a stance in this new age of "Black Power," Jones had written, "Roywilkins is an eternal faggot. / His spirit is a faggot," and concluded: "if i ever see roywilkins on the sidewalks / imonna stick half my sandal up his ass."

Hughes summarily recorded what he learned from the holiday party about how Wilkins and the rest of his peers felt. He wrote, "SNCC is now nix."[8] Contrary to the stance of those leading competing organizations, Hughes signaled his own sympathies in clear terms by affixing a SNCC sticker by his name on a letter narrating these events he sent to his friend Arna Bontemps. SNCC's cries of "Black Power" had put the NAACP on the outside looking in. SNCC was inspiring new up-and-coming poets such as Jones to show unrestrained disdain for anyone who lacked a perceived militancy equal to the current moment.

Hughes's death provided a rare window in time for Wilkins to try and regain some lost status by shouting to the world that only the moderate NAACP could publicly proclaim Hughes as their own. He did this despite the poet already having worked directly with SNCC, SCLC, and CORE. Wilkins moved swiftly to reestablish the long-standing tradition of the NAACP as the cornerstone of the civil rights movement as rival Martin Luther King Jr. suffered irrevocable damage eight weeks earlier for speaking out publicly against the Vietnam War. Wilkins's strongest brick was the NAACP's early support of Hughes. Hughes's death was indeed personally tragic—Wilkins had known Hughes for nearly thirty years—but it also provided a moment not to be missed.

To drive home the desired link, so that anyone seeing the name "Langston Hughes" would unconsciously think "NAACP," editor Henry Lee Moon tied the June 1967 volume of the *Crisis* with unmistakable cords binding Hughes to his publication. He included a full-page photo of Hughes smoking a cigarette, reprinted "The Negro Speaks of Rivers," and featured a three-page "Farewell to Langston Hughes," with a tasteful—but purposeful—mention of his long connection to the NAACP in the sixth paragraph. Reprinting Hughes's poem was not without precedent; the *Crisis* had marked the twentieth anniversary of the poem in its 1941 edition. However, the most dramatic choice came when "The Backlash Blues" was featured in the 1967 issue in such a way that it bookended Hughes's life in letters. As it was concurrently becoming his most definitive song, "The Backlash Blues" was significantly framed here as Langston Hughes's final artistic statement. It was the *Crisis* that published the poem immediately following Hughes's death. Key footnotes accompany each of these two seminal poems, and in revisiting them, it becomes clear that the narrative the NAACP created was built on this key motivation, not historical accuracy.

The first footnote, to "The Negro Speaks of Rivers," forecasts the marriage the *Crisis* wanted to establish in codifying how Hughes had been vocationally wed to the NAACP from start to finish. An asterisk at the end of the poem's title leads us to the small print at the bottom of the page, where we find a forced inaccuracy: "This poem was originally published in the June 1921 CRISIS and was the first of Mr. Hughes' poems to be published other than in school magazines."[9] This is not true.

Hughes first published nationally in *Brownies' Book* in early spring of 1921. Though it may seem excusable enough to overlook the three poems that appeared there, what is being created in the *Crisis* is something with lasting implications. This is much more than an act that erases the editorial expertise of Jessie Redmon Faucet, the woman who accepted all four of these pieces for both magazines. Rather, the NAACP wanted to assertively claim the famous Hughes as a writer who has been in constant step with its moderate politics without ever breaking stride. Such framing has lasting implications. It stands at the start of a long process of tinting Hughes so that his measurable work with groups such as CORE and SNCC suddenly dimmed to anyone searching without a compass in the many years to come.

The lengths of this successful persuasion might be traced to a dangerous point of origin located on the next page. The first footnote having seemingly birthed Hughes's career, the second footnote, accompanying "The Backlash Blues," now claimed that only the NAACP was kneeling at his deathbed: "Mr. Hughes sent this poem to NAACP Executive Director Roy Wilkins three weeks before his death, in appreciation of one of Mr. Wilkins' columns. It is the last poem submitted by Mr. Hughes for publication."[10] Like Wilkins, we also want this statement to be true. However, it seems far too serendipitous and convenient. And in fact, this would not even be the final new poem by Hughes to be published in the *Crisis* over the next twelve months.

Having publicly proclaimed that "The Backlash Blues" was Hughes's last submission in 1967, the *Crisis* forged ahead by publishing two new poems by Hughes. Nine months after Hughes's death, "Freedom" appeared in February 1968—profoundly placed immediately beside an article recognizing the continuing civil rights efforts of Mississippi's Charles Evers. With Hughes's poem defiantly denying that when "Some folks think / By killing a Man, They kill Freedom," astute readers were intended to see that Charles Evers was continuing in the struggle despite the infamous murder of his brother Medgar in 1963.

Not nearly as startling as this powerful juxtaposition, the Hughes poem that appears in the outlet's combined June–July 1968 issue is even more perplexing. The top of the page features a simple drawing of a broken board to match the poem's title, "Flotsam"—a word that denotes the strewn remains from a wrecked boat. Hughes's final poem published in the *Crisis* was strategically timed to coincide with the first anniversary of his death. The poem reflects on the fact that the cargo of his ruined ship is "songs" that now feel "wasted." Invoking the word "songs" is prescient to animate the idea of both poems by Hughes and all the songs he tried to get recorded. Yet one singular sign of hope remains: They will be "taken by the sea wind / And blown along." The art Hughes created did end up on unexpected shores where the initial journey never intended. Editor Henry Lee Moon wisely recognized that the collective imagery in this work should stand as the final metaphor for all of Langston Hughes's verse. As we will see, the weather system that encircled Hughes's works after he died included a long and powerful season of la Niña.

The reflective tone of "Flotsam" is quickly usurped by an unmistakable contradictory fact included at the bottom of the page. Eschewing the assertion beside the previous year's asterisk, the footnote following "Flotsam" provides contradictory information: "Editor's Note: This is the last of seven poems Mr. Hughes submitted to *The Crisis* for publication, prior to his death on May 22, 1967." Counting in reverse order through Hughes's final set of seven submissions, the *Crisis* published "Flotsam" (June 1968), "Freedom" (February 1968), "The Backlash Blues" (June 1967), "Suburban Evening" (April 1967), "Metropolitan Museum" (December 1966), "Question and Answer" (December 1966), and "Black Economics" (December 1966). Excluding the first three poems, all published in December 1966, and another appearing in April 1967, Hughes submitted the remaining poems sometime before May 1967. In other words, Moon still had three of these seven poems in hand in June 1967, a month after Hughes's death. Given its personal connection to Wilkins, "The Backlash Blues" appeared after Hughes died, and Moon held back the other two for a later date. Though "Flotsam" arrived earlier than "The Backlash Blues," the poem's content made it a perfect choice to save for the one-year anniversary of Hughes's death. As such, the *Crisis* concocted and then seized a second opportunity in 1968 to double the cultural capital of the NAACP. The organization was now asserting that both "The Backlash Blues" *and* "Flotsam" marked the final iconic works of Langston Hughes. In this way the NAACP had found a way to first sanctify Hughes as he died and then worship him again later in resurrection.

After fully interrogating what read like dubious claims in the *Crisis*, "The Backlash Blues" was indeed the final poem that Langston Hughes submitted for publication. A closer look at the poem Hughes submitted in early May 1967 reveals something dramatically startling: This is the version Nina Simone revised as she made changes about how to perform the finalized copy of Hughes's poem. The version of "The Backlash Blues" published in the *Crisis* in June 1967 lacks the repeating blues structure of the version Hughes completed in October and sent in to Knopf the next month to be published in *The Panther and the Lash*.

Moreover, this iteration in the *Crisis* has the new ending Simone inserted. It reads: "*Wait and see*." Hughes did not revise this line on his own. Although Hughes could have simply received a printed copy of Nina's finalized lyrics, precedent suggests another source. More likely—sometime between late January and the end of April 1967—Hughes was loaned an audio tape of Nina's studio recording before the album was released. Hughes commonly previewed musicians' songs on tape before they appeared on vinyl. He had done this with both the live Newport Jazz Festival recording of Muddy Waters in 1960 and Randy Weston's album *Uhuru Afrika*. Absent any new drafts of the poem in his archive, Hughes seems simply to have retyped Nina's lyrics *exactly* as he heard them and then submitted *her* improvements to the *Crisis* in May 1967.[11] This means that the final poem Langston Hughes ever submitted for publication—mere days before his death—was simultaneously his most important song *and* a poem with verses collaboratively created by Nina Simone. In his final months on earth, after a nearly fifty-year career as a published poet, Hughes had finally written a song suitable to be sung by Nina. It was one he coauthored with Simone. This uncanny truth calls into focus notions of fate and destiny.

BEYOND THE CRISIS

"The Backlash Blues" was featured in one of the first lesson plans about Hughes distributed nationally to schoolchildren. Hughes's second biographer, Milton Meltzer, summarized the poet's life before including the final Hughes–Simone version of the poem in a five-page lesson that featured ten multiple-choice questions for children to answer. Meltzer had worked closely with Hughes, and this biography was a National Book Award finalist for children's literature. Meltzer's teaching lesson provided a reproduction of the final iteration of "The Backlash Blues" straight from Hughes's personal files. Completed in early 1967, the lesson educated schoolchildren all across the United States about Hughes as a political force active in their contemporary world, not an abstract figure who shaped the Harlem Renaissance. In a lesson used before and after he died in May of the same year, children and their teachers had no idea the words they were reading in the poem included in their lesson had been collaboratively composed with the help of singer Nina Simone.[12]

Even more visible in the world of literature, this collaborative version of "The Backlash Blues" was further linked to Hughes's death in that it also served as the thirteenth number in poet Dudley Randall's highly visible Broadside Press. When it appeared in July 1967, this stand-alone poem was featured on an alluring thick cardstock of sky-blue paper in what is known as a broadside.

Based in Detroit, Randall was committed to publishing the radical verse that would soon be labeled as a defining part of the Black Arts Movement. His choice to include this work reminds us as much of the versatility of this new Simone-Hughes poem as it does about the highly contested nature of what camp Hughes actually represented. Was he a hot revolutionary or a calm moderate? "The Backlash Blues"—coauthored by Nina Simone and Langston Hughes—is simultaneously evidence for both: It was claimed by the NAACP within weeks of also becoming an irremovable artifact of the Black Arts Movement. Though Simone's obvious connections to the Black Arts Movement stand uncontested, in 1967, Langston Hughes stood stretching one foot on each side of the divide between grounds surveyed by the NAACP and now hoping to be annexed by Broadside. Literary scholar James Smethurst defined Hughes as a "key midwife of the Black Arts Movement," noting that Amiri Baraka "proudly kept a framed letter from Hughes on the wall of his house in Newark."[13] Endorsing his revolutionary work, Hughes told students at Spelman College during his appearance in early 1960 that they should read Baraka's poetry.[14]

One way or another, Randall was in tune with exactly when Hughes first started to compose his radical poem. More than happy to acknowledge the poem's official copyright from the book published by Knopf in 1967 (rather than the moderate publication the *Crisis*), Randall nonetheless countered the self-serving narrative created by the *Crisis*. Randall captures the earlier moment in history when the white backlash emerged in response to calls for Black Power as he accurately dates the first drafts of the Hughes poem in large letters as 1966. Without the rise of "Black Power," Hughes's poem could not have countered what emerged with its defiant threats against the white backlash.

That Hughes had encouraged Simone with his own lyrics to "Power," and that Simone reenergized that concept in her updated version of "Sinnerman," shows us that Hughes was now in effect in a dialogue with himself. He knew a powerful Simone needed to assert exactly what she wanted on behalf of the cause, and he was there to put down the backlash it brought when Stokely Carmichael accessed the emotional language of that call and made it overtly political.

SIMONE'S TRIBUTE TO HUGHES: THE NEWPORT JAZZ FESTIVAL, 1967

"Backlash Blues" truly became iconic only because of Nina Simone's repeated live performances and continual improvements to its coauthored words. With Hughes himself in attendance, Nina performed their song on November 22, 1966, at Lincoln Center's Philharmonic Hall. Using an RCA telegram, the same company she was now recording for, Hughes wired Simone the day of her concert:

HAPPY HOURS IN THE PHILHARMONIC
TONIGHT AND MANY TIMES AGAIN.
AFFECTIONATELY!
LANGSTON[15]

Whatever Hughes felt must have been amplified tenfold when he heard it live in person: By all accounts, their song "Backlash Blues" was the standout moment of Nina's set. Though Hughes would never spin the released album on his turntable at home, he had personally witnessed its unquestionable success. Hughes was able to revel in the rise of Nina's star without having to absorb the fall. Simone left Lincoln Center with full confidence to perform their song again: "Backlash Blues" was the only tune from the entire evening that received a standing ovation.[16]

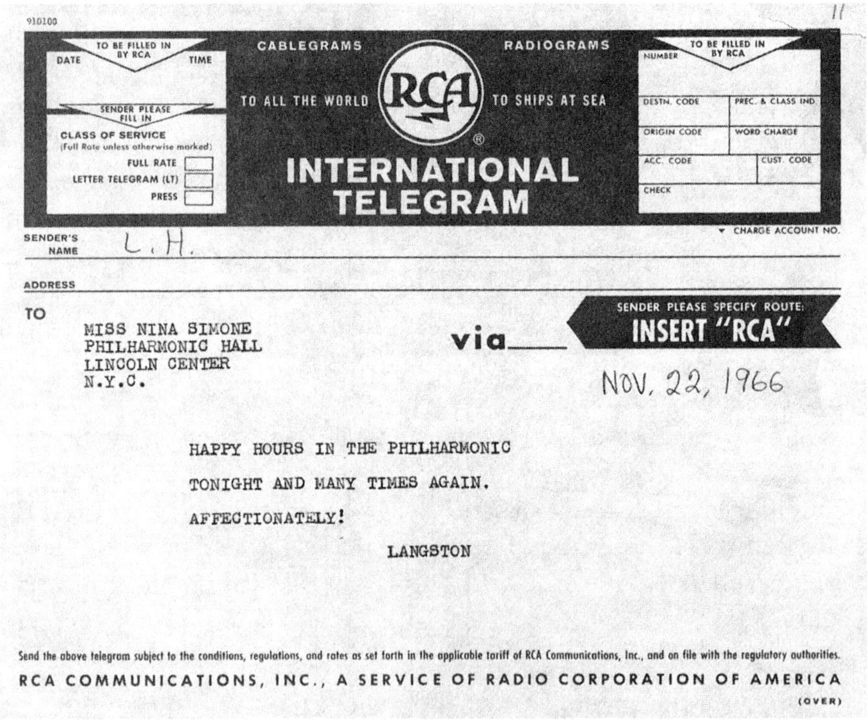

910100 11

DATE TO BE FILLED IN BY RCA TIME

SENDER PLEASE FILL IN

CLASS OF SERVICE (Full Rate unless otherwise marked)

FULL RATE
LETTER TELEGRAM (LT)
PRESS

CABLEGRAMS RADIOGRAMS

TO ALL THE WORLD RCA TO SHIPS AT SEA

INTERNATIONAL TELEGRAM

NUMBER TO BE FILLED IN BY RCA

DESTN. CODE PREC. & CLASS IND.
ORIGIN CODE WORD CHARGE
ACC. CODE CUST. CODE
CHECK

CHARGE ACCOUNT NO.

SENDER'S NAME L. H.

ADDRESS

TO

MISS NINA SIMONE
PHILHARMONIC HALL
LINCOLN CENTER
N.Y.C.

via ___ SENDER PLEASE SPECIFY ROUTE: INSERT "RCA"

NOV. 22, 1966

HAPPY HOURS IN THE PHILHARMONIC
TONIGHT AND MANY TIMES AGAIN.
AFFECTIONATELY!
LANGSTON

Send the above telegram subject to the conditions, regulations, and rates as set forth in the applicable tariff of RCA Communications, Inc., and on file with the regulatory authorities.

RCA COMMUNICATIONS, INC., A SERVICE OF RADIO CORPORATION OF AMERICA

(OVER)

Fig. 13.1. The RCA telegram Langston Hughes sent to Nina Simone the night he watched her perform "Backlash Blues" for the first time in her career. (James Weldon Johnson Memorial Collection in the Yale Collection of American Literature, Beinecke Rare Book and Manuscript Library, Yale University.)

Another critical moment in the long history of their song came at a venue Nina would forever associate with Hughes. The version of "Backlash Blues" she delivered July 1 at the 1967 Newport Jazz Festival offers a rare glimpse into a song still being altered and refined.[17] As Nina came softly into her ending of "Don't Let Me Be Misunderstood," she tried to transition straight into an important tribute. Not realizing that the audience's response to her second song would draw such loud applause, she began to address the crowd for the first time that evening: "Langston Hughes was . . ." A full fifteen seconds later, the roar subsided, and she could continue by stumbling through a plethora of warm memories: "In 1950, 1960, I think it was, I met Langston Hughes here." As Nina stumbled on the date, perhaps she was simply conveying that it felt as if she had known Hughes forever. Or was she unconsciously recalling having met him in Asheville, North Carolina, in 1949? Either way, it was immediately clear that, "deeply affected by his death, Nina turned her set at the Newport Jazz Festival July 1 into a tribute."[18] Given the time and place, it is interesting to ask: To what degree was Nina thinking of Hughes's passing with her opening song, "Just in Time"? Unlike her typical live versions (from both 1960 and 1968), tonight the pulsing rhythm was replaced by a pace and tone that was tired and somber. The song addressed someone who "changed my life" so there was

> No more fear
> I done found my way
> That lucky day.

If the whole song did not apply to her feelings about Hughes, perhaps at least key phrases such as these informed the depth with which she sang. Gene Taylor's bass and Charles Crosby's drums set a slow blues tempo. Not a rhythm to dance to, this turtle pace was best grooved to with a casual snap of the fingers. Nina continued her quiet tribute to the mentor who had died six weeks earlier:

> And he used to sit on the board here. He was here when it began, you know. And he wrote this tune, he wrote the poem . . . "Backlash" just before he died, and gave it to me to put some music to. It was his final slap in the face of the white backlash of this country. So we're going to do his tune. And of course he's gone from us, but not really, he's out there somewhere.

Nina riffed a bit on the piano through a full twelve bars and then addressed the congressman who was "Mister Backlash." This seven-minute performance offers a startling way to measure how the song was originally received. No one at the festival had heard it before. Though Nina had recorded it in studio in January 1967, the recording was not released until August, a month after this performance in Newport. The photo of Nina taken in the studio the day she recorded the song captures her moments after as she turns away from her piano in a posture of deep reflection, her frustration uncoiled. Sheet music is resting on the piano as, seated on her stool, she looks down with a despondence that her lit cigarette tries to ease. By contrast, the audience response at Newport offers a sonic record documenting how loudly this slap struck the cheek of Mister Backlash before the song ended.

After Nina delivered the opening reference to taxes, wages, and Vietnam, the crowd started cheering immediately. She sang about teaching Mister Backlash the blues before she left him. After "second-class fools," added shouts of surprised shock and defiance mixed to form a complete approval for the tone of this brand-new song.

The deep groove continued with an early morning pace to match the energy of someone still in need of their first cup of coffee. Though the words pronounced clear anger, Nina kept the music light. Perhaps she was trying to capture the often-perplexing tension in Hughes's own work. Here was a poet who could wag his finger even as he laughed. After she sang, "When I try to find a job," she snapped her fingers before finishing the idea "to earn a little cash." The volume of the tune rose after the fourth verse as Rudy Stevenson entered with a guitar solo featuring a single-string picking technique that treated his electric guitar as if it were a mandolin.

Nina likely wanted to continue to stretch the length of this song out on this occasion for at least two reasons. First, with the final lyrics still missing an appropriate punch, the song's ending needed some rhetorical work. Second, this was a tribute to Hughes, and Nina wanted to be sure that his legacy was being honored rather than rushed to closure. Hence, when she reached the fifth verse, she combined a few ideas about the "world":

> It's big and bright and round
> And there's some more like me
> Who are Black, Yellow, Beige, and Brown.

Simone understood the song's idea of expanding the national idea of revolt into world revolution. In returning to this notion a second time in this performance, she was spelling out that she was far from alone. There were "some more like me" who would leave Mister Backlash black-eyed and bruised. For such emphasis, she added extra vibrato here to "Beige" and then eventually let the final word of the song, "blues," linger long enough to signal to her loyal

Newport following that the song's apparent ending was now at hand. Moreover, this new ending nods directly to the fact that Langston Hughes indeed left this world by giving Mister Backlash these blues.

The next day's Newport newspaper singled out the crowd's reaction as singular for the evening's full set of performances when it called the song "a Negro protest number which got tremendous applause." However, in playing straight through twenty seconds of continuous applause, Nina had no intention of stopping. The song restarted. Three iterations of "da da da Dah" suddenly gave way to moving from future vindication to italicizing the empowerment felt by speaking directly into the face of power. Circling back emotionally to a line in her first song, "Just in Time," Simone now connected the two songs to twice declare, "Got no more fear," to model how it felt to sing the truth about the kind confidence Hughes instilled. Eschewing fear was a cornerstone of Simone's personal philosophy. Her pairing it so emphatically with Hughes reminds us of the crucial role he played in removing it from her life and music. Perhaps she was indeed reflecting on Hughes from the moment she took the stage? Either thinking of what such a revolution might cost her or recalling that Hughes himself was no longer here, she testified, "Gotta tell ya how I feel / 'cause I might not be here tomorrow." But in innocently trying to repeat an idea from the song, many in the audience mistakenly feared that Nina's three-song set might suddenly be over. Perhaps unaware of the implications, she repeated, "I'm gonna leave you, now" four times. After several loud pleas of "No!," someone in the crowd shouted, "You can't do it now." Enjoying this suspense, Nina assured them she had more to give. "Not yet," she told the crowd. "Not yet."

As Nina moved into performing "You Can Have Him," her onstage playfulness reemerged. It was as if Hughes's own famous sense of humor needed to be honored tonight as well. In speaking facetiously about a man she really wants, the singer asserted, "I could never make him happy. Nancy Wilson made him happy." The reference to singer Nancy Wilson is a gesture toward the fact that Wilson recorded this song after Nina included it on her album *Broadway-Blues-Ballads* in 1964. The callout of Wilson drew a massive response of laughter. When Simone's performance at the 1967 Newport Jazz Festival aired on Voice of America, on December 14, 1967, Willis Conover's radio broadcast omitted Nina's version of "Backlash Blues." Perhaps the simple fact that it had not yet been released on vinyl meant that the studio version of the album *Nina Sings the Blues* might be carried by this new tune and have a life of its own.

Before Nina sang her seventh and final song at Newport, she returned the evening's focus back to Langston. Introducing "Four Women" included one last reminiscence that preserved Hughes rather than bidding him farewell. Nina spoke to the audience: "We don't have much time, so we're going to have to leave you with this one. Again, we want to say, just say hello to Langston, and hope that you remember him. Keep him with you always. He was, he was beautiful. Beautiful man. And he's still with us of course." "Hello" is the word Nina invoked, suggesting that their friendship was too deep to ever really say "goodbye." After all, Hughes, his influence, and now his most defining song were going to be forever associated with Nina Simone. Along with "Just in Time," this was a perfect bookend. In the middle, Mr. Hughes's lyrics to "Backlash Blues" anchored her set. Nina's personal assessment of how she honored her friend Langston Hughes was definitive: "I could feel it. It's your most dramatic moment."[19] Yes, though this performance is not available on any CDs or streaming services (even today), Nina Simone delivered her most decisive set on this evening at Newport in 1967. She was inspired by the place and all her intimate memories of first appearing there in 1960. As a result, she channeled a deep desire to honor none other than Langston Hughes, the dear friend who first invited her to its stage.

14

Where It's At

THE WESTBURY MUSIC FAIR, APRIL 7, 1968

Three days after Martin Luther King Jr.'s assassination, an emotionally exhausted Nina Simone had to be coaxed into taking the stage in Long Island, New York, at the Westbury Music Fair. Perhaps because of these incredible tribulations, her concert on April 7, 1968, turned out to be one of the most memorable performances in musical history.[1] She presented an epic tribute memorializing the life of King, improvised a new ending to what would become *the* defining version of "Don't Let Me Be Misunderstood," and updated her already iconic "Mississippi Goddam!"

But perhaps most importantly, she debuted a newly created verse for "Backlash Blues." That verse would be forever embedded within the song as a tribute to her friend Langston Hughes. Before mapping exactly how the song's cultural impact continued to grow as Nina performed "Backlash Blues" over the next nine years, it is illuminating to revisit these four songs from her April 7, 1968, performance in detail. This iconic concert established the context that surrounds the emergence of the new verse that eventually allowed Nina to earn her official title as coauthor of "Backlash Blues."

"WHY?"

Having just finished singing a song hurriedly written and rehearsed especially in response to Dr. King's death, Nina now started speaking from the heart after ending "Why (The King of Love Is Dead)." Still sitting at the piano, she tried to introduce the song "Take My Hand, Precious Lord." As part of King's final conversation across the balcony of the Lorraine Motel, this was the song King had requested that musician Ben Branch play later in the evening. Of course, King never heard Branch play the song on his saxophone. Nina faltered in making the turn and instead offered her thoughts. "A year ago, maybe more, longer than that now," she told the crowd, "Lorraine Hansberry left us, and she was a dear friend. She had her favorite song. And then Langston Hughes left us, Coltrane left us, Otis Redding left us, you can go on. Do you realize how many we have lost?"

After a long, exasperated breath, caught by a sensitive microphone, she implored her audience to think. "Then it really gets down to reality doesn't it? Not a performance, not microphones and all that crap." She continued, "We have lost a lot of them in the last two years."

But, seemingly to turn the tide of sadness, she added, "But we have remaining, Monk." When she paused, someone shouted the name *Miles*. Nina repeated the name approvingly just when someone else in the crowd said *Cannonball*. A third name rang from the crowd, one equal to jazz pianist Thelonious Monk, trumpeter Miles Davis, and saxophonist Cannonball Adderley: Someone shouted a loud *Nina*.

"I love you, too!" she told the crowd.

But Nina was hardly done. "They're shooting us down one by one. Don't forget that. 'Cause they are." Nina whispered, pausing for emphasis between each of her final three words: "Killing us *one by one*."

Though the song had been performed in honor of the nonviolent Dr. King, Nina was reflecting on the incident with a militant attitude. "Well, all I have to say is that, those of us who know how to protect those of us that we love, stand by them, and stay close to them," she told the crowd. "And I say that if there'd been a couple of more a little closer to Dr. King he wouldn't a got it. Really. Just a little closer to him." Nina's appeal to self-defense hinted toward an armed resistance she fully endorsed. In this way, her posture was in firm step with California's Black Panther Party leaders Huey P. Newton and Bobby Seale. Before the Panthers had come into visibility, the Student Nonviolent Coordinating

Committee itself had ensured that the March for Freedom through Mississippi in 1966 had armed protection from a group known as the Deacons for Defense and Justice.

At this concert, Nina took the moment singing about King to also remember the stature of Langston Hughes. It was far from out of place to link the two, as Dr. King's famous "I Have a Dream" speech has its origins in Langston Hughes's poem "I Dream a World."[2] In fact, as Lerone Martin has found, the preacher had been acting out memorized versions of Hughes's poems since seventh grade, "under the guidance of Miss Lemon," as a young King "imbued the words of Langston Hughes, and learned to be a dreamer."[3] A look at the evening's themes of violent uprising reveals how much more Simone's ideology was in step with the poet than it was with the preacher. To contextualize Nina's unparalleled approach, no other singer even considered responding in music to the deaths of playwright Lorraine Hansberry, Langston Hughes, Martin Luther King Jr., Jimmie Lee Jackson, James Meredith, and the four girls killed in Birmingham, Alabama, while attending Sunday school. Her two responses on this night reveal how she successfully applied the strategies of resistance Hughes had pioneered during the Harlem Renaissance to properly honor the dead with elegies that celebrated their lives. One of the most important of his strategies was documenting the cultural and emotional history of the moment at hand.

Simone's bassist Gene Taylor wrote the song "Why?" to honor King in the wake of his assassination three days before this concert. Nina's performance of Taylor's lyrics documents a ravaged and torn moment in American history, as cities across the nation burned. Known as the Holy Week Uprising, the violent days leading up to Easter Sunday in 1968 were the most sustained and widespread moment of social unrest of the century in the United States. "Why?" gestured first toward the mass confusion of how a nonviolent minister could be murdered, but the song also served as an empathetic explanation for addressing *why* whole street blocks were on fire. Historically, when a king is killed, anarchy reigns until a successor is named. Nina riffed on the lyrics she had struggled to memorize in such short time. Though spoken softly, Nina's extemporaneous questions had a loud impact. "Don't you know how we got to react?" she sang. "Don't you know what it will bring?"

Nina's anger seemed to also be directed toward her instrument. After she wondered aloud if murders like these would ever cease, her right hand rolled a loud arpeggio up the keyboard that was punctuated with a stunning strike to a single key. Her movements sounded like attacks on the keys.

With lyrics that suggested the country was on the brink of exploding, she improvised from the heart of her frustrations, her true emotions coming through as she issued a sinister warning about people rising in the streets. Unfiltered, Nina was endorsing the riots as an appropriate response when she twice declared: "Even if they have to die." Lost when we approach the song with the assumption that it only celebrates King, Nina asserted unequivocal affirmations to the rioters when she asserted: "If you have to die, it's alright!"

The theme was highlighted again later in the evening's version of "Mississippi Goddam." Nina underlined her stance in this song with personal testimony. She had fresh targets for her rage that summoned old memories, and only two verses in, she removed "Tennessee" and instead sang, "Lurleen Wallace has made me lose my rest." When Alabama's laws forbade George Wallace from running for another term as governor, his wife, Lurleen, won the election of 1966, allowing George to continue as the de facto leader of Alabama. The second time Nina arrived at "Tennessee," she sang instead, "Memphis has made me lose my rest." The striking coincidence that Memphis was a city in Tennessee made it feel that she was indeed a high priestess singing a song first performed four years earlier that had somehow proved to be prophetic.

"The time is too late, now. Good God. You know?" she sang. "The King is dead. The King of love is dead."

She then hollered, "I ain't 'bout to be *nonviolent,* honey!" Merging laughter into what sounded like a threat, she blurred her words together into an unspellable example of something you might hear at a religious revival.

"*Ahh ah ah ah ooooohhh,* No!" Few in the Long Island audience cheered this declaration of violence delivered in the midst of honoring the passive approach that defined Dr. King.

But the most personal trigger for Simone's hidden rage is almost imperceptible. Simone delivered the following lines, then hesitated before continuing, as if she was visibly remembering a specific injustice about the derogatory label "Aunt Sadie." Not in either the concert or the studio versions of this song from 1964, the unexpected reference to Simone's mother, Kate, surfaces something that Simone is nearly on the verge of sharing. Five years later, Simone finally revealed why this reference to "Aunt Sadie" drew such personal ire. Performing "Four Women" at Berkeley in 1969, Simone explained sections of her own song with several key breaks that sound like long annotations. The song reads like a T. S. Eliot poem, complete with footnotes.

The most profound moment of the electrifying Berkeley concert occurred when Simone ended the first section of "Four Women" and introduced Aunt Sarah. Planning to "leave her there," Nina could not resist the palpable atmosphere she sensed from the politically charged city. She started back in slowly: "I could tell you a story about my mama in the South. They called her 'Auntie.' In these grocery stores. I only wish I had been there when they called her

'Auntie.' No 'Missus.'" Furious at the thought, Nina then voiced a wordless disgust that sounded like *eehhh* once she defaulted to the self-sustaining idea that such anger was only wasted energy. Then, as if literally seeing a scene before her, Nina was compelled to continue as if she were speaking mystically to historical racists only she could see: "No, don't don't do that, don't do that."

After signaling that she was now introducing "the second woman," Nina suddenly realized she was still not ready to move on. In 1969, she proclaimed: "You see, I know Berkeley's on fire. I know that anyway, you see, I say that in a positive way. But I kind of have to hold myself down here because the vibrations are so strong." Then she exploded, rattling off words fast as machine-gun fire. "But I tell you this, if I'd have been there when they called my Mama 'Auntie' I'd have burned the whole goddamn place down, I tell you that!" For the next nine seconds, an explosive mixture of applause and laughter erupted from the crowd, returning to Nina in a way found nowhere else throughout her discography. At the 1968 concert dedicated to Dr. King's passing, this image of her mother being so publicly belittled was the incident felt but not shared at the Westbury Music Fair.

"DON'T LET ME BE MISUNDERSTOOD"

Nina sincerely hoped she had not been misunderstood at Westbury the way she had when she first released "Mississippi Goddam." In 1964, the second word of her title had to be double bleeped just to get played on the radio. Many civil rights advocates felt that such overt blasphemy went too far. And her just mentioning that she had stopped believing in prayer put her further at odds with the long religious tradition of successful protest dominating the direction of a movement that was on the verge of passing the Civil Rights Act of 1964. Tonight, she calibrated accordingly by immediately following "Mississippi Goddam" with a version of "Don't Let Me Be Misunderstood" so genuine the audience response surprised even Simone. Instead of gesturing toward the song's inherent subject of two lovers reconciling, tonight Nina fully appropriated the lyric so that it was an undeniable statement about her own challenging role as a protest singer. The crowd instantaneously recognized the approach and applauded her after the first chorus. Encouraged, Simone eased quietly into the second verse as if she were confessing deep truths to the audience about what worried her most: "Oh, Lord, please don't let me be misunderstood."

Nina started scatting now as if calling to an unknown muse. Her unspellable words offered direct access to feelings no one could name. She also used the space to retune her soul. Nina avoided singing the phrase "ink-come-a" that she usually used here. Invoked first in "My Man" and later on *Nina Sings the Blues* in the song "House of the Rising Sun," "ink-come-a" became a Simone-ized amalgamation Nina personally compressed to communicate the frustration that results from realizing that your waiting is in vain. "Ink-come-a" became a head-shaking and self-muttering realization as her tongue eventually blurred the full thought into words: "Ain't comin' back."

Again, more applause in the middle of the song pushed her further until she was fully riffing. In place of the expected bridge of the song that addressed the lover most directly through the idea of being "edgy," Nina took the song a completely different direction from which it never returned. Rather than being received by the artist, the muse had surrendered to Nina's chanting: "Too much hatred. Too much of everything. The people, strange Lord, Strange Now. Don't want to come here no more, Lord." Facing an audience she had to lead while she herself was so emotionally unsteady was a painful burden. Pointing back to "Mississippi Goddam," she sang, "Don't want to be misunderstood this time around. Give me the words to say it like it is. Like you want me to say it." Instead of eschewing God as she had four years earlier, this historic moment ended with an earnest prayer as Simone concluded with eight consecutive incantations of "use me, use me, use me . . ."

Nina thought the song was finished. She struck the first chord for the next song, "Peace of Mind," then suddenly realized the applause was sustained. The audience was not ready to move on. Nina had been transported so far inward that she had nearly forgotten the crowd was out there. This affection prompted a reprise. Following guitarist Rudy Stevenson's lead, the band returned to the song's groove. An unsure Nina joined them. Another minute more passed, where the audience clapped on beat to share in the collective experience of what felt like Nina Simone's public confession. At the very end, she earned another well-deserved applause, the fourth of the song. It coincided with an ineffable sigh from Nina, one that communicated equal parts fatigue and exasperation. Better than any words, it expressed how tired Nina was of having to explain her anger.

This sigh, and the resistance to white supremacy through artistic creation, shows how Nina's sincerity had touched an audience of generous listeners who were fully willing to bestow their absolution. Or were they merely telling Nina, in the spirit of Black Power, that they themselves were sorry for misunderstanding her when she understandably raged against Mississippi?

"BACKLASH BLUES"

Before the evening reached the levels of emotional intensity where breaths held as much weight as words, Nina's earlier rendition of "Backlash Blues" arrived after a wonderful moment of playfulness. Just before she started into the opening chords of "Backlash Blues," the third song of the evening, Nina's six-year-old daughter, Lisa, audibly asked for a hot dog. After the crowd laughed at the tone of the earnest (and not precocious) request, Nina added to a moment of collective levity: "I hope you got that on that tape." More laughter eased the tension on what was going to become a very emotional night. Once Nina started into the fourth verse of "Backlash Blues," asserting that the world was filled with other colors of people, it would have been hard to miss the night's first suggestion of revolution. It would soon be revisited and amplified in "Why?," where she would declare, "My people are rising."

A statement made to introduce "Mississippi Goddam" serves as context for what Nina was about to add here tonight to "Backlash Blues." Before singing "Alabama's got me so upset," Nina spoke over the opening piano chords to tell the audience she hoped "we will have songs that go down in history for these wonderful brave people who are no longer with us." Swapping out the original stanza that appeared both in Hughes's poem and on her recent record, Nina added a new fifth verse to "Backlash Blues" this evening. She literally sang the praises of Langston Hughes as one of the militant heroes of the Black Power movement, invoking her coauthor's name, "When Langston Hughes died," before ending with his final directive to her: "Make sure you tell 'em exactly where it's at / So they'll have no place to hide." The crowd's applause at this new verse drowned out the sound of the band, which was still playing. Nina was not only claiming Hughes as a dear friend but elevating him to the class of a fallen Black hero.

More than this, Nina was voicing her true mentorship from Hughes. He was the encouragement to keep her "workin'" to gain the respect she deserved. Suggesting that Hughes imagined a day when Nina could tell white racists "exactly where it's at" codifies Hughes as an overlooked arbiter ready and willing to express the unredemptive vengeance of Black Power. Moreover, the phrase "where it's at" clearly has its origins here well before Simone used it in her iconic song "To Be Young, Gifted, and Black" (1969). Given this unmistakable connection, Hughes's words to Nina eventually became the same unforgettable advice Simone in turn gave to all the talented Black youth of America. This is how a mentee becomes a mentor.

Finally, it is startling to hear in this iteration that Mister Backlash himself will eventually have "no place to hide." The "Sinnerman" Simone once sang of was a Black protester who could not find any symbolic protection from rock, river, sea, Lord, or devil. Here, in this reimagined futurity, the white sinnerman, dressed in a tie and suit, is Mister Backlash himself. No unofficial lobbyists or judicial pardons can protect a congressman who has consistently legislated against a Black populace that has nonetheless grown powerful enough to finally tell him off.

Nina physically embodied the idea of rising up against white power in the calculated way she ended "Backlash Blues." It was a true warning about the expectant failures of gerrymandered elections, the war in Vietnam, the imminent threat of a worldwide proletariat revolution, and an assertion of the success, longevity, and impact of the rich tradition of blues music itself. She told Mr. Backlash: "*I'm* gonna leave you with the blues."

To overenunciate this final line of the song, Nina stood up and roared *I'm*, sending the sound of her voice out well above her microphone before she then sat back down. All her audience had to do, she showed, was rise up and follow her. For the next twenty years, Nina's concerts consistently featured this personal tribute to Hughes as the song began to model what it meant to stand up against white power with a hope that others would be inspired by the example Simone and Hughes had forged together.

Beginning with the new verse about Langston Hughes's advice added to the cowritten "Backlash Blues," Nina was now strategically building a musical history by memorializing the era's passing heroes in song. With "To Be Young, Gifted, and Black," Nina's 1969 tribute to Lorraine Hansberry, she inspired the next generation to embrace the wonderful exuberance of their youth, burgeoning expertise, and proud racial history as things to merge collectively as they shaped their American identities. "Why?" unintentionally documented the moments of violence surrounding Dr. King's death, ensuring that the events of the Holy Week Uprising survived to become a history published in vinyl that sharply contrasts with nonviolent protest. In this way, history becomes the news we never forget. With "Backlash Blues," Hughes is forever named as Simone's mentor. To Nina, Hughes embodies artistic perseverance, unrelenting confidence in her talents, and a sublimated hope for vengeance. Such retribution returns in varying doses every time a white politician loses an election, realizes a defeat on the battlefield, or continues to underestimate the international presence of the proletariat. Even if some or all of these are belated, such racist leaders consistently fail to understand the global reach of blues music, which has simply become America's signature form of artistic expression. These three songs are ones only Nina Simone could sing as she created the soundtrack to the civil rights movement.

THROUGH THE YEARS

Remarkably, Nina Simone's repeated live performances of "Backlash Blues" (from 1967 to 1987)—not her original studio recording—made the song a legitimate addition to the Black Arts Movement. If Black Power was an idea as much

Fig. 14.1. Nina Simone's album featuring live versions of "Why (The King of Love Is Dead)," "Backlash Blues," and "Don't Let Me Be Misunderstood." *'Nuff Said* (RCA, 1968).

as it was a political goal, its best artifacts are the art it produced as compensation for a lack of real social change. Nina's various performances of "Backlash Blues" offer unique insights into how this ever-evolving song became an inextricable pillar in her repertoire. By extension, "Backlash Blues" is a key, but consistently overlooked artifact of the Black Arts Movement, a loose coalition of works and authors from which Hughes and his poems have too often been excluded. Yet Hughes and this song held lasting and immense sway throughout the very era the moniker earnestly seeks to bracket and name. Because each performance is so profound—and intricate—Nina Simone's songs deserve the same attentiveness we bring to poetry.

Though the television special "Sound of Soul" would air nationally in the United Kingdom on September 14, 1968, Nina had filmed her London performance earlier in June. The program audience could tell by the way she introduced “Backlash Blues.” After the band started playing its opening bars of blues while she played her piano, Nina offered a personal prologue that was both accurate and sincere. “Now, last year at this time,” she said, fingers over the keys, “Langston Hughes left us. And he told me to make sure that I sang this song everywhere I went. And I told him that I would ’cause he wasn’t gonna be here to say it anymore. My good friend.”[4]

Nina’s performance of “Backlash Blues” is highlighted by a wardrobe that features a stunning black crocheted outfit that mirrors the white full-length version she wore at Newport the year before. Simone’s long, dangling earrings swayed in such a way that they were always on the offbeat. Oversized earrings such as these had gained popularity in America in the mid-1960s after more and more Black women stared wearing their natural hair very short. Historian Tanisha C. Ford, who has written books on style and Black history, says that “Afro-inspired earrings were an appealing accessory because they allowed Black women to make a subtle statement about their cultural politics while they maintained and projected their femininity.”[5]

In the brief interlude in the middle of the song, Nina raised both of her hands up high before dropping them onto the keys of the Steinway and Sons grand piano. She hammered the song’s most basic chord changes this way with the precision of an accomplished blacksmith. Immediately after the interlude, she delivered her newly added tribute verse. Similar to her concert at Westbury two months before, Nina altered only two phrases. First, she substituted “times” in place of the expected “months” she invoked earlier in April: “When Langston Hughes died, he told me many times before.” Second, in Nina’s mind, Mister Backlash was already on the run. As a result, he was now told he would have “no other place to hide.” Like Nina’s “Sinnerman,” it seemed as if rock, river, and sea had each already denied him refuge.

A country that deeply valued its poets saw Nina smile wide as she defiantly stood up among all the mod English hipsters to deliver her final line. She said, “I’m gonna leave you with the blues.” Nina left, then returned to the stage after a thoughtful wardrobe change. Wearing a full sarong and stunning turban (whose matching colors of bright azure and Egyptian gold were completely lost in the black-and-white film footage), Nina stared down into the black abyss of her closed piano lid to conjure a truly dark and mesmerizing (though abridged) version of “I Put a Spell on You.” As if channeling her mentor’s directives, she sang that she “went to Alabama and got me a mojo.” Simone signaled she was now fully embracing Hughes’s concept of incantation and spell binding—from head to toe—as two of Hughes’s song ideas appeared back to back. Each was one of the signature emblems defining exactly who Nina Simone was as an artist Europe was ready to embrace.

An image of Nina Simone at the Harlem Cultural Festival of 1969 was overtly used to promote Questlove's Academy Award–winning film *Summer of Soul* (2021). Blurred in many promotional materials, the color footage highlighted Nina's dramatic look as a priestess who had already been crowned. Performing outdoors before an audience so hot that they sheltered under umbrellas, Nina wore a dramatic print dress that featured spots and flowers against a bright ocher. It was fully open in the back. Her triumphant hairdo ended in two giant circles, suggesting the very interstellar planets where she presumably already ruled. Other moons she had merely visited rotated in orbits like mobiles from her ears. Her earrings communicated confrontation. Silver in color, the largest outer rings attached to themselves in ways that almost suggested a pair of handcuffs.

Before she performed on that hot August day, Nina took the stage alone. To warm up the crowd, she recited David Nelson's poem "Are You Ready?," adding to a long line of poets she engaged—Nina would at one time recite or sing poems such as Waring Cuney's "No Images," Paul Laurence Dunbar's "When Malindy Sings," and David Nelson's "Today You Are a Killer." With limited time to perform, Nina played only six songs. This speaks to the place of privilege "Backlash Blues" held at the time Nina was at her most assertive politically. With makeshift notes and scrap papers fluttering distractedly in front of her on the top of her piano, Nina repeated, "Yes I am," three times at the end of the first proclamation that she would leave Mister Backlash with the blues. Then she added unexpected vibrato to her voice in extending the words "find" and then "world." Here in Mount Morris Park, located in Hughes's home of Harlem, the guitar solo was reinserted before Nina shared that Hughes had told her to keep on working not "months" but "many *years* before he died." Before she riffed that she had to leave Mister Backlash with the blues, "Got to do it in the hot sun, if necessary," Simone both intensified and updated Hughes's expression for retribution when she declared his directive: "Make sure you sock it to 'em where they live." Was Simone thinking of punching or hitting Mister Backlash? Where would this blow land?

In her opening rendition of Nelson's poem, Nina asked the crowd in no uncertain terms, "Are you ready?" In many ways, the poem choice signaled her desire to start a literal riot. *Really*. Rather than building up to what being ready might entail, she opened very early with the most direct query possible: "Are you ready to kill, if necessary?" This was followed by interrogating the audience to identify if they were ready to "smash white things" and "burn buildings"? The High Priestess posited an alternative way forward that was not invoked by mere mortals. She asked if they were ready to call on "the wrath of Black gods, Black magic, to do your bidding"? Truly bewitched, she repeated,

"Ready, ready, ready, ready," over and over at an excited, ever-increasing pace, encouraging others that their consent would be a choice to follow her on a path she was already marching.

Nina's famous concert at Fort Dix, New Jersey, on November 18, 1971, featured a rendition of "Backlash Blues" not included when the album of the show was released as *Emergency Ward* (1972). Not released until 1973, Nina's equally electric performance of "Backlash Blues" before about five thousand students at the University of California, Berkeley, on April 26, 1969, mirrored her delivery at the Harlem Cultural Festival.[6] After hearing that Hughes had told Nina to "sock it to 'em where they live," the crowd also learned—after the song ended—why it appeared so early in the set: "I sang 'Backlash' because I knew I was going to get a request for it later, so we did it now." Clearly, audiences had been imploring Nina to sing this song, and she was happy to preempt their demands before answering them felt like acquiescence.

Nina's set at the Lincoln Center's Philharmonic Hall on October 26, 1969, included "Backlash Blues," but the song was left off the album *Black Gold* when it was released in early 1970. (The same occurred with the 1974 live album *It Is Finished.*) Nonetheless, Hughes remained a visible presence on the vinyl. Ed Williams, future president of the Joint Center for Political and Economic Studies in Washington, DC, began the Philharmonic Hall show by introducing Nina's band. He quoted a poem from 1923 by Langston Hughes that was newly available in his posthumous collection *The Panther and the Lash*. The short lyric was titled "Justice." After imaging justice as a goddess, Williams told the crowd:

> We black are wise
> Her bandage hides two festering sores
> That once perhaps were eyes.

Immediately afterward, Williams welcomed "the High Priestess of Soul, Miss Nina Simone," to the stage. Although many scholars and editors would later regard Hughes as less revolutionary and radical than other writers of the Black Arts Movement, that clearly was not how Simone, Ed Williams, or this audience regarded him in 1969.

While Nina's new tune "To Be Young, Gifted, and Black" meant that her dear friend Lorraine Hansberry was featured extensively in her introduction to the song, Hughes was prominently invoked when Nina reprised the language of another song, "West Wind," in the middle of this newly released single. Channeling the muse of wind, inspiration for Greek and Romantic poets alike, her spoken words in Miriam Makeba's song "West Wind" led to a touching and personal plea spoken to those who were physically absent but spiritually present: "Hear me Miriam. Hear me Stokely. Hear me momma. Hear me daddy. Hear me everybody. I'm calling on Lorraine. Hear me. Langston, hear me, and help me." Singer Miriam Makeba, her new husband Stokely Carmichael, Kate and J. D., Lorraine, and Langston: These six figures were the centers of Nina Simone's consciousness as an artist who was expanding the soundtrack to the civil rights movement with each and every live performance.

Philharmonic Hall itself must have felt a bit haunted by the recently departed Hughes. It was here on November 22, 1966, that Nina debuted "Backlash Blues" with Hughes in the audience. Neither Hughes nor Simone could have known this would be the last time Hughes heard Nina perform in person.

On May 24, 1970, *King: A Filmed Record* raised over $3 million (about $23 million in 2026) in a single day for the cause of civil rights in America. The one-off event is still unprecedented in film history. With over six hundred movie theaters participating, the producers set their archival footage of King against a convincing soundtrack of the movement's music. This meant that King's presence at the Selma to Montgomery March in 1965 was incomplete without Nina's stirring performance of "Mississippi Goddam." When it came time for the most moving images of King's funeral, nothing captured the somber feeling better than Nina's live version of "Why? (The King of Love Is Dead)." In fact, the track was so apt that it was reprised as the final credits rolled so that every viewer left their seats with Nina's stirring song haunting their ears.

Though retrospective framing of the Black Arts Movement might lead us to imagine a fierier personality such as James Baldwin contextualizing King's life and times in 1970, no literary figure loomed larger in the three-hour epic film than Langston Hughes. Even three years after his death, Hughes still represented the most assertive and visible voice for civil rights in America. The film also added Hollywood stars to ensure both transitions within its topics and a larger attendance at the box office. Actor James Earl Jones descended a set of stairs to recite Hughes's poem "Who but the Lord?" to introduce the police violence and attack dogs used in Birmingham in the spring of 1963. Jones spoke Hughes's lines of having the law "beat the living hell / out of me!" He ended by anticipating a weapon more powerful than prayer:

> So who but the Lord
> can protect me?
> *We'll see.*

Jones was an ideal voice to recite Hughes's works: His father, Robert Earl Jones, had performed both Hughes's poems and acting roles at the Harlem Suitcase Theater in the 1930s.

To summarize the horrific death of the four girls attending Sunday school on September 15, 1963, Joanne Woodward read Hughes's "Birmingham Sunday." She stared into the camera as church bells rang in the background. Later, Paul Newman presented Hughes's poem "The Face of War" while seated sternly in a chair. With this, audiences across the United States were prepared to revisit Dr. King's controversial stance against the Vietnam War. Seemingly uncanny if we did not understand their intense collaboration, the poet and singer had each addressed both this bombing and war with "Mississippi Goddam" and their collective venture "Backlash Blues." It is illuminating to recall that Nina and Langston framed how King's life was first presented on film to the world. This was not a coincidence. One had modeled for the other how documentary strategies could best respond to racism—one going first in poetry, the other following his example in song.

Epilogue

RED, WHITE, AND (BACKLASH) BLUE: THE 1976 MONTREUX JAZZ FESTIVAL

When Nina Simone took the stage in Switzerland on July 3, 1976, New York City was only ten hours away from its bicentennial celebration on Sunday, July 4. The subject of freedom was also very much on Nina's mind. She opened the concert altering "Little Girl Blue" so that the subject was named throughout the song (for the only time) as "liberated little girl blue."[1] Her fourth song, "I Wish I Knew How It Would Feel to Be Free," ended with a declaration Nina could not make when she sang the song here in 1968. Having lived overseas in Monrovia, Liberia, since 1974, she could now safely say that she knew what freedom meant. As only Nina could, she also used the image of a bird in the song to connect freedom to spirituality by declaring, "*Jonathan Livingston Seagull* ain't got nothing on me." The allegorical book by Richard Bach had broken through to become a cult classic just a few years earlier. In between these two tunes, "Backlash Blues" offered a startling glimpse into how the land of the free was faring two hundred years after its founding.

Fig. 15.1. Nina Simone's Montreux Jazz Festival performances include her 1976 version of "Backlash Blues." *Nina Simone: The Montreux Years* (BMG, 2021).

Nina's only previous appearance at the festival, in 1968, resulted in a memorable interaction between her and a cameraman. Having just started the second song of her extensive fourteen-song set, Nina offered a gentle "shhhhh" forty-five seconds into "Just in Time." When a cameraman continued to snap photos, the noise from the shutter interrupted Nina's mood. He was both silenced and embarrassed when Nina quickly repeated "click" eight times in a row before swerving away from singing her vocals to instead veer off into a long and unexpected piano solo.[2]

Complicating Nina's inherent level of uncommon intensity, Simone played the 1976 Montreux Jazz Festival high from something she had either swallowed or smoked. It showed most when she insistently queried the crowd believing her new private fan David Bowie might be present. Confessing to the audience that she was "half high" during the final song only partially accounted for the bizarre events of the evening. Having watched the documentary film *Janis* the night before during her five-day stay in Switzerland, Nina started writing a song about the deceased singer Janis Joplin before settling on the idea that the living singer Janis Ian's song "Stars" already metaphorically addressed the subject of fleeting fame. It was an important topic that mirrored Nina's reflective mood at this stage of her now fully dormant career, and Nina decided to include it in her set. Nina would soon share with the crowd how it felt to use a name you never owned.

Following a set list written on a single piece of paper placed to her left on the piano, Simone started "Stars." Nina had sweat dripping down the left side of her brow. Using her left hand, she wiped it back up into her hair. Just then she spotted someone moving in the crowd. Looking straight ahead across the onyx Yamaha baby grand, she finished singing one of the early lines of "Stars." Just as she ended an early verse about musicians who "go like the last light of the sun all in a blaze," both hands suddenly stopped playing. Simone raised her right hand and pointed. Without blinking, she locked on a young woman, saying, "Hey girl, sit down." An interminable moment passed, and Nina seemed to welcome the tension.

"Sit *down*," she repeated.

With her hand still aiming, Simone raised her voice a final time at someone who could not believe they had been noticed on their way to step out quietly for a bathroom or smoke break.

"Sit Down!"

With the young woman returned to her seat, Nina started "Stars" over from the beginning, certain everyone knew who was in charge.

Though startling, this exchange with an audience member midway through her set should not have been the most memorable moment of her first return to the Swiss festival since 1968. Rather, Nina's alarming—and convincing—assertion near the end of a meandering rendition of "Feelings" seemed to go completely unnoticed. Turning both eyes toward the audience, Nina declared with remarkable transparency, "I wish I'd never lived this long." This dire thought went mysteriously ignored or forgotten (the track was never released).

Wearing a sheer black dress with an open back, Nina could move freely. Eventually, she convincingly displayed some traditional African dance moves. The High Priestess cast herself this evening as an African queen who had decided not to wear earrings. This choice strategically drew full attention to the dazzling Greek necklace recently bestowed upon her by festival organizer Claude Nobs. Wearing her hair very short and naturally styled, Nina proudly fondled the stunning diamonds hanging in a tight collar at her neck, asserting that they were "made for a queen, and I'm a queen." With her full spiritual ambiguity on display, she then understood that some might believe she really was royalty: "It just occurred to you it might be true."

Nina's rendition of "Backlash Blues" represents much more than an updated version of the song. As the longest version she recorded, it stands as one of the most enduring accomplishments of her career. After some mic issues, she was now fully relaxed in her performance, and she announced, "And I think we'll get to 'Backlash Blues' and pay Langston Hughes a tribute." Tonight's delicate version placed Nina's restrained prowess at the keyboard on full display. In an odd turn, the bicentennial year of 1976 turned "Mister Backlash" into a version of Uncle Sam. Rather than a politician responding to Black Power, he was now a figure who defined America to the greater world.

Stripped down to piano and drum kit, the barebones approach countered the metaphorical Uncle Backlash with the sounds of actual blues music. Though Nina clumsily repeated a few words at various times, she signaled how much things had changed since 1968 when she referenced Vietnam: "You send my only son to son to Vietnam (you see what happened there)." Her eye wink to the crowd immediately afterward suggested that Hughes had been correct that the war would become one way Mister Sam would learn about the collective power of a larger world.

Nina continued annotating her song with asides best printed in parentheses. Did the reference here to a country filled with "second-class fools" apply to those living in America or in Switzerland? In calling those who stayed behind "fools," Nina was almost agreeing with Mister Backlash as she then immediately continued: "That's the truth now." Having moved to Liberia in 1974, Nina could now distance herself intellectually and emotionally from those who stayed behind in the United States. Unlike her, they did not know the power and freedom of living in what she considered her ancestral homeland of Africa.

Nina's first of two trips through her third verse updated the lyric to emphasize the global impact of Uncle Sam. Mister Backlash is now given a new face: "Backlash (and Kissinger), I'm gonna leave you, and you already *got 'eeemmmm*, the blues." Raising the contraction a full octave and extending it for emphasis, Nina's "got 'em" ended with the last syllables vibrating inside her closed mouth to drive home America's definitive loss in Vietnam. The United States had a kind of blues the whole world recognized as it faced an unmitigated defeat. As Hughes forecast, that defeat came at the hands of a wide world filled with others labeled Yellow among an earth full of Black, Beige, and Brown. Henry Kissinger's uncommon complicity as the face of America's humiliating withdrawal from Vietnam resulted from serving simultaneously as both secretary of state and national security adviser under President Richard Nixon. In years to come, his disgrace would become eclipsed by Robert McNamara as the face of a US government that continued to send citizens to fight (and die) in what it knew would ultimately be a failed campaign.

Nina engaged the audience by talking to them. Her emphasis on the idea of not having "much time" followed the distinctive nasal cadences of Bob Dylan. Having recorded such Dylan tracks as "The Times They Are a Changin'," "I Shall Be Released," and others, Nina echoed Dylan's signature moan most unmistakably this evening when she sang the consecutive lines that end with the words "sea," "sing," "know," "feels," and "free" in her rendition of "I Wish I Knew How It Would Feel to Be Free."[3]

Voicing protest inside the Montreux casino, she reprised the third verse of "Backlash Blues" to raise the stakes for what was on the table. Dropping her poker face, Nina asserted that this was very personal: "When my daughter tries to find a little job to earn a little cash." A vein bulged in her neck and both arms pointed straight down to suggest that the issues were still immediate and inescapable. The rising defiance was calling. Both the singer and her listeners now had to show their cards. The world Nina had already "seen" was not full of people who were "yellow" but instead "Japanese."

Nina's aside that she has seen this world speaks to a growing maturity that now channels the international perspective of Langston Hughes. Having traveled to Europe and Africa, and now living in Liberia, her worldview is one that knows the United States better for having left it. With the war in Vietnam ended, Hughes's "Yellow" is updated to index the new rising power of Japan. Finally, her fourteen-year-old daughter Lisa's emerging aspirations to one day practice linguistics already felt blocked because of white academic gatekeepers. With applause now rising as she delivered these lines midsong, Nina backed the volume down to a softer set of whispers that culminated with a verse that was hummed, not spoken. Obedient as well-trained pets, the audience both cheered on cue and sat quietly on command.

Before testifying about what Hughes had once told her, she thoughtfully allowed her drummer to settle in by easing back on her keys for two percussive-centric passes through these twelve-bar blues. It was a wise move. After all, Simone had met her lone accompanist, Doug Hammond, only the day before.

When "Backlash Blues" ended with a whispered final line followed by two gentle chords from Nina's left hand, Mister Backlash had just experienced what Roberta Flack meant by "killing me softly."[4] The song over, Simone stood up and posed with her left hand on the piano. As she walked to the microphone, she bowed deeply in full knee bend, clasping each of her hands in a position of greeting that felt more Asian than African. The applause lasted well beyond the twenty-five seconds now captured on streaming services. Only two songs into her program, the crowd began clapping in unison. It was a preview of the way it would eventually implore Nina to return for one of her three encores.

One of only six songs she shared, "Backlash Blues" was much more than a critical staple in Nina's repertoire: Its signposts allowed Simone to critique America in an updated way that offered fresh commentary. Vietnam, Kissinger, and a fifteen-month bicentennial celebration provided images and allusions that educated Europe in ways of seeing a very different version of the United Sates that countered the one being patriotically projected at home.[5] Nina's version was not merely asserted; it was so convincing that it became accepted to everyone present that evening, to say nothing of the thousands of eventual listeners. Outdistancing formal diplomacy, Nina's music was a more believable and permanent ambassador.

With the civil rights movement over, "Backlash Blues" had a rejuvenated political relevance. Written only two years after "Mississippi Goddam," Hughes's song forecast Black artistic success and US failure on the world stage as concurrent truths. "Mississippi Goddam" would always represent a critical historical moment; "Backlash Blues" projected a futurity. The signature collaboration of Mr. Hughes and Miss Simone forever codified the very idea of "Backlash" itself into the American lexicon. Beginning quietly in conservative circles, the white backlash soon remerged emphatically in the long wake after the election of President Barack Obama in 2008. Even now, 250 years old, America is the home of the red, white, and blues.

ACKNOWLEDGMENTS

This project began in February 2020 while I was promoting my new biography of Langston Hughes. After telling a well-received story at the Busboys and Poets bookstore about Hughes serving as busboy at the Wardman Park Hotel in Washington, DC, I decided to add local color about the poet's ties to North Carolina for my next event, in Raleigh. After I informed the patrons at Quail Ridge Books that Hughes was asked to write the liner notes for a Nina Simone album, the audience gasped. I immediately knew I had to learn about every possible event connecting the Poet Laureate of Harlem and the High Priestess of Soul.

The previous seven biographies of Hughes—including the one I just finished—contained exactly one sentence referencing their relationship. Personal conversations with Simone biographer Nadine Cohodas established the frame, and I immediately began stretching the canvas. Now that the paint has dried, I have a host of people to thank beyond the incredibly gracious and kind Nadine.

My graduate seminar "Langston Hughes: From Popular Culture to the Civil Rights Movement" encourages local archival research. Researchers such as Kristina Beek, Jennifer Curry, Corey Foard, Isaac Green, Madison Lloyd, Madeline Preiss, Garrett Simco, and Maya Sinclair overcame the limitations of lockdown in the spring of 2020 to take up valuable explorations. Two scholars extended this work in significant ways. Austin Horne and Maj. Kelli Pryor uncovered new approaches to Hughes's typography and documented Simone's presence at the 1960 Newport Jazz Festival. Xavier Searle, Hannah Gaitlin, and Shelby Weisberg deserve equal praise for later exploring "Goodbye Newport Blues," as well as Nina's visits to Raleigh (1968) and Nigeria (1961). Mary Burnette's stories about rooming with Eunice Waymon on high school glee club trips were profoundly insightful. Thomas Calder's generosity enabled Lauren McKenzie to document and share the first set of Mary's remarkably clear memories. I thank Clare Grant for drawing my attention to the full correspondence between Langston Hughes and Claire Lennon. Kacey Cooper's MA thesis and ongoing PhD work on Hughes's visit to Wilson, North Carolina, in 1949 continues to inspire me. All the above-mentioned work is celebrated online in the digital humanities project *Backlash Blues: Nina Simone and Langston Hughes*, supported by funding provided by NC State University's Provost Professional Experience Program (2020–22). I also offer deep thanks to *Backlash Blues* site creators and contributors Carolin Benack, Patrick Elliott, Savannah Kirchner, Anne Marie Mullis, Sara Pinkowski, and Mandy Stacy.

My dear friend Mignon Durham gladly accompanied me to Tryon, North Carolina, for the groundbreaking of the Nina Simone Archive on May 1, 2021, where Beverly Kelly and John Wilkins shared stories with me of Nina. Crys Armbrust was kind enough to show me the original copy he owns of "Spotlight on Nina Simone," which Langston Hughes sent to Nina in November 1960.

Florence Blackwell and Dr. Akeia de Barros Gomes have deepened my understanding of events surrounding Newport. It was an honor to both formally consult for and learn from Florence as she completed her research at Brown University on Charles Mingus's and Max Roach's still-understudied Rebel Festival of 1960.

I was honored to receive a yearlong fellowship at the National Humanities Center in 2022–23. Robert Newman facilitated unparalleled scholarly resources as Matthew Booker provided continuous interest and support in shaping and publicizing this project. Librarians Brooke Andrade and Joe Millillo tracked down autographed editions of Carnegie Hall programs, hard copies of the *Philadelphia Tribune*, first pressings of Nina's albums, and the rare first promotional single for "Mississippi Goddam." Indispensable insights about Kurt Weill's music, Haiti, sound, hair, icons, *Star Trek*, "Gin House Blues," sound, color, and CIA agents were provided by NHC fellows Naomi André, Raphael Dalleo, Irving Goh, Blair LM Kelley, Martha M. F. Kelly, Elena Machado, Tricia Matthew, Umrao Sethi, and Cedric Tolliver. The first draft of this book was written at the NHC in 2022–23, fueled by these discussions, James Getkin's meals, and Thomas Reed's cookies.

Gregg Hecimovich and Jon Eig provided crucial feedback on drafts and energetic support for this project during definitive moments in its development. The works of David Cecelski and Greil Marcus complement efforts made by Jeff Arnal, Thomas Edward Frank, Mary Emma Harris, Kim Kowalke, Alice Sebrell, David Silver, and Everett B. Ward that also inform this project. David Garrow, Keith Miller, and Patrick Parr collectively provide an eminent source of constant intellectual and personal support.

At NC State, Sylvia Adcock, Vicki Cumbee, Marc Hall, and Chris Saunders brought this emerging research to several alumni channels. In addition to print, I thank the video work of Molly Donovan and Evan Kidd. For deep archival work and Nina's performance history on my campus, Todd Kosmerick and Mark Tulbert expertly supported this research.

Archivist Matthew Rowe was essential to the most recent research I conducted at the Beinecke Rare Book and Manuscript Library at Yale University in August 2022. My thanks to Douglas Remley at the National Museum of African American History and Culture.

I also thank Amelia Chase at the Alabama Department of Archives and History, and those who stored and then provided research into the American Society of African Culture Collection at the Moorland-Spingarn Research Center at Howard University. Coming in during the height of Covid, the masked Jan Grenci heroically searched the Prints and Photograph Collection for me at the Library of Congress. Other, equally important images were secured by Owen Kirchner and Gabriel Graña. Thank you.

Access to the Carnegie Hall Rose Archives in New York and SNCC documents cached at the Wisconsin Historical Society and the Center for Documentary Studies at Duke University were as valuable as rare audio shared from wax cylinders by Phillip MacDonald at the Repository, Collections and Archives at Duke University Libraries. As for Hughes's visit to North Carolina in 1949, very special thanks go all the way back seventy-five years to the full staffs of Irene Hendrick of the Asheville Negro Library, Mollie Huston Lee of the Richard B. Harrison Library in Raleigh, and Mary Hairston of the George Moses Horton Branch Library in Winston-Salem. I extend current thanks to Lisa Y. Henderson of Black Wide Awake, Kathy Hill of Buncombe County Special Collections at Asheville's Pack Memorial Library, Monica Lucas of Wake Country Libraries, Elizabeth Jenkins and Tammy Medlin at the Wilson County Public Library, and Heather South of the Western Regional Archives.

Musician Sandra Dubose and North Carolina legend Jaki Shelton Green provided unforgettable insight when I shared this emerging research during a series of performance outreach events with them at the North Carolina Museum of Art under the unequaled vision of Moses T. Alexander Greene.

I thank Austin Miller for his diligence and expertise in once again preparing critical elements of these reference materials.

Not only is it an honor to be included in editor David Menconi's *American Music: New Roots* series, but one could not imagine the joy I felt from working with Executive Editor Lucas Church and the full team of professionals at UNC Press, including Thomas Bedenbaugh, Laura Jones Dooley, Erin Granville, Helen Kyriakoudes, and Lindsay Starr.

To my darling wife, Sherri, once again—please know you have my deepest gratitude. So often breathed, these thanks are set in ink.

NOTES

PROLOGUE

1. The Reverend C. T. Vivian kindly shared this story with me in person when he visited Raleigh, NC, on October 27, 2013.

2. King's address to the crowd can be viewed at the 25 sec. mark of "Stars for Freedom Rally, Third Selma March, 1965," posted on August 5, 2021, by HuntleyFilmArchives, YouTube, www.youtube.com/watch?v=GJynHdBkGLI.

3. Gordon, "Al Schackman on Nina Simone."

4. Light, *What Happened, Miss Simone?*, 114.

5. Simone, *I Put a Spell on You*, 103.

6. Wald, *This Is Rhythm*, 179, 8.

7. Miller, *Langston Hughes and American Lynching Culture*, 1.

8. Miller, "Turnarounds in Langston Hughes's Poetry," 150–51.

9. Simone, *I Put a Spell on You*, 96.

10. Eig, *King*, 322.

CHAPTER 1

1. "Langston Hughes Reads Poems Before Large Audience Here," *Winston-Salem (NC) Journal*, February 7, 1949, 5.

2. For a complete account of Hughes's time at Black Mountain College, see Miller, "Poet Langston Hughes's Unknown."

3. For a complete summary of Hughes's week of events, see "Timeline: Langston Hughes in North Carolina," Biography section, Backlash Blues: Nina Simone and Langston Hughes (website), accessed October 31, 2025, www.backlash-blues.com/allen-school-1949.

4. Hughes's itinerary for the trip can be found in Box 480, Folder 12048, Langston Hughes Papers, Beinecke Rare Book and Manuscript Library, Yale University, New Haven, CT (hereinafter LHP).

5. At home in Harlem, Hughes signed books in green ink. He used black only while traveling.

6. For more on rural literacy and Hughes's full trip to Wilson, NC, in 1949, see Kacey Cooper's digital humanities project Welcome to Wilson, NC, Mr. Hughes!, https://kaceykcoop.wixsite.com/freedomsplow.

7. Hughes notes these performers in LHP, Box 480, Folder 12048.

8. Langston Hughes, "Poetry Buys a Ticket for Little Trip South During History Week," *Chicago Defender*, February 26, 1949, 10.

9. "Langston Hughes Reads Poems Before Large Audience Here," *Winston-Salem (NC) Journal*, February 7, 1949, 5.

10. Miller, *Langston Hughes*, 10–13.

11. Jennifer Schuessler, "Langston Hughes Just Got a Year Older," *New York Times*, August 9, 2018, C1.

12. Rampersad, *Life of Langston Hughes*, 1:12–13.

13. Rampersad, *Life of Langston Hughes*, 1:13.

14. Miller, *Langston Hughes*, 14.

15. Miller, *Langston Hughes*, 19–20.

16. Hughes, *Big Sea*, 47.

17. Sharpley-Whiting, *Bricktop's Paris*, 27.

18. Berry, *Langston Hughes*, 62.

19. Langston Hughes, "The Negro Artist and the Racial Mountain," *Nation*, June 23, 1926, 692.

20. Rampersad, *Life of Langston Hughes*, 1:78.

21. Rampersad, *Life of Langston Hughes*, 1:78.

22. Maxwell, *F. B. Eyes*, 237.

23. Miller, *Origins of the Dream*, 1.

24. Ferris, "Interview with Margaret Walker," 54.

25. Rampersad, *Life of Langston Hughes*, 2:107–9.

26. Rampersad, *Life of Langston Hughes*, 2:107–9.

27. Hughes, *Selected Letters*, 306.

28. Rampersad, *Life of Langston Hughes*, 2:124–25.

29. The following summary of Hughes's exhaustive drive to have his songs recorded comes from his own files, LHP, Box 511, Folders 12668–76.

30. Hughes's personal notes to "Blueberry Hill" can be found in LHP, Box 511, Folder 12680.

31. For more, Hughes's personal notes to "Blueberry Hill" can be found in LHP, Box 511 Folder 12680.

32. "Hughes Reads Poems Before Large Audience."

CHAPTER 2

1. Unless otherwise noted, all Mary Burnette quotations in this chapter are from her interview by Lauren McKenzie, June 26, 2021, in the author's possession.

2. Lords, dir., *Nina Simone*.

3. Cohodas, *Princess Noire*, 45–46.

4. For more about M. W. Warren performing, see "Langston Hughes Reads Poems Before Large Audience Here," *Winston-Salem (NC) Journal*, February 7, 1949, 5. Hughes references Delores Fullman in his personal itineraries, LHP, Box 480, Folder 12048.

5. My deep thanks to Claire Grant for locating the correspondence between Hughes and Claire Lennon. The three Hughes songs were "The Negro Speaks of Rivers," "At the Feet of Jesus," and "This Is My Land." As he did in his correspondence with the folks in Wilson, NC,

Hughes also sent a chapbook of his long poem "Freedom's Plow." Though it was performed by students in Wilson at the St. Alphonsus Catholic School, there is no indication that the students at Allen performed Hughes's historical poem. For more on the poem and songs, see Langston Hughes to Claire Lennon, December 10, 1948, LHP, Box 5, Folder 101.

6. "Poet to Appear at School on Tuesday," *Asheville (NC) Citizen-Times*, February 4, 1949.

7. "Negro Library Will Observe History Week," *Asheville (NC) Citizen-Times*, February, 6, 1949, 3.

8. "Negro Library Will Observe."

9. "Negro Library Will Observe."

10. Hughes received the check for this performance fee by mail on January 3, 1949, a full month before he appeared. For more, see Nate White to Lennon, November 22, 1948, LHP, Box 5, Folder 101.

11. Lennon to Hughes, December 6, 1948, LHP, Box 5, Folder 101.

12. For more on Hughes's housing in Asheville and the school's excitement, see Lennon to Hughes, February 1, 1949, LHP, Box 5, Folder 101.

13. Langston Hughes, "Poetry Buys a Ticket for Little Trip South During History Week," *Chicago Defender*, February 26, 1949, 6.

14. Hughes to Lennon, January 27, 1949, LHP, Box 5, Folder 101.

15. Hughes to Lennon, January 5, 1949, LHP, Box 5, Folder 101.

16. Bolden, "Retrospective View of Soul," 130.

17. London, dir., *Disappearance of Miss Scott*.

18. For more, see Kyle Macdonald, "Nina Simone Plays a Stunning Bach-Style Fugue in the Middle of One of Her Classic Songs," ClassicFM.com, updated January 20, 2022, www.classicfm.com/discover-music/instruments/piano/nina-simone-improvises-bach-fugue-classic-song/.

19. Maya Angelou, "Nina Simone: High Priestess of Soul," *Redbook*, November 1970, 132.

20. Mary Burnette, email correspondence with author, September 29, 2022.

21. Anne Hunter Jenkins, "News Polices of Papers Criticized," *Asheville (NC) Citizen-Times*, February 13, 1949. 5.

22. Halsey Leavitt, "Reader Criticizes Langston Hughes," *Asheville (NC) Citizen-Times*, February 20, 1949, 5.

23. Julia Titus, "Recalls Address by Langston Hughes," *Asheville (NC) Citizen-Times*, February 27, 1949, 5.

24. Titus, "Recalls Address by Langston Hughes."

25. Titus, "Recalls Address by Langston Hughes."

26. Lennon to Hughes, February 24, 1949, LHP, Box 5, Folder 101.

27. Lennon to Hughes, February 24, 1949.

28. Lennon to Hughes, March 5, 1949, LHP, Box 5, Folder 101.

29. Langston Hughes, "Langston Hughes Answers Critics," *Asheville Citizen-Times* (NC), April 3, 1949, 5.

30. Claire Lennon to Langston Hughes, April 18, 1949, LHP, Box 5, Folder 101.

31. "Dupes and Fellow Travelers Dress Up Communist Fronts," *Life*, April 4, 1949.

32. Hughes, "Langston Hughes Answers Critics."

33. Langston Hughes, "A Portent and a Warning to the Negro People from Hughes," *Chicago Defender*, February 5, 1949, 6.

34. Millender, *Martin Luther King, Jr.*, 118.

35. "Dr. William Holmes Borders Gives Resume of Negro History in His Poem That Will Eventually Become a Classic in American History and Literature," *Pittsburgh Courier*, February 20, 1943.

CHAPTER 3

1. Hughes's calendar noting this appointment can be found in LHP, Box 491 [no folder].

2. This list is found in LHP, Box 512, Folder 12722.

3. This first meeting between Hughes and Simone likely occurred on the night of one of Simone's performances at the Village Gate on either April 27 or May 11, 1959.

4. Nelson, dir., *Miles Davis*.

5. Ben H. Bagdikian, "Jazzmen in Revolt," *Evening Bulletin* (Providence, RI), July 1, 1960, 1.

6. Studs Terkel, "Langston Hughes, John Sellers, James Cotton, and Otis Spann Discuss Blues Music," aired July 15, 1960, on WFMT radio, available at Studs Terkel Radio Archive, https://studsterkel.wfmt.com/programs/langston-hughes-john-sellers-james-cotton-and-otis-spann-discuss-blues-music. The error in attribution stems from the fact that Hughes included this song in *The Big Sea* (1940), and many then assumed it was an early unpublished poem of his own.

7. Langston Hughes, "Gloomy Day at Newport," *Chicago Defender*, July 30, 1960, 10.

8. Langston Hughes, "Gloomy Day at Newport," 1.

9. "Armstrong, Mulligan Top Tonight's Jazz Program," *Newport (RI) Daily News*, July 1, 1960, 1.

10. Terkel, "Langston Hughes, John Sellers."

11. Saul, *Freedom Is, Freedom Ain't*, 99.

12. Saul, *Freedom Is, Freedom Ain't*, 100.

13. Hughes, "Gloomy Day at Newport," *Chicago Defender*, July 30, 1960, 10.

14. Saul, *Freedom Is, Freedom Ain't*, 100.

15. Saul, *Freedom Is, Freedom Ain't*, 101.

16. This prepared script can be found in LHP, Box 482, Folder 12193.

17. Smith, *Albums That Changed Popular Music*, 59.

18. This series of events can be seen near the 27 min., 44 sec., mark of "Muddy Waters Newport Jazz Festival 1960," posted on July 23, 2017, by Huck Finn, YouTube, www.youtube.com/watch?v=fLTCIqfsefc.

19. Terkel, "Langston Hughes, John Sellers."

20. A copy of this comment from the October 1961 edition of *Audio and Record Review* (London) can be found in LHP, Box 564, Folder 13521.

21. Hughes's drafts to "Newport Blues" can be found in LHP, Box 393, Folder 7477.

22. "Newport Jazz Festival Closed Because of Rioting," *New York Times*, July 4, 1960, 1.

23. Festival organizer George Wein reportedly "bawled like a baby" when he heard the lyrics to Hughes's song being performed. For more, see "Music: Newport Blues," *Time*, July 18, 1960.

24. Both the typed lyrics and Hughes's note can be seen in LHP, Box 393, Folder 7477.

25. A copy of this laudatory comment from the October 1961 edition of *Audio and Record Review* (London) has been highlighted in yellow (and underlined in red pencil) by Hughes. See LHP, Box 564, Folder 13521.

26. Simone, *You've Got to Learn*.

CHAPTER 4

1. This notebook can be found in LHP, Box 271, Folder 4453.

2. This notebook can be found in LHP, Box 271, Folder 4453.

3. The location for these engagements was the Village Gate, Nina's home base in Greenwich Village. For more, see Brun-Lambert, *Nina Simone*, 72.

4. Cohodas, *Princess Noire*, 110.

5. Saul, *Freedom Is, Freedom Ain't*, 142.

6. This editorial change can be found in LHP, Box 272, Folder 4467. Using the gorgeous first edition of *Ask Your Mama* as a reference, I have softened the "ALL CAPS" to small capital letters throughout to capture the way it was originally intended to be experienced.

7. This editorial change can be found in LHP, Box 272, Folder 4467.

8. Langston Hughes to W. E. B. Du Bois, May 22, 1956, LHP, Box 57, Folder 1073.

9. As scholar Kevin Thomas Miles notes, this confrontation with a page of written music becomes "the site at which one form of knowing confronts another and finds no passage for itself as itself beyond the site for confrontation." For more, see Miles, "Haunting Music, 206.

10. Miles, "Haunting Music," 202.

11. This sheet music can be found in LHP, Box 272, Folder 4467.

12. This note is on a slip of paper in LHP, Box 272, Folder 4470.

13. Hughes's files concerning what he learned about "playing the dozens" by speaking to Harlem resident Charles McCoy and reading both a 1939 article by John Dollard and a 1958 academic article by William Elton can be found in LHP, Box 271, Folder 4452.

14. This intended press release is housed in LHP, Box 272, Folder 4472.

15. Hughes to LeRoi Jones, April 27, 1961, LHP, Box 12, Folder 268.

16. The red pencil marks omitting this section from his script are in LHP, Box 272, Folder 4465.

17. Hughes, *Black Verse*.

18. Priestley, *Mingus*, 115.

19. This hand-drawn map is located in LHP, Box 482, Folder 12184.

20. "Cliff Walk Manor's Jazz Concert Well-Attended at Midnight Session," *Newport (RI) Daily News*, July 2, 1960, 3.

21. Reed, *Soundworks*, 72.

22. I visited Newport in July 2025 to stay at the Hotel Viking and map this route by foot. The former Cliff Walk Manor where Mingus stayed is the Chanler hotel today.

23. Mingus confronted Wein at the Hotel Viking (where Hughes was staying) sometime on June 30, 1960. Ben H. Bagdikian, "Jazzmen in Revolt," *Evening Bulletin* (Providence, RI), July 1, 1960, 10.

CHAPTER 5

1. Langston Hughes to Nina Simone, October 2, 1960, LHP, Box 147, Folder 2724.

2. Hughes's consecutive calendar entries from 1960 can be found in LHP, Box 491 [no folder].

3. Hughes to Simone, October 2, 1960.

4. Hughes's calendar entry can be found in LHP, Box 491 [no folder].

5. Simone to Hughes, October 6, 1960, LHP, Box 147, Folder 2724.

6. Hughes to Simone, October 4, 1960, courtesy Dr. Crys Armbrust, Tryon, NC.

7. Betsy Schlabach, "The Love Between Langston Hughes and Gwendolyn Brooks," Black Perspectives, February 13, 2017, www.aaihs.org/the-love-between-langston-hughes-and-gwendolyn-brooks/.

8. Langston Hughes, "Ballad in Black and White," *Chicago Defender*, September 1, 1945, 12.

9. This draft can be found in LHP, Box 416, Folder 9064.

10. Cohodas, *Princess Noire*, 106. I also thank Nadine Cohodas for her helpful insights about this project over several conversations.

11. Langston Hughes, "Spotlight on Nina Simone," *Chicago Defender*, November 12, 1960, 10.

12. Cohodas, *Princess Noire*, 62.

13. Rampersad, *Life of Langston Hughes*, 2:330.

14. Hughes, *Langston Hughes and the South African Drum Generation*, 128.

15. This draft can be found in LHP, Box 416, Folder 9064.

16. It is uncertain whether Hughes watched this performance, though Eartha Kitt's appearance on the same Sunday evening episode raises that likelihood (as she was also being mentored by Hughes).

17. This draft can be found in LHP, Box 416, Folder 9064.

18. This draft can be found in LHP, Box 416, Folder 9064.

19. This draft can be found in LHP, Box 416, Folder 9064.

20. Langston Hughes, "Nina Simone," *New York Post*, June 29, 1962.

21. Cohodas, *Princess Noire*, 151.

22. This letter can be found in LHP, Box 416, Folder 9064.

CHAPTER 6

1. Letter from Langston Hughes, November 10, 1961, in Hughes, *Langston Hughes and the South African Drum Generation*, 133.

2. Memo from Evelyn Lincoln, October 27, 1961, John F. Kennedy Library, Boston, Sanford L. Fox Papers, 8.8, Series 2.

3. I thank Cedric Tolliver for so astutely bringing the connections between AMSAC and the CIA to my attention across multiple conversations.

4. Wilford, *Mighty Wurlitzer*, 24–25.

5. Rampersad, *Life of Langston Hughes*, 2:400.

6. Tolliver, *Vagabonds and Fellow Travelers*, 41.

7. The outline of these events is located in LHP, Box 483, Folder 12208.

8. Rampersad, *Life of Langston Hughes*, 2:343.

9. Simone, *I Put a Spell on You*, 79.

10. Simone, *I Put a Spell on You*, 77. Though heretofore ignored, Simone alludes to being abused just once in her entire discography. In her 1968 performance at the Montreux Jazz Festival, the song "The House of the Rising Sun" includes three biographical details that do not appear in any other known performance of the song as recorded by any artist as she once again takes on the persona of a sex worker. First, Nina references her "baby sister" who is "in Detroit" at 2 min., 19 sec., of the song. (It is unclear whether this is also the person she is referencing in the same concert performance of "I Wish I Knew How It Would Feel to Be Free" when she later says, "Because my second soul is coming 'round now / 'bout

July 7, she's comin' 'round now"). Second, Simone sings with further biographical accuracy in "The House of the Rising Sun" that her mother (Kate) is a "a preacher" (3 min., 55 sec., into her live performance). Third, and finally, Nina sings of a lover who may stand in for how she perceives her husband, Andy: "My sweetheart is a drunkard he always hits hits" (repeated twice by Simone).

11. Cohodas, *Princess Noire*, 118–19.

12. Cohodas, *Princess Noire*, 119.

13. These seating placements and travel arrangements are documented by two photographs featured in the film *The Amazing Nina Simone* (2015).

14. Nina Simone to Andy Stroud, December 17, 1961, National Museum of African American History and Culture, Washington, DC (hereinafter NMAAHC), https://nmaahc.si.edu/object/nmaahc_2011.132.3a-e.

15. I thank the research librarians at the National Humanities Center who secured so many of these documents during my yearlong fellowship in 2022–23 so that I could provide the first-ever full account of this overlooked festival.

16. Simone to Stroud, December 17, 1961, NMAAHC.

17. Hughes notes these activities in his personal papers located in LHP, Box 463, Folder 11245.

18. Olabode Festus Omojola, "Victor Olaiya: Stadium Hotel, Highlife, and Nostalgia," *The Conversation*, April 27, 2020, https://theconversation.com/victor-olaiya-stadium-hotel-highlife-and-nostalgia-136072.

19. Simone to Stroud, December 17, 1961, NMAAHC.

20. Washington, "Desegregating the 1950s," 28.

21. De Santis, *Let America Be America Again*, 177, 182.

22. Wilford, *Mighty Wurlitzer*, 30.

23. This correspondence can be found in LHP, Box 484, Folder 12207.

24. Washington, "Desegregating the 1950s," 28.

25. Miller, "Langston Hughes and Martin Luther King," 30.

26. Miller, "Langston Hughes and Martin Luther King," 22.

27. Simone to Stroud, December 17, 1961, NMAAHC.

28. "The Nights Benson Stole the Show," *Daily Express*, December 21, 1961, 5.

29. "Nights Benson Stole the Show."

30. "AMSAC Presents a Stupendous Display," *Africa* (Lagos, Nigeria), February 1962, 11.

31. For the definitive account of Weston's lifelong engagements with Africa, as well as his friendship during this 1961 trip with Bobby Benson, see chapter 2 of Robin D. G. Kelley's superb *Africa Speaks*.

32. April Sizemore-Barber, "The Voice of (Which?) Africa," 266.

33. This original December 5, 1961, agenda can be found in LHP, Box 463, Folder 11245.

34. Rampersad, *Life of Langston Hughes*, 2:348.

35. Pan, "Stop Faking African Culture."

36. "Nigerians Ridicule AMSAC Production," *New York Amsterdam News*, February 10, 1962, 2.

37. Keefe, "America's Secret Weapon."

38. Rampersad, *Life of Langston Hughes*, 2:348.

39. "AMSAC Presents a Stupendous Display,"12.

40. Cohodas, *Princess Noire*, 124.

41. "AMSAC Presents a Stupendous Display," 12.

42. "Nights Benson Stole the Show."

43. For more on Brock Peters, see "Why AMSAC Festival Was a Flop," *Daily Express* (Lagos, Nigeria), December 22, 1961, 3. Disparaging remarks about Italian arias and Babatunde "Michael" Olatunji can be found in Sango Africanus, "The Shortcomings of AMSAC Show," *Morning Post* (Lagos, Nigeria), January 2, 1962, 13.

44. "Nigerians Ridicule AMSAC Production."

45. "AMSAC Presents a Stupendous Display," 13.

46. Wilford, *Mighty Wurlitzer*, 32.

47. Questionnaires, Langston Hughes and Nina Simone, January 31, 1962, Box 4, Folder 5, AMSAC Collection, Moorland-Spingarn Research Center, Howard University.

48. Memo, Lagos Festival Participants, October 21, 1961, Box 30, Folder 7, AMSAC Collection, Moorland-Spingarn Research Center, Howard University.

49. Nina Simone to Andy Stroud, December 17, 1961, NMAAHC, https://nmaahc.si.edu/object/nmaahc_2011.132.3a-e.

50. Hughes's and Simone's room numbers at the Federal Palace Hotel are recorded carefully (along with those of most of the other thirty-three AMSAC delegates); however, they are inadvertently misfiled as the last entry in Hughes's Yale files concerning his earlier November 1960 visit to Nigeria. LHP, Box 482, Folder 12189.

51. Rampersad, *Life of Langston Hughes*, 2:349.

CHAPTER 7

1. Andy Stroud to Langston Hughes, February 18, 1964, LHP, Box 147, Folder 2724.

2. Langston Hughes to Nina Simone, telegram, March 21, 1964, LHP, Box 147, Folder 2724.

3. The creative tack in this chapter seeks to blend "books" one and two of the approach expertly employed by Tracy Sharpley-Whiting in *Bricktop's Paris*. It also follows the kind of imaginative play with photography that shapes Rachel Cohen's equally engaging *A Chance Meeting: American Encounters*.

4. Simone to Hughes, card, October 20, 1961, LHP, Box 147, Folder 2724.

5. Simone, *I Put a Spell on You*, 96.

6. Hughes to Simone, June 18, 1963, LHP, Box 147, Folder 2724.

7. The memo sheet with these two phone numbers can be found at LHP, Box 509, Folder 12634.

8. Hughes to Simone, June 18, 1963.

9. Hughes to Simone, June 18, 1963.

10. Hughes to Simone, January 31, 1964, LHP, Box 147, Folder 2724.

11. Cohodas, *Princess Noire*, 312.

12. Cohodas, *Princess Noire*, 157.

13. Langston Hughes, "Simple's Prize," *New York Post*, October 19, 1962, 44.

14. For the first full (and exemplary) discussion of this connection, see Brooks, "Nina Simone's Triple Play."

15. Feldstein, *How It Feels to Be Free*, 28.

16. Langston Hughes, "Jim Crow's Funeral," *New York Post*, November 30, 1962, 50. There is no indication that any of these references by Hughes are in any way related to Simone's performances of the song "Go to Hell."

17. Langston Hughes, "Thorns," *New York Post*, April 26, 1963, 38.
18. Feldstein, "I Don't Trust You Anymore," 1352.
19. Hughes, *Selected Letters*, 395.
20. The original text is in all caps. It can be found in the LHP, Box 509, Folder 12637.
21. This invitation is located in LHP, Box 147, Folder 2724.
22. Cohodas, *Princess Noire*, 157.
23. Simone to Hughes, June 28, 1964, LHP, Box 509, Folder 12637.
24. Stroud to Hughes, November 19, 1964, LHP, Box 509, Folder 12637.

CHAPTER 8

1. Margaret Bonds to Langston Hughes, March 27, 1962, Georgetown University, Maragaret Bonds Papers, Box 4.
2. Hamn, "Popular Adaptations of Weills' Music," 61, 76. My deep thanks to Naomi André for putting me in touch with Weill expert Kim Kowalke, who generously led me to this wealth of information.
3. Brooks, "Nina Simone's Triple Play," 179.
4. For more about the impact of this song on Bob Dylan, see Dylan, *Chronicles*, 272–76; and Marcus, *Folk Music*, 98–100. Given the content of the song, it seems highly relevant that Joan Baez remembers Dylan writing the song immediately after he had issues at the front desk while trying to check into a hotel. Baez had to vouch for Dylan (given his hobo aesthetic and slovenly look that day).
5. Stein, *Fantasies of Nina Simone*, 87.
6. Liberman, dir., *Amazing Nina Simone*.
7. Hamn, "Popular Adaptations of Weill's Music," 41–42.
8. Nina played the Brecht–Weill song "Mr. Smith" in 1984 at Ronnie Scott's. She also played an all-Brecht program at the Brooklyn Academy of Music on January 14, 1973. For more, see Cohodas, *Princess Noire*, 275.
9. Cohodas, *Princess Noire*, 68.
10. I thank Naomi André for loaning me her expertise to talk me through the musical intricacies of these two songs. The best ideas that follow are thanks to her.
11. Weill and Brecht, *Threepenny Opera*, album liner notes.
12. These appointments with Baker are located in Hughes's personal calendars in LHP, Box 491 [no folder].
13. Hughes, *Arna Bontemps-Langston Hughes Letters*, 472.
14. Hughes, *Selected Letters*, 401.
15. Hughes's list of song suggestions for Simone is in LHP, Box 403, Folder 8127.
16. For more on Hansberry, see these excellent biographies: Colbert, *Radical Vision*, and Perry, *Looking for Lorriane*.
17. This list of song suggestions for Simone is in LHP, Box 403, Folder 8127.
18. Hughes to Nina Simone, telegram, January 15, 1965, LHP, Box 147, Folder 2724.
19. Hughes to Simone, January 26, 1965, LHP, Box 147, Folder 2724.
20. Hughes received a book about Haitian practices from Hermina Dumont Huswood in 1947. For more, see Dalleo, *American Imperialism's Undead*, 111.
21. Hughes, *Troubled Island*, act 2, scene 1.

CHAPTER 9

1. Nina Simone to Langston Hughes, July 6, 1965, LHP, Box 147, Folder 2724.

2. "Seeing the Color of the Soul," *St. Louis (MO) Globe Democrat*, May 8, 1904, 54.

3. "Wife Names 122 'Other Women,'" *Oklahoma Leader* (Oklahoma City), December 30, 1922, 2.

4. "Sharon," *Palm Beach (FL) Post*, July 28, 1974, 32.

5. Leonard Feather, "Nina: High Priestess of Soul Heads for Vegas," *Melody Maker*, March 11, 1967, 13.

6. "High Priestess of Soul," *New York Evening Post*, September 16, 1968, 2.

7. Hugh Wyatt, "Nina's 'Soul' Reigns 6th Year," *New York Daily News*, July 5, 1968, 38.

8. Garland, *Sound of Soul*, 22.

9. "Educational Programming Scheduled on Channel 35-ETV Columbia," *Times and Democrat* (Orangeburg, SC), February 14, 1971, 8.

10. Roy Kohler, "The 'Sound of Soul' Strikes Right Chord," *Pittsburgh Press*, November 16, 1969, 14.

11. Garland, *Sound of Soul*, 202.

12. Garland, *Sound of Soul*, 123.

13. Lieberman, dir., *Nina Simone: The Legend*, film.

14. This song can be heard on the album *It Is Finished*.

15. As for the Caribbean, Nina had been to Barbados twice. In 1970, she went after permanently leaving her husband, Andy Stroud. Later, in 1974, Nina was in a deep love affair with the country's prime minister, Errol Barrow.

16. This song can also be heard on the album *It Is Finished*.

CHAPTER 10

1. John Kruth, "Rickie Havens Revisited," *Please Kill Me*, February 28, 2022, https://pleasekillme.com/richie-havens/.

2. Kruth, "Rickie Havens Revisited."

3. Browne, *Talkin' Greenwich Village*, 42.

4. This riff is extremely similar to what Nina plays instead with her left hand on the song "God, God, God," *Live at Ronnie Scott's*, 1985.

5. Tillet, "Strange Sampling," 129.

6. White, "No Hidin' Place."

7. It may be noteworthy that Nina sang a poignant version of another, perhaps related song when she took to the piano and sang with both her mother, Kate, and daughter Lisa. The documentary *Nina Simone: The Legend* (1991) captures the three together in Tryon, NC, singing the refrain: "Take Me to That Hiding Place."

8. The lyrics to "Power" can be found in LHP, Box 403, Folder 8127.

9. These three performances are recorded in Hughes's personal calendars in LHP, Box 491 [no folder].

10. These lyrics are located in LHP, Box 403, Folder 8127.

11. John F. Kennedy, "Address at Rice University on the Nation's Space Effort, September 12, 1962," John F. Kennedy Presidential Library and Museum, www.jfklibrary.org/archives/other-resources/john-f-kennedy-speeches/rice-university-19620912.

12. Hughes's complete lyrics to "Power" can be found in LHP, Box 403, Folder 8127.
13. Hughes's reference to "Swanee River" can be found in LHP, Box 403, Folder 8127.
14. Hughes's complete lyrics to "Power" can be found in LHP, Box 403, Folder 8127.

CHAPTER 11

1. Cohodas, *Princess Noire*, 174.

2. These songs can be viewed at "Nina Simone Live in Holland 1965," posted on June 24, 2020, by 22over7guy, YouTube, www.youtube.com/watch?v=fMZKhPN4N8s.

3. *Eyes on the Prize.*

4. During his life, the name "De Lawd" was applied to King in many contexts. For more, see both "Civil Rights: The Law and De Lawd," *Time*, November 5, 1965; and "Martin Luther King, Jr., Mentors and Allies," People section, SNCC Digital Gateway (website), accessed November 5, 2025, https://snccdigital.org/people/martin-luther-king-jr/.

5. Lomax, *When the Word Is Given*, 199.

6. Parr, *Malcolm Before X*, 199.

7. Langston Hughes, "If Simple Went to Selma," *Chicago Defender*, April 24, 1965, 8.

8. Charles Barron, "Black Power! Still Needed! Still Relevant!," *New York Amsterdam News*, October 31, 2019, https://amsterdamnews.com/news/2019/10/31/black-power-still-needed-still-relevant/.

9. Minnis, *Care and Feeding of Power Structures*, 7.

10. Yerkey, *He's Coming to Start Riots*, 70.

11. Yerkey, *He's Coming to Start Riots*, 57.

12. Light, *What Happened, Miss Simone?*, 101–2.

13. Light, *What Happened, Miss Simone?*, 92.

14. Light, *What Happened, Miss Simone?*, 129.

15. For more, see "Inside SNCC," SNCC Digital Gateway, https://snccdigital.org/inside-sncc/sncc-culture/.

16. Cohodas, *Princess Noire*, 153–54.

17. "Willie Ricks Interview for Voices Across the Color Line Oral History Project (Part 2 of 2), posted on June 27, 2016, by Atlanta History Center, YouTube, www.youtube.com/watch?v=kZpUak4YLyA&t=669s (10 min. mark).

18. Stokely Carmichael, "Stokely Carmichael," *The Movement: SNCC Newsletter*, June 1966, 7.

19. Carmichael, "Stokely Carmichael," 7.

20. Yerkey, *He's Coming to Start Riots*, 79.

21. This quotation is an outtake from an interview with Carmichael conducted on November 7, 1985. It was intended for the film *Eyes on the Prize: America at the Racial Crossroads, 1965–1985*. Washington University Libraries, Film and Media Archive, Henry Hampton Collection, Eyes on the Prize Interviews. It can be viewed here: https://vimeopro.com/crma/eyes-on-the-prize-interviews/video/1000139232.

22. I thank the devoted research librarians at the National Humanities Center for providing me two months' worth of copies of the *Philadelphia Tribune*, a hard-to-find newspaper that can be accessed only in hard copy.

23. It appears that Nina was first introduced to Stokely by her friend (and his later wife) singer Miriam Makeba. For more, see Hampton, *Nina Simone*, 40.

24. Chet Coleman, "'Black Power,' Beauty Unity Rally Themes," *Philadelphia Tribune*, July 19, 1966, 1.

25. Coleman, "'Black Power,' Beauty."

26. Ray McGann, "Hail Singer Nina Simone as 'Black Power' Princess," *Philadelphia Tribune*, December 20, 1966, 3.

27. McGann, "Hail Singer Nina Simone."

CHAPTER 12

1. "Statement by Dr. Martin Luther King, Jr.," Southern Christian Leadership Conference press release, October 14, 1966, Wisconsin Historical Society, Student Nonviolent Coordinate Committee, MSS 577, image #6610.

2. John J. Waggy Jr., "Black Power and the Disrobing of White Liberality," sermon, Church of the First Unitarian Society, Schenectady, NY, October 23, 1966, Wisconsin Historical Society, Student Nonviolent Coordinate Committee, MSS 577, image #661023.

3. Donald Szantho Harrington, "What's the Matter with Black Power?," sermon, the Community Church of New York, October 2, 1966, Wisconsin Historical Society, Student Nonviolent Coordinate Committee, MSS 577, Folder 661002.

4. Henry Golden, "Black Power Brought Out White Backlash," *Chicago Defender*, December 17, 1966, 12.

5. Cathy Aldridge, "Langston Hughes Mourned; Memorial Monday: Schedule Hughes Memorial Mourned," *New York Amsterdam News*, May 27, 1967, 1.

6. Hamn, "Popular Adaptations of Weill's Music," 69.

7. De Santis, *Let America Be America Again*, 171.

8. This and all quotes that follow are my transcriptions from "Black Power, White Backlash, Documentary (CBS 1966)," posted November 29, 2020, by thepostarchive, YouTube, www.youtube.com/watch?v=otMQeJFOAzM.

9. All of Hughes's drafts to this poem (cited throughout this chapter) can be found in LHP, Box 373, Folder 6135.

10. Jackie Robinson, "'White Backlash' Threatens Black Hopefuls at the Polls," *Philadelphia Tribune*, November 8, 1966, 7.

11. "People Are Talking About," *Jet*, June 1, 1967.

12. I thank the research librarians at the National Humanities Center who kindly secured every album missing from my discography of Simone's work during my yearlong fellowship in 2022–23.

13. "Langston Hughes Speaking at UCLA 2/16/1967," posted on December 2, 2014, by UCLA Irv and Xiaoyan Drasnin Communication Archive, YouTube, www.youtube.com/watch?v=Px5hwNCs9ss.

14. Miller, "Dreams of Hughes and King," 35.

15. "Composers and Musicians for Peace Chamber Orchestra and Chorus," May 24, 1968, Carnegie Hall Rose Archives, Programs Collection.

16. Jelks, *My America*, 64.

CHAPTER 13

1. Brun-Lambert, *Nina Simone*, 159.

2. Langston Hughes, "The Negro Speaks of Rivers," *Crisis*, June 1967, 246.

3. Langston Hughes to Roy Wilkins, September 9, 1939, LHP, Box 170, Folder 3128.

4. Wilkins to Hughes, December 18, 1939, LHP, Box 170, Folder 3128.

5. Hughes to Wilkins, March 22, 1941, LHP, Box 170, Folder 3128.

6. Wilkins to Hughes, November 10, 1955, LHP, Box 170, Folder 3128.

7. Wilkins to Hughes, May 6, 1964, LHP, Box 170, Folder 3128.

8. Hughes, *Selected Letters*, 415.

9. Hughes, "Negro Speaks of Rivers," 250.

10. Langston Hughes, "The Backlash Blues," *Crisis*, June 1967, 251.

11. "The Backlash Blues" was also published in a journal based at San Francisco State College entitled *Etc.: A Journal of General Semantics*. Though the issue is dated June 1967, the quarterly journal did not appear in print until July. It is unclear exactly how or why the poem was published in this unusual place by editor S. I. Hayakawa.

12. Milton Meltzer, "Langston Hughes: Poet of the People," *Springboards* lesson plan, Portal Press, 1967, LHP, Box 169, Folder 3106.

13. Smethurst, "Langston Hughes and the Black Arts Movement," 256–57. Randal Jelks also concurs, noting, "Langston vehemently opposed Africanness and Blackness as being abject long before the stridency of the Black Arts Movement or James Brown." Jelks, *My America*, 206.

14. Miller, W. Jason, "The Long Shadow of Langston Hughes," 182.

15. Hughes to Nina Simone, telegram, November 22, 1966, LHP, Box 147, Folder 2724.

16. Robert Shelton, "Nina Simone Casts Her Moody Spells," *New York Times*, November 23, 1966.

17. I thank Nadine Cohodas for loaning me her copy of this entire 1967 NJF performance, which she secured from the Library of Congress during research for her exacting and insightful biography *Princess Noire* (2010).

18. Cohodas, *Princess Noire*, 200.

19. Cohodas, *Princess Noire*, 201.

CHAPTER 14

1. This evening's performance was heavily edited when it first appeared on Nina Simone's album *'Nuff Said!*

2. Eig, *King*, 322.

3. Martin, *Young King*, 59.

4. This performance can be viewed in its entirety at "Nina Simone Live in England," posted on October 17, 2013, by FistQLturko, YouTube, www.youtube.com/watch?v=t_Fi_tnTbNs.

5. Ford, *Liberated Threads*, 89.

6. Simone, *Live at Berkeley*.

EPILOGUE

1. This entire concert performance is captured on the film *Nina Simone: Live at Montreux 1976*.

2. Simone, *Nina Simone: The Montreux Years*.

3. For more on how Simone first heard Dylan's music from cover recordings by Judy Collins and Roberta Flack, see Elliott, *Nina Simone*, 92.

4. Performing on July 3, 1976, Simone is likely suggesting something very insightful at the very end of the song when she oddly references "strange hats." From April 1975 through July 4, 1976—a full fifteen months—the United States of America celebrated an idealized version of its past with historical costumes, particularly hats. Many parades featured pioneers in cowboy hats, women in bonnets, minutemen wearing colonial tricorns, and newly popular trucker hats featuring the official bicentennial logo. Queen Elizabeth II visited President Gerald Ford at the White House in a well-publicized luncheon and dinner and wore a distinctive blue Scottish tam-o'-shanter. The Dallas Cowboys, known as "America's team," added the color red for the season, making the stripe on their helmets red, white, and blue. The most visible of all the "strange hats" associated with the 1976 celebration included skimmer hats and the ubiquitous Uncle Sam top hat. Interrogating strange hats at this time meant Nina Simone was giving Mister Backlash a dose of the red, white, and blues.

5. Miller and Bolden, "Soul Talk," 227.

BIBLIOGRAPHY

MANUSCRIPT AND SPECIAL COLLECTIONS

Alabama Department of Archives and History, Montgomery
Alabama Media Group Collection
Atlanta History Center, Atlanta, GA
Voices Across the Color Line (Oral History Transcriptions)
Beinecke Rare Book and Manuscript Library, Yale University, New Haven, CT
Bruce Nugent Papers
Langston Hughes Papers
Carnegie Hall Rose Archives, New York City
Programs Collection
John F. Kennedy Library, Boston
Papers of John F. Kennedy
Presidential Papers
National Security Files
Sanford L. Fox Papers
Newport Historical Society, Newport, RI
Newport Jazz Festival and Folk Festival Ephemera
Wisconsin Historical Society, Madison
1964 Freedom Summer Project
Student Nonviolent Coordinating Committee

North Carolina

Center for Documentary Studies, Duke University, Durham, NC
SNCC Civil Rights Digital Archive
David M. Rubenstein Rare Book and Manuscript Library, Duke University, Durham, NC
Frank Clyde Brown Collection of Field Recordings
Nina Simone Project, Tryon, NC
Crys Armbrust Collection
Southern Historical Collection, Wilson Library, University of North Carolina, Chapel Hill
Southern Folklife Collections

Washington, DC

Booth Family Center for Special Collections, Georgetown University
Margaret Bonds Papers
Library of Congress
Recorded Sound Reference Room
Moorland-Spingarn Research Center, Howard University
AMSAC Collection
National Museum of African American History and Culture
Photographs and Still Images

NEWSPAPERS AND MAGAZINES

Africa (Lagos, Nigeria)
Asheville (NC) Citizen-Times
Audio and Record Review (London, UK)
Austin (TX) American
Chicago Defender
Crisis
Daily Express (Lagos, Nigeria)
Dayton (OH) Daily News
Dispatch (Moline, IL)
Evening Bulletin (Providence, RI)
Jet
Life
Melody Maker
Morning Post (Lagos, Nigeria)
Newport (RI) Daily News
New York Amsterdam News
New York Daily Press
New York Evening Post
New York Post
New York Times
Oklahoma Leader (Oklahoma City)
Palm Beach (FL) Post
Philadelphia Tribune
Pittsburgh Courier
Pittsburgh Press
St. Louis (MO) Globe Democrat
Time
Times and Democrat (Orangeburg, SC)
Winston-Salem (NC) Journal

BOOKS AND PAMPHLETS

Berry, Faith. *Langston Hughes: Before and Beyond the Harlem Renaissance*. Wings Books, 1983.
Browne, David. *Talkin' Greenwich Village: The Heady Rise and Slow Fall of America's Bohemian Music Capital*. Hachette, 2024.
Brun-Lambert, David. *Nina Simone: The Biography*. Aurum, 2005.
Cohen, Rachel. *A Chance Meeting: American Encounters*. New York Review of Books, 2024.
Cohodas, Nadine. *Princess Noire: The Tumultuous Reign of Nina Simone*. University of North Carolina Press, 2010.
Colbert, Soyica Diggs. *Radical Vision: A Biography of Lorraine Hansberry*. Yale University Press, 2021.
Dalleo, Raphael. *American Imperialism's Undead: The Occupation of Haiti and the Rise of Caribbean Anticolonialism*. University of Virginia Press, 2016.
De Santis, Christopher C., ed. *Let America Be America Again: Conversations with Langston Hughes*. Oxford University Press, 2022.
Dylan, Bob. *Chronicles: Volume 1*. Simon and Schuster, 2005.
Eig, Jonathan. *King: A Life*. Farrar, Straus and Giroux, 2023.
Elliott, Richard. *Nina Simone*. Equinox, 2013.

Feldstein, Ruth. *How It Feels to Be Free: Black Women Entertainers and the Civil Rights Movement*. Oxford University Press, 2013.

Ford, Tanisha C. *Liberated Threads: Black Women, Style, and the Global Politics of Soul*. University of North Carolina Press, 2015.

Garland, Phyl. *The Sound of Soul*. H. Regnery, 1969.

Hampton, Sylvia, and David Nathan. *Nina Simone: Break Down and Let It All Out*. Sanctuary, 2004.

Hughes, Langston. *Arna Bontemps–Langston Hughes Letters, 1925–1967*, edited by Charles H. Nichols. Dodd-Mead, 1980.

Hughes, Langston. *Ask Your Mamma: 12 Moods for Jazz*. Alfred A. Knopf, 1961.

Hughes, Langston. *The Big Sea*. Hill and Wang, 1993.

Hughes, Langston. *The Collected Works of Langston Hughes*. 16 vols. University of Missouri Press, 2001–4.

Hughes, Langston. *Langston Hughes and the South African Drum Generation: The Correspondence*, edited by Shane Graham and John Walters. Palgrave Macmillan, 2010.

Hughes, Langston. *The Panther and the Lash: Poems of Our Times*. Alfred A. Knopf, 1967.

Hughes, Langston. *Selected Letters of Langston Hughes*, edited by Arnold Rampersad and David Roessel. Alfred A. Knopf, 2015.

Hughes, Langston. *Troubled Island*. Play, 1949.

Jelks, Randal Maurice. *My America: Langston Hughes on Democracy*. Broadleaf Books, 2026.

Kelley, Robin D. G. *Africa Speaks, America Answers: Modern Jazz in Revolutionary Times*. Harvard University Press, 2012.

Light, Alan. *What Happened, Miss Simone?* Canongate, 2016.

Lomax, Louis. *When the Word Is Given . . . A Report on Elijah Muhammad, Malcolm X, and the Black Muslim World*. World Publishing Company, 1963.

Marcus, Greil. *Folk Music: A Bob Dylan Biography in Seven Songs*. Yale University Press, 2022.

Martin, Lerone. *Young King: The Making of Martin Luther King Jr*. Amistad, 2026.

Maxwell, William J. *F.B. Eyes: How J. Edgar Hoover's Ghostreaders Framed African American Literature*. Princeton University Press, 2015.

Millender, Dharathula H. *Martin Luther King, Jr: Boy with a Dream*. Bobbs-Merrill, 1969.

Miller, W. Jason. *Langston Hughes*. Reaktion Books, 2020.

Miller, W. Jason. *Langston Hughes and American Lynching Culture*. University Press of Florida, 2010.

Miller, W. Jason. *Origins of the Dream: Hughes's Poetry and King's Rhetoric*. University Press of Florida, 2015.

Miller, W. Jason. "The Long Shadow of Langston Hughes." In *The Cambridge History of African American Poetry*, edited by Keith Leonard. Cambridge University Press, 2026.

Parr, Patrick. *Malcolm Before X*. University of Massachusetts Press, 2024.

Perry, Imani. *Looking for Lorriane: The Radiant and Radical Life of Lorraine Hansberry*. Beacon Press, 2018.

Priestley, Brian. *Mingus: A Critical Biography*. Da Capo, 1984.

Rampersad, Arnold. *The Life of Langston Hughes*. 2 vols. Oxford University Press, 1986, 1988.

Reed, Anthony. *Soundworks: Race, Sound, and Poetry in Production*. Duke University Press, 2021.

Ritz, David. *Respect: The Life of Aretha Franklin*. Little, Brown, 2014.

Saul, Scott. *Freedom Is, Freedom Ain't: Jazz and the Making of the Sixties*. Harvard University Press, 2003.

Sharpley-Whiting, Tracy. *Bricktop's Paris: African American Women in Paris Between the Two World Wars*. SUNY Press, 2015.

Simone, Nina. *I Put a Spell on You*. Da Capo, 1991.

Smith, Chris. *101 Albums That Changed Popular Music*. Oxford University Press, 2009.

Stein, Jordan Alexander. *Fantasies of Nina Simone*. Duke University Press, 2024.

Stroud, Andy. *Nina Simone: Black Is the Color . . .* Xlibris, 2005.

Tolliver, Cedric. *Of Vagabonds and Fellow Travelers: African Diaspora Literary Culture and the Cultural Cold War*. University of Michigan Press, 2019.

Wald, Gayle F. *This Is Rhythm: Ella Jenkins, Children's Music, and the Long Civil Rights Movement*. University of Chicago Press, 2025.

Wilford, Hugh. *The Mighty Wurlitzer: How the CIA Played America*. Harvard University Press, 2009.

Yerkey, Gary G. *He's Coming to Start Riots: On the Road to Black Power with "The Reverend" Willie Ricks*. GK Press, 2016.

JOURNAL ARTICLES AND ESSAYS

Bolden, Tony. "A Retrospective View of Soul—Langston Hughes as Forerunner." *Langston Hughes Review* 29, no. 2 (2023): 119–49.

Brooks, Daphne A. "Nina Simone's Triple Play." *Callaloo* 34, no. 1 (2011): 176–97.

Feldstein, Ruth. "'I Don't Trust You Anymore': Nina Simone, Culture, and Black Activism in the 1960s." *Journal of American History* 91, no. 4 (2005): 1349–79.

Ferris, William. "Interview with Margaret Walker: 'My Idol was Langston Hughes.'" *Southern Cultures* 16, no. 2 (2010): 53–70.

Hamn, Charles. "Popular Adaptations of Weill's Music for Stage and Screen, 1927–1950." In *The Kurt Weill Edition*, ser. 2, vol. 2, edited by Charles Hamn, Elmar Juchem, and Kim H. Kowalke. European American Music, 2009.

Hughes, Langston. "The Backlash Blues." *Etc.: A Review of General Semantics* 24, no. 2 (1967): 176.

Miles, Kevin Thomas. "Haunting Music in *The Souls of Black Folk*." *Boundary 2* 27, no. 3 (2000): 199–214.

Miller, W. Jason. "The Dreams of Langston Hughes and Martin Luther King, Jr." *Re-Markings* 21, no. 1 (2022): 28–38.

Miller, W. Jason. "Langston Hughes and Martin Luther King: Together in Nigeria." *South Atlantic Review* 83, no. 1 (2018): 22–41.

Miller, W. Jason. "Poet Langston Hughes's Unknown 1949 Visit to Black Mountain College," *Journal of Black Mountain College Studies* 17, *Time Cycles* (2026). www.blackmountaincollege.org/journal-of-bmc-studies-home/.

Miller, W. Jason, and Tony Bolden. "Soul Talk—Langston Hughes and Nina Simone's Friendship: A Conversation with Jason Miller." *Langston Hughes Review* 29, no. 2 (2023): 217–27.

Miller, W. Jason. "Turnarounds in Langston Hughes's Poetry: Re-Listening to Four of His Most Performative Poems." *Langston Hughes Review* 30, no. 2 (2024): 137–57.

Pan, Peter. "Stop Faking African Culture: An African Editor Warns American Negroes." *Negro Digest* 12, no. 1 (1962): 16–20.

Sizemore-Barber, April. "The Voice of (Which?) Africa: Miriam Makeba in America." *Safundi* 13, no. 3–4 (2012): 251–76.

Smethurst, James. "Langston Hughes and the Black Arts Movement." In *Langston Hughes in Context,* edited by Vera M. Kutzinski and Anthony Reed. Cambridge University Press, 2023.

Tillet, Salamishah. "Strange Sampling: Nina Simone and Her Hip-Hop Children." *American Quarterly* 66, no. 1 (2014): 119–37.

Washington, Mary Helen. "Desegregating the 1950s: The Case of Frank London Brown." *Japanese Journal of American Studies,* no. 10 (1999): 15–30.

RECORDINGS AND LINER NOTES

Back to the Bible Quartet. "No Hidin' Place," and "Cert'ny Lord." *What You Are.* Singspiration Sacred Recordings, [195–?].

Big Miller. *Did You Ever Hear the Blues?* LP. United Artists Records, UAL 3047, 1959.

Ellington, Duke, Mahalia Jackson, and the Duke Ellington Orchestra. *Black, Brown and Beige.* LP. Columbia, 1958.

Exuma. *Exuma I.* LP. SR-61265. Mercury, 1970.

Hughes, Langston. *The Black Verse: 12 Moods for Jazz.* LP. Buddah Records, BDS 2005, 1969.

Mingus, Charles. *Mingus Ah Um.* LP. Columbia, 1959.

Simone, Nina. *Emergency Ward!* LP. RCA, 1972.

Simone, Nina. *Live at Berkeley.* LP. Stroud, 1973.

Simone, Nina. "Mississippi *%??**&%." 45 Single. First Richmond Pressing [Promo]. Philips, 1964.

Simone, Nina. *Nina Simone: Live at Ronnie Scott's.* LP. DRG Records, 1984.

Simone, Nina. *Nina Simone: The Essential Collection.* CDs. Metro Doubles, 2003.

Simone, Nina. *Nina Simone: The Montreux Years.* LP. CAT461DLP. BMG, 2021.

Simone, Nina. *Nina Simone at Newport, at the Village Gate, and Elsewhere.* CD. Westside, 1998.

Simone, Nina. *Nina Simone Sings the Blues.* LP. RCA Records, 2016.

Simone, Nina. *'Nuff Said.* LP. RCA Victor, LSP-4065, 1968.Simone, Nina. *Pastel Blues.* LP. PHS 600-187. Verve, 1965.

Simone, Nina. *To Be Free: The Nina Simone Story.* 3 CDs and 1 DVD box set. RCA/Legacy, 2008.

Simone, Nina. *You've Got to Learn.* LP. B0037882-01. Verve, 2023.

Weill, Kurt, and Bertolt Brecht. LP. E3121. *The Threepenny Opera,* adapted by Marc Blitzstein. MGM Records, 1954.

White, N. E. White. "No Hidin' Place." Wax cylinder, ca. 1922. Duke University Collections and Archives.

OTHER MEDIA: FILM | RADIO | PODCAST | TELEVISION | VIDEO

Edwards, Harvey. *Dream Deferred.* Produced for SNCC, 1964.

Eyes on the Prize: America's Civil Rights Movement. American Experience, Blackside, 1987. Film.

Gold, Joel, dir. *Nina.* Peter Rodis, 1970. Streaming video.

Gordon, Jason Thomas, host. *The Singers Talk Podcast,* season 1, episode 19, "Al Schackman on Nina Simone," August 28, 2024. Podcast.

Juassi, Raymond, dir. *Nina Simone: Live at Montreux 1976.* Eagle Eye Media, 2005. DVD.

Keefe, Patrick Radden, host. *Wind of Change*, season 1, episode 3, "America's Secret Weapon," May 25, 2020. Podcast.

Lieberman, Jeff, dir. *The Amazing Nina Simone*. Re-Emerging Films, 2015. Streaming video.

London, Nicole, dir. *American Masters: The Disappearance of Miss Scott*. Aired February 21, 2025, on PBS.

Lords, Frank, dir. *Nina Simone: The Legend*. Quantum Leap, 2002. DVD.

Lumet, Sidney, and Joseph L. Mankiewicz, dirs. *King: A Filmed Record . . . Montgomery to Memphis* (1970). Richard Kaplan Productions, 2009. DVD.

McTiernan, John, dir. *The Thomas Crown Affair*. United Artists, 1999.

Mort, Cynthia, dir. *Nina*. RLJ Entertainment, 2016. DVD.

Nelson, Stanley, dir. *Miles Davis: Birth of the Cool*. Sony, 2019. DVD.

Nina Simone: Live at Ronnie Scott's. Wadham Films, 1985. DVD.

Sherlock, season 2, episode 3, "The Reichenbach Fall." Aired January 15, 2012, on BBC.

Simone, Nina. *Nina Simone: Live in '65 and '68*. Produced by David Peck, Phillip Galloway, and Tom Gulotta. San Diego: Reelin' in the Years Productions, 2008. DVD.

Terkel, Studs. "Langston Hughes, John Sellers, James Cotton, and Otis Spann Discuss Blues Music." *Studs Terkel Radio Archive*, July 15, 1960. Radio show.

WEBSITES

Backlash Blues: Nina Simone and Langston Hughes, www.backlash-blues.com

The Official Home of Nina Simone, www.ninasimone.com

INDEX